Time, Reality, and Transcendence in Rational Perspective

Edited by Peter Øhrstrøm

Aalborg University Press
2002

Time, Reality and Transcendence in Rational Perspective

Peter Øhrstrøm (editor)

ISBN 87-7307-644-9

© 2003 The authors and Aalborg University Press

Publisher: Aalborg University Press
Niels Jernes Vej 6B
9220 Aalborg Ø
Phone +45 96357140
Fax +45 96350076
E-mail: aauf@forlag.auc.dk
http://www.forlag.auc.dk/

Printed by BookPartner, Copenhagen, Denmark

English language editor: Ulrik Petersen
Interior design by Ulrik Petersen
Cover design by Aksel Sørensen
Cover illustration:
Messier 104, the Sombrero galaxy, NGC 4594
© 1993-2002, Anglo-Australian Observatory, photograph by David Malin.

Table of contents

Peter Øhrstrøm: Introduction	5
Steinar Thorvaldsen: Kepler, Galileo, Newton and the Constructive Ideas of Modern Science	11
Nicolai Winther-Nielsen: Reading for the Creator's Discourse: Speech Acts and Transcendence in Genesis 1-3	39
Mogens Wegener: God, Time and Creation: An Essay in Metaphysics	75
William Lane Craig: Relativity and the 'Elimination' of Absolute Time	91
William Lane Craig: On the Mind-dependence of Temporal Becoming	129
Søren Holm: Christian Ethics in a Secular World	147
Per Hasle: Truth, Time and Mythos in Cicero, St. Paul and St. Jerome. An Essay in the Relation between a Rhetorical and an Early Christian Conception of Truth and Communication	161
Peder A. Tyvand: The Rhetorical Pyramid	193
William Lane Craig and Lennart Nørreklit: Is Being a Theist More Rational than Being an Atheist? - A Debate	227

Introduction

PETER ØHRSTRØM

This book deals with the relations between rationality and religious faith. In particular, it takes into consideration various perspectives on the idea of an intellectual approach to the Christian faith.

Some of the key questions in this book will be: Are some world views more rational than others? Is it rational to believe in a transcendent dimension of reality? Is being a theist more rational than being an atheist? Are there limits to what questions we can hope to answer by rational and scientific reasoning and investigation? What role can rationality play in the study of time and reality? How can we settle questions about transcendence and metaphysics?

It is sometimes claimed that rationality and logic are more or less opposed to the very ideas of metaphysics and transcendence. This is, however, not at all the case. On the contrary, notions such as validity and truth very easily give rise to ideas of the transcendent and supernatural. As an illustration of this point we can mention the Aristotelian view.

It is common to consider Aristotle to be the founding father of Western logic, although elements of logic can certainly be pointed out in pre-Socratic thought and in the writings of Plato.

One of the basic concepts in Aristotle's thinking on logic was the syllogism. Aristotle's problem was the following: Which of the many possible syllogisms are valid and which are not? Aristotle provided very clear answers to this question. In fact, it is most interesting that it is possible in any group of people to reach a very high degree of agreement on the question of validity of syllogisms. For instance, everybody will agree that the syllogism:

> some S are M
> all M are P
> ergo: some S are P

is valid whereas the structure e.g.

> some S are M
> some M are P
> ergo: some S are P

is certainly not a valid syllogism. But what is the origin of this agreement? The same fundamental question could be asked with respect to many other kinds of logical reasoning. Aristotle himself formulated the question in a very precise way:

> And the starting-point of reason is not reason, but something superior to reason. What then could be superior even to knowledge and to intellect, except God? [Eudemian Ethics VIII. II, 22]

Aristotle obviously considered the origin of logic to be transcendent. Although he did not present any detailed exposition of the nature of logic, he was obviously aware of the fact that the question of validity of logical arguments is related to the problem of the semantic structures of natural language. His interest in language and semantics becomes evident when one considers his famous ten categories, which can be used in order to explain the meaning of a sentence. The categories can be viewed as basic components of meaning.

Thus following the Aristotelian line of thinking it seems that logic and rationality is given to humans, and that the validity of logic and rationality comes from something superior. A similar thought can be found in the writings of the great Polish logician Jan Łukasiewicz (1878-1956), who beautifully formulated his view in the following way:

> Now, whenever I work even on the least significant logistic problem, for instance, when I search for the shortest axiom of the implicational propositional calculus I always have the impression

> that I am facing a powerful, most coherent and most resistant structure. I sense that structure as if it were a concrete, tangible object, made of the hardest metal, a hundred times stronger than steel and concrete. I cannot change anything in it; I do not create anything of my own will, but by strenuous work I discover in it ever new details and arrive at unshakable and eternal truths. Where is and what is that ideal structure? A believer would say that it is in God and is His thought. [Jan Łukasiewicz: *Selected Works*, 1970, p.249]

In this way the very study of logic, understanding and communication can provide useful insights indicating that it seems it is rather reasonable to assume the existence of a supernatural or transcendent reality.

Something similar can be said about natural science as such. The very fact that we may gain reliable and meaningful information about reality from our senses and our reason suggests that this possibility is given to human beings by the Creator of everything. As **Steinar Thorvaldsen** argues in his paper in this volume, this is at least the way in which the pioneers of natural science understood their work. One may say that this is how they understood why understanding is possible at all.

It appears that the notion of creation is crucial. The world has become meaningful and understandable by creation. If this is so, we have every reason to look into the content of this notion. In this volume, **Nicolai Winther-Nielsen** offers a careful study of the Biblical creation story. He suggests that this text is relevant in a modern context, pointing out that it clearly contains important statements about time, reality, and transcendence. In reflecting upon what it would mean to understand such crucial features and what it means for the world to be meaningful, the very notions of verbal explanation and human language become important. Nicolai Winther-Nielsen points out that the Creator of the universe according to the text illuminates his own being as a speaking and acting God who crowns his work by creating man, whom he endows with the capacity of speech.

In his paper, **Mogens Wegener** analyses the notion of creation from a perspective slightly different from that of Nicolai Winther-Nielsen. Mogens Wegener points out that the divine creation should not be conceived of as an act in the past. He suggests that God's act of creation may also be interpreted in accordance with the contingency of the present as the preservation of nunc stans, a standing Now, in the midst of the river of time. Understood in this way, the fact that a Now is standing is a sign of divine creation.

William Lane Craig in his paper *On the Mind-dependence of Temporal Becoming* supports a similar conclusion, arguing that we should not dismiss the common experience of mankind with respect to temporality, but we should understand that it shows that the world in fact becomes, and that the Now is real. In his paper *Relativity and the Elimination of Absolute Time*, Craig argues that this conclusion can be maintained even if Einsteinian theories of relativity are accepted. He argues that in God's temporal experience, there is a moment, which is present in metaphysical time, wholly independently of physical clock times. He says: "God would know, without any dependence on clock synchronization procedures, or on any physical operations at all, which events were simultaneously present in metaphysical time - and He would know this simply in virtue of His knowing at every such moment the unique set of present-tense propositions true at that moment, without any need of a sensorium or any physical observation of the universe."

In this way the Now as the common experience of mankind with respect to temporality may be seen as an indication of something superior, a condition in life given by the Creator.

Taking transcendent reality for granted, the Christian intellectual has to face a number of challenges. Some of them have to do with ethics. Arguing from Christian belief, ethical truth is grounded in the will of God. But how can the Christian intellectual discuss ethical questions with other intellectuals who have different basic beliefs? In his paper in this volume, **Søren Holm** has tried to identify a number of different roles that a Christian ethics can assume in the modern secular world.

A similar challenge arises in relation to the notion of truth and relativism. In his paper, **Per Hasle** discusses among other things how a "rhetorical relativism" relates to ideas of fixity of meaning, absolute truth, and the idea of a privileged Mythos. He also analyses how Roman Rhetoric met with early Christianity, exemplified especially by the case of St. Jerome, what points of difference, respectively contact, exist between Christianity and Roman Rhetoric, and where this may leave us in an increasingly rhetorical culture.

Being very much engaged in the intellectual debate in Norway about Christianity and materialism, **Peder A. Tyvand** has a very special background for characterising the crucial features of this kind of debate. In his paper, he maintains that in some cases, i.e. at some levels in the discussion, what matters is not arguments, whether good or bad, but rather power or brute force. He himself has borne the brunt of some of the latter in the Norwegian public debates.

Peder Tyvand does not exclude the possibility of a rational debate about religious questions. On the contrary, he would be very much in favor of such a debate. In fact, there is every reason to believe that a rational debate about religious questions could be very useful and interesting. The final paper in this volume is a transcription of a debate which took place at Aalborg University on March 20, 1999, between **William Lane Craig** and **Lennart Nørreklit**. The theme of the debate was formulated in the following way: *'Is Being a Theist More Rational than Being an Atheist?'* The debate is a nice illustration of the fact that a rational debate of religion and metaphysics is possible. It should also be noted that there is no clear winner of the debate. No final proof of God's existence or non-existence was given. Obviously all the arguments used in the debate had to be based on some premises. The question of which premises should be accepted and which ones should be rejected has to be left to the reader.

Peter Øhrstrøm

Kepler, Galileo, Newton and the Constructive Ideas of Modern Science

STEINAR THORVALDSEN

Abstract

Nowadays science and Christianity are mainly seen as two completely separate contributions to our daily life and culture. In this paper I intend to argue that historically and conceptually, science and Christianity should in fact be seen as very closely related entities. The new kind of science, which was introduced about 400 years ago, was very much inspired by the Christian world-view which all the important pioneers in science accepted.

The modern attitude has its roots in problems which arose more than one hundred years ago. When we in this lecture shall go even further back, it will be somewhat strange for us to see how close Christianity and science were linked together at that early time.

But the fact is that modern science grew up in Europe around the beginning of the 17th century, and Christianity had the function of being some of the soil from which it grew. In the last thirty years we have witnessed a reorientation among scholars in the question of the relation between religion and science [Merton & Trenn 1979, Lindberg & Numbers 1986, Brook 1991, Henry 1997]. Investigations in the history of science have contributed to casting new light upon the relationship between religion and science after the Middle Ages. The American sociologist Robert Merton, for instance, claims to find evidence that the Protestant ethics in the English culture had created a positive attitude to scientific work in the 16th and the 17th century. Merton interpreted this religious mandate as a necessary condition for the origin of modern science. For him there was a causal connection between Christianity and science. The old conflicts have thereby gradually lost their dominance in favour of other ways of understanding the relationship between religion and science.

Why did the scientific revolution happen in Europe only, and why did it occur in the 17th century? From where did the new ideas develop? What is the origin of the new challenges, and all the new scientific knowledge? - These questions will probably never be answered completely. Historians of science should be content if they will be able to identify the principal factors, which they will then have to evaluate relative to more or less subjective considerations. However, it appears to be evident that in order to discuss these questions in a proper way we have to involve considerations on topics outside of the subject of traditional science and history of science. Only a precise analysis of cultural ideas of the East and the West will eventually clarify why modern science and technology arose just in Europe, and not in other cultures.

Even if relations of philosophical and intellectual character have played the main role for the growth of science, we must not forget that there without any doubt also exist important social and economical causes. Only given a certain cultural level of advancement (penmanship, book printing, school system and so on) is a scientific revolution possible. Most cultures perished prior to its possibility to start developing a scientific revolution at all.

Some have attempted to explain the scientific revolution as a result of interplay between the demands and progress in technology (where technology again is a function of the social requirements). Such attempts, however, have never been particular convincing. Social structures and technological development may be necessary as prerequisites for a scientific revolution, but they are far from sufficient prerequisites. Chinese culture is a very interesting example. In the 16th century, China was in many respects far ahead of Europe. Joseph Needham, who has a comprehensive knowledge of China, says in the beginning of his book *The Grand Titration*:

> "The more you know about Chinese philosophy, the more you realize its profoundly rationalistic character ..... I believe that the more you know about Chinese civilization, the more odd it seems that modern science and technology did not develop there." [Needham, 1969]

In his attempt to give an explanation Needham writes:

> "There was no confidence that the code of Nature's laws could ever be unveiled and read, because there was no assurance that a divine being, even more rational than ourselves, had ever formulated such a code capable of being read." [Needham, 1969]

Gradually it looks as if the Chinese, as people of many other large cultures, lost their interest in science. When Albert Einstein was asked to analyse the development behind Western science, he answered in a well-known letter:

> Dear Sir,
>
> The development of Western science has been based on two great achievements: the invention of the formal logical system (in Euclidean geometry) by the Greek philosophers, and the discovery of the possibility of finding out causal relationships by systematic experiment (at the Renaissance). In my opinion one need not be astonished that the Chinese sages did not make these steps. The astonishing thing is that these discoveries were made at all.
>
> Sincerely yours, Albert Einstein.
> [*Letter to J. E. Switzer* 1953, quoted from Needham 1969, p. 43]

The Middle Ages (500-1500)

When modern humans today look back to the Middle Ages, with its cultural and religious life, we may either be filled with a longing after the unified culture that gave life stability and safety, or with an abhorrence for the suppression that existed to maintain the same cultural unity. Science and world view in the Middle Ages were bound to the Roman Catholic teaching, without any great stress on the significance of studying the real world around ourselves. The church had such a great influence and power over life, that it did not tolerate any other authority than its own spiritual authority. It actually lifted itself up in God's place. Meditation instead of action got the greatest importance in human life. The world was seen as a picture of divine goodness only to show man the possibility of salvation upon doing good deeds. But with such a separation between daily existence and the real world-to-come, what existed now had no true interest. Life and the universe were only considered areas for moral test.

However, this worldview of the Middle Ages also had positive sides. From our modern point of view we should not automatically or uncritically despise it. A positive side was that during the Middle Ages, man understood himself to live in a personal universe. He did not primarily need to find his identity in the impersonal matter around himself. Humans knew that they existed in a personal universe that started with a personal creator: The God of the Church.

Moreover they had a uniform way of thinking, where everything was integrated in a unified and sensible understanding of the universe. They worked within a united philosophy, in contrast to the specialized and fragmented view on knowledge that modern humans often have to live with.

Further, they expressed their concepts through the wish of harmony, 'a harmony of the spheres.' The stars were not studied so much in order to understand how they moved, but more to discover some of the harmony in creation itself. Astrology was also studied to understand some of the deep harmony in the universe. It was supposed that the stars had influence on terrestrial incidents. This was not primarily regarded as destiny, such as Arab astrology taught when introduced into western thinking around one thousand years ago, but rather as an attempt to increase harmony between everything existing.

In fact, quite a complicated construction arose out of the synthesis of the early Middle Ages between Christian theology and Neo Platonic philosophy. Through the work of the church fathers, including Augustine's comprehensive theology, a framework was made uniting all forms of knowledge in a grand hierarchy with theology as 'The Queen of Sciences,' and the other sciences as companions and helpers to theology. The result was a united and integrated worldview that was religious all through.

However, the worldview of the Middle Ages also had several negative consequences. Since the Church demanded the right to dictate the correct teachings, it accepted no testing in the universe outside, and therefore made itself a deity. The church was often so occupied with the spiritual sides of existence, that it tolerated much cruelty in practical life. With reputable exceptions, such as the Franciscan monks, little was done to combat illness and better the health among people. This embracement of nature could only be sustained if part of reality, with its particularities and information, was kept down and given little meaning. This worldview broke down under the hard pressure which an irresistible reality exerted. It ended with a collapse of man's great idea of being the centre of the universe. In addition, the brutal Black Death raged in Europe around 1350 and raised the question of the actual harmony and unity in nature. All this contributed to abolishing the assumption - and it was nothing else than an assumption - of a harmonic nature and a harmonic management from the Church above reality.

A fresh ideal for science was gradually born. One could no longer let scientists stay passive with the knowledge they had. Their knowledge had to be expanded into new areas, and the present situation should be changed for the better for the coming generations. The Renaissance in Southern Europe and The Reformation in the North both bore a philosophy that "made wonders of scientific progress."

When great breakthroughs take place in science, it often is the result of the effort of a few people. Science is - more so than other subjects - the workshop of the geniuses and pioneers. This fact points to the reasons for which we in the following take a closer look at three of the principal founders of modern science and their efforts.

Johannes Kepler (1571-1630)

Kepler is one of pioneers of the new science. He was born in Weil der Stadt, a small town west of Stuttgart. Thirteen years old he entered the evangelical convent school in Adelberg. Two years later he moved to another convent school where he was to stay until he was ready for university. Bible studies had a central place in school, but also mathematics and astronomy were among the subjects. Eighteen years old, Kepler entered the university in Tübingen where he some years later passed the magisterial degree with honors. In 1594 he was called to be a teacher in mathematics at the protestant gymnasium in Graz. Life went on step by step for Kepler, and in 1601 he was appointed Imperial Court astronomer and mathematician in Prague.

Fig 1. Johannes Kepler

Kepler wanted to provide a philosophy or physics of celestial phenomena in place of the theology or metaphysics of Aristotle. In his 59 years of life,

Kepler published about ten major scientific works. In the 15th and 16th century, a profound change in the philosophical and scientific thinking was going on in Europe. Aristotle and his reigning philosophical system were falling down from the throne. Scientists began to look at reality and the facts to be concluded from these in a new way. Here Kepler made significant contributions both to astronomy, optics and mathematical analysis. He is best known for his three laws of planetary motion around the Sun. These were found on the basis of data collected by the Danish astronomer, Tycho Brahe, roughly after 22 years of intensive calculations. They were the first *Natural Laws* in the modern meaning of word. The path Kepler went through towards his goal is considered a masterpiece in the history of science. With these laws he contributed to building a bridge from the old picture of the universe as an unalterable cosmos, to the new idea of a dynamic system subject to mathematical laws. Kepler's first law published in his work *New Astronomy* (1609), indicates as an example what the new laws looked like:

> "The planets move around the sun in elliptical orbits, with the sun in one of the focal points." [Kepler 1929, chap. 59]

Prior to Kepler's time, quantitative calculations by and large were used as a support for geometrical a priori assumptions. In Kepler's works, however, the quantitative aspect found a fundamental meaning, an attitude that has influenced the scientific method and comprehension of the world for all posterity. Kepler solved the problem of circular versus elliptical orbits by claiming that it was not the geometrical figures themselves that were to be conclusive for the harmonic regularities in nature, but the quantitative harmonies that could be deduced from nature itself. His vision was a solar system where the changing velocities of the planets formed a basis for a symphonic harmony to the honor of the Creator.

A concrete example of Kepler's quantitative understanding of harmony is found in his so-called second law, the area law. It was quite a shock for Kepler to discover that the planets did not move with even velocity in their orbits around the Sun, but the velocity changed according to how close the planet was to the Sun. Kepler was still capable of maintaining harmony because he found that in the same amount of time, *equal areas* was swept out by the movements of the planet. The area is defined by the line from focus in the ellipse, where the Sun is located, and to the planet at the edge of the ellipse. Thereby the concept of harmony is still valid, although formulated in a more complex mathematical form. This was quite a new idea, with far-reaching consequences ahead.

Kepler's detection of elliptical planetary orbits undermined to some extent the ideal world that the contemporary scientist had inherited from the old Platonic and Pythagorean worldview. Still Kepler found that he could maintain the basic idea in his worldview, namely that nature itself reveals regularity and constancy that may be acknowledged by humans. This idea was united with the Christian faith in God as the source of law and regularity, because God was the same from eternity to eternity. But he made progress in unifying Greek cosmology and Christian theology by pointing out that the law and constancy in nature was of a quantitative character.

The following quotation from 1597 indicates Kepler's own opinion of his scientific activities, and also expresses hope that humans in an even better manner might acknowledge the Creator in nature:

> "My God make it come to pass that my delightful speculation the *Mysterium Cosmographicum* have everywhere among reasonable men fully the effect which I strove to obtain in the publication, namely that the belief in the creation of the world be fortified through this external support, that thought of the creator be recognized in its nature, and that his inexhaustible wisdom shine forth daily more brightly. Then man will at last measure the power of his mind on the true scale, and will realize that God, who founded everything in the world according to the norm of quantity, also has endowed man with a mind, which can comprehend these norms. For as the eye is for color, the ear for musical sounds, so is the mind of man created for the perception not of any arbitrary entities, but rather of quantities." [*Letter to Masterlin*, April 19, 1597. See Caspar 1930, band I, p. 44]

Here something more is involved than the pure Platonic principle of God as the first cause in geometry. Kepler's God has given humans possibilities to communicate directly with their divine origin through recognizing the laws of nature. Recognition of the order of nature expressed in mathematical language with its possibility of quantitative calculation is to have a share in God's own thoughts. Kepler's mathematical astronomy was a way to realize the thought that mathematics is a symbolic interpretation of the nature of the Universe. The mathematical language 'reflects' realities in such a way that it is a basic correspondence between the human acknowledgment and nature itself. This understanding of the relation between reality and language turned out to be founding for science and later for the triumph of technology in the centuries to come.

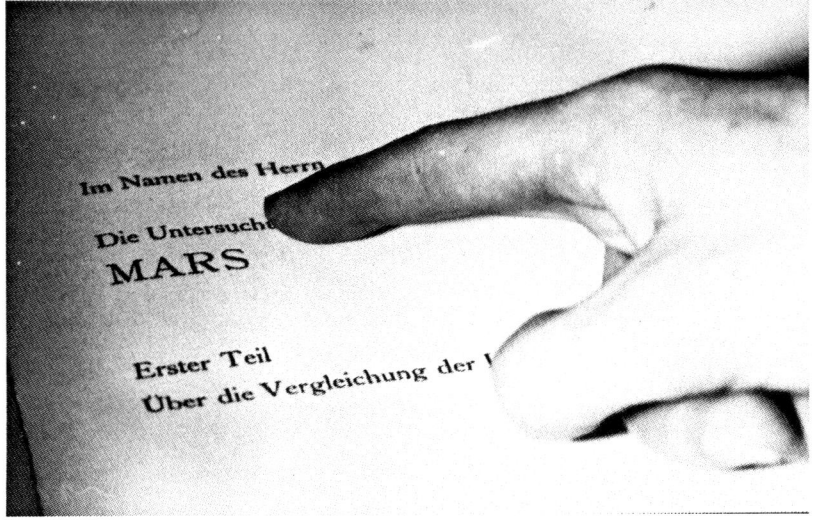

Fig 2. The first page of Kepler's book New Astronomy

Eight years later, when the theory in *Mysterium Cosmographicum* was rejected and the new book *New Astronomy* was under construction, he still has his aim clear in mind:

> "My aim is to show that the heavenly machine is not a kind of divine, live being, but a kind of clockwork (and he who believes that a clock has a soul, attributes the maker's glory to the work), insofar as nearly all the manifold motions are caused by a most simple, magnetic, and material force, just as all motions of the clock are caused by a simple weight. And I also show how these physical causes are to be given numerical and geometrical expression." [*Letter to Herwart von Hohenburg*, February 10, 1605. See Caspar 1930, band I, p. 219]

If we shall try to sum up Kepler's basic ideas, we may find that his understanding varies somewhat through his life. But the following subsequent factors were of great importance to Kepler's science:

Firstly, his basic idea was that universe was an *ordered universe*. The universe had a God-given order for Kepler. He was enthusiastic of the idea that God had created the world as beautiful as possible. The harmony and correspondence in nature was the 'signature' from the Creator himself: Such he wanted it to be.

Secondly, Kepler held that this order could be expressed *mathematically*. He believed, as the Greeks, that the creator worked according to mathematical models when he created the world.

Thirdly, Kepler thought that *man could acknowledge this mathematical order*. In his own words:

> "Those laws [which govern the material world] lie within the power of understanding of the human mind; God wanted us to perceive them when He created us in His image in order that we may take part in His own thoughts..." [*Letter to Masterlin*, April 19, 1597]

Furthermore, Kepler held that in order to grasp the right laws, man had to take the physical creation under investigation. *Physical observations* were necessary and decisive. Here Kepler differs consistently from the Greek way of thinking. The Greeks had postulated that the ideas in mathematics never could be implemented in full scale in matter - they only had a weak 'reflection' there. But Kepler considered matter as given directly from God's creative hand, and often talked about the necessity of *"reading the book of nature."* Here an error of eight arc minutes between observations and computations for the orbit of planet Mars, made Kepler reject the two thousand years old postulate of circular planetary orbits, to introduce elliptic orbits. The main thing was to be precise and absolutely true in the scientific work. All errors and simplifications would offend God's majesty.

Finally, we should mention that Kepler, like the famous composer J.S. Bach, always wanted to *give God the glory*. Science was a part of his worship. Kepler represented a kind of 'praising scientist,' who together with the apostle Paul, could worship with his mind.

Galileo Galilei (1564-1643)

Galileo was born in the town of Pisa in Italy. After completing his studies, he was appointed professor of mathematics in 1589. Galileo was the first to use the telescope to study the sky. He also studied how bodies move here on Earth, and thereby he laid the foundation of experimental mechanics.

In Galileo's scientific theory, nature itself was presented as a *single, ordered system* - even stronger than in Kepler's mind. Secondly, Galileo maintained that nature itself was composed as a *mathematical language*:

> "Philosophy is written in that great book which ever lies before our eyes - I mean the universe - but we cannot understand it if we do not first learn the language and grasp the symbols, in which it is written. This book is written in the mathematical language, and the symbols are triangles, circles, and other geometrical figures, without whose help it is impossible to comprehend a single word of it; without which one wanders in vain through a dark labyrinth."
> [Drake 1957, *The Assayer*, p. 237]

The universe was for Galileo a book written in a foreign language. Therefore it also had to be interpreted and explained in this language. After many misunderstandings humans now had begun to discover this language - which is the principles and concepts of mathematics. Any part of mathematics could always be applied in the material world. Physical bodies, for example, were always geometrical figures, even if they did not have a regular form as in geometry. When one was trying to understand an unknown aspect of nature, the method was to make use of the language of nature and thereby decompose the system in mathematical terms. The physical world, Galileo conjectured, was identical with Euclid's geometrical space. Thereby mathematics had validity in the material world.

Fig 3. Galileo Galilei

Furthermore, according to Galileo, the validity of the theorems in mathematical language was guaranteed by the divine intellect:

"Extensively, that is, with regard to the multitude of intelligibles, which are infinite, the human understanding is as nothing even if it understands a thousand propositions; for a thousand in relation to infinity is zero. But taking man's understanding intensively, in so far as this term denotes understanding some proposition perfectly, I say that the human intellect does understand some of them perfectly, and thus in these it has as much absolute certainty as Nature itself has. Of such are the mathematical sciences alone; that is, geometry and arithmetic, in which the Divine intellect indeed knows infinitely more propositions, since it knows all. But with regard to those few which the human intellect does understand, I believe that its knowledge equals the Divine in objective certainty, for here it succeeds in understanding necessity, beyond which there can be no greater sureness." [*Dialogue concerning two chief World Systems*, 1970, p. 103].

The development of mathematical physics showed that mathematics is far more than just a tool. This insight led to the main turning point between old and new science. The quantification of nature was the key to understanding the world, and without this mathematical approximation of reality, modern science would have been unthinkable. With Galileo, science therefore took the great leap towards the implementation of the mechanistic worldview. Furthermore, Gary Deason [cf. Lindberg & Numbers, p. 167-191] has argued that there is a connection between the theological underlining of God as the absolute and sovereign majesty, and the growth of a mechanical interpretation of the world. As an aside, we may mention that the famous conflict between Galileo and the Catholic Church was not a collision between two opposite worldviews. The trial was rather the result of personal conflicts and provocations (cf. Arthur Koestler: *The Sleepwalkers*). The philosophical confrontation had to do with the relation between Galileo's physics and Aristotle's physics. Aristotle's was at this time the authorized tutoring at the universities, and it was in reaction to this that Galileo stated the following:

> "They wish never to raise their eyes from those pages - as if this great book of the universe had been written to be read by nobody but Aristotle, and his eyes had been destined to see for all posterity." [Drake 1957, Galilei: *Letters on Sunspots*, letter 3].

Therefore, it is a misunderstanding and a twist of the historical relations, to give a picture of a Galileo who never was able to get the Pope to take a look in his telescope; and a Copernicus who waited till after his death to publish his work, because he was afraid of reactions from the church. The historical fact is that Copernicus met little or no resistance from the church against his theory. Even Galileo had friends high up in the church hierarchy sympathizing with his ideas. Galileo's first publication and following visit in Rome was an immediate success, and the Jesuits at the Vatican's public bureaucracy mentioned his discovery and the new equipment, the telescope, in inspiring words. The first dispute with the censors was not at all on his scientific discovery, but on the theology he used to legitimate his scientific activity.

The principle of "neutrality of hypotheses" was a basic and important part of the position which the ecclesiastic authorities held. Galileo's book, *Dialogue concerning two chief World Systems*, was approved by Pope Urban in 1630 and printed two years later. To keep the claim of neutrality, Galileo had consequently included the central words, dictated by the Pope himself, that the Copernican theory was no categorical or ultimate truth. He had, however, laid these words in the mouth of a person named Simplicio, who in the book is a rather weakly equipped character. Censors of course discovered this, and when the Pope was notified, he took it as a personal offence. But it was hardly the Pope himself Galileo had in mind when he created the Simplicio character. The historian Stillman Drake asserts that it rather was Galileo's first opponent, Lodovico delle Colombe, an autodidactic and otherwise amateur in scientific affairs, who was portrayed as Simplicio.

It may also be of interest to mention that Galileo often used an atomic theory of matter. Galileo found it useful to suppose that matter was decomposable in "*infinite small, indivisible atoms*" (cf. *Two New Sciences*, p. 40). Perhaps this theory has connection to the mathematical indivisibles, but otherwise they may also derive from the Greeks. Galileo's student, the monk Bonaventura Cavalieri (1598-1647), applied this concept frequently in mathematics.

With such visions of a mathematical reading of the material world, Galileo could state one of his well known headlines:

> "Let us measure everything that is measurable, and let us make measurable everything that not yet is measurable." [Drake 1957]

Isaac Newton (1642-1727)

Sir Isaac Newton is considered to be among the very greatest in the history of science. He stands out as one of the driving forces forming the whole of our Western science and culture. During his own lifetime he reached such an authority and influence that he challenged and defeated even Aristotle. Posterity has, so to speak, unanimously chosen him as the greatest scientific intellect that has ever lived. According to an interesting anecdote, his contemporary competitor Leibniz said:

> "Taking mathematics from the beginning of the world to the time when Newton lived, what he did was much the better half." [Brewster 1965, vol. 2, p. 406]

In contrast to all this stands Newton's own words towards the end of his life:

> "I do not know what I may appear to the world; but to myself I seem to have been only like a boy playing on the seashore, and diverting myself in now and then finding a smoother pebble or a prettier shell than ordinary, whilst the great ocean of truth lay all undiscovered before me." [Quoted in Brewster, 1965]

The University of Cambridge early became aware of Newton's capacity, and in 1669 he took over a professorship. The years 1684-86 are among the most important in the history of science. Then Newton finally had been convinced by a friend to publish his astronomical and physical discoveries. Working almost day and night with this for two years, the project *Philosophia Naturalis Principia Mathematica* (in short: *Principia*) was realized. This book at once had a great influence in the whole of Europe. The presentation is elegant. It is characterized by an enormously systematic, and impressive penetration and width in the problems dealt with. He starts with the laws for the motion of bodies, and from this he explains a whole row of phenomena (among other things the tides) known for the Earth, the moon and the rest of our solar system. The work was a synthesis of Kepler's and Galileo's theories, and it represents the first and greatest triumph for the new mathematical analysis (the calculus) that Newton himself had discovered. Here Newton marks the introduction of a completely new epoch of science.

Fig 4. Isaac Newton

It is beyond doubt that Newton did not have an utterly materialistic worldview. Voltaire, who knew him, said:

> "Sir Isaac Newton was firmly convinced of God's existence, with whom he understood not only an infinite, almighty and creative being, but also a Lord that had established a covenant between himself and his creation." [Royal Society 1947]

Newton could go as far as to regard *Principia* and his other scientific works as useful because they gave external help to make the laws of The Creator visible. All discovery of scientific law underlined the order and structure that was implemented in creation. Studies in nature were for Newton a question of interpreting the marks of God's hand, and thereby decipher the puzzle of the Universe. Such richness, entity and width were above Newton's intense research.

In Principia he also puts up some rules for scientific work, the so called *Regulae Philosophandi*. In his famous *General Scholium* in *Principia*, Newton states this:

> "This most beautiful system of the sun, planets, and comets, could only proceed from the counsel and dominion of an intelligent and powerful Being... This Being governs all things, not as the soul of the world, but as Lord over all; and on account of his dominion he is wont to be called Lord God, or Universal Ruler... And from his true dominion it follows that the true God is a living, intelligent, and powerful Being; and, from his other perfections, that he is supreme, or most perfect. He is eternal and infinite, omnipotent and omniscient; that is, his duration reaches from eternity to eternity; his presence from infinity to infinity; he governs all things, and knows all things that are or can be done. He is not eternity and infinity, but eternal and infinite; he is not duration or space, but he endures and is present. He endures forever, and is everywhere present; and, by existing always and everywhere, he constitutes duration and space." [*Principia*. A Revision of Motte's Translation by Cajori, 1946, p. 545]

These reflections Newton terminates with the following words: *"So much on God. To think about him on the basis of the phenomenon we can observe in the universe, naturally belongs to science."* This is a very strong claim. We can also sense a Christian excitement behind it! Newton did not consider faith and science as two separated areas. His religious conviction was so strong that he had to give expression to it, even in his deep scientific treatise. We must add that after Newton's time, 6-7 theories on the origin of the solar system have appeared. But up to this day the problem is an unsolved one.

What was the driving force for Isaac Newton in his intensive activities? In a letter to Dr. Bentley, he gave us at least a part of his answer:

> "Sir; When I wrote my treatise about our system, I had an eye upon such principles as might work with considering men, for the belief of a Deity; and nothing can rejoice me more than to find it useful for that purpose. But if I have done the public any service this way, it is due to nothing but industry and patient thought...." [Cohen, 1958, p. 280].

Newton's view on the interaction between faith and science made him stress the importance of two matters: *mathematics* and *experiments*. The order and regularity resident in creation made it possible to formulate exact knowledge about it. Mathematics was the language that in the best way could express this exact order. But the mathematically formulated theory always had to build upon an experimental basis. In such a way Newton made the common rendezvous of the two main streams in science: the *empiric experimental* and the *deductive mathematical*. Science was to him the exact mathematical formulation of phenomena in space and time in God's universe.

The mathematical analysis

I have elsewhere [1979] discussed the origin of the area of mathematics which we today call Calculus. This is a very important subject, especially for engineers. I have argued that it is possible to find three creative factors that contributed to establish the new subject. A *creative factor* may be understood as an element or aspect that enriched mathematics with fertile ideas, which can lead to further progress.

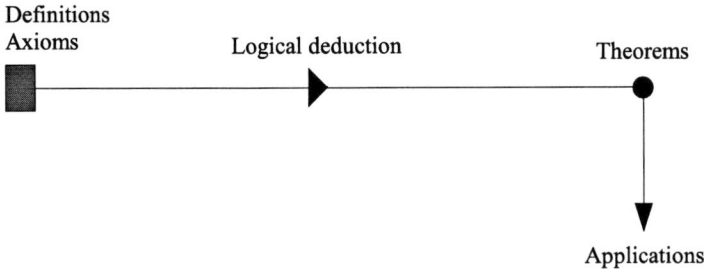

Fig. 5. Context of justification

When we today present a subject of mathematics at the universities, we follow a quite strict deductive form, presenting axioms, definitions, theorems with proofs, and at the end applications. This can be called a *context of justification* (cf. Suppe 1974, p. 125). But the *context of discovery* may be completely different. New areas of mathematics often start on an intuitive basis. After this intuitive phase, however, there must follow a critical reshaping of the subject, where the whole presentation is made exact and deductive. This formalization removes all vague notions, and conserves only concepts and symbols that represent the abstract mathematical relations. Such a formalization-process gives up the link between the concepts and the original relations they where conceived from. One forgets that the axiomatic structure was constructed upon, for example, an empirical basis.

Regardless of this, logical thinking is a necessary substance in any mathematical project. The first creative factor is therefore logic. This is something we have inherited from the Greeks. They were engaged in deducing truth, and especially the Platonic school stressed that truth only could be reached upon mathematical abstraction and reasoning. Leibniz and his *characteristica generalis* may specially be seen in connection with the Greek way of thinking. But all mathematicians that contributed in making the new mathematical analysis made use of the Greek way of thinking as an important part of their 'mental tools.'

The Greeks, however, had been so consistent in their demand for exactitude, that all imprecise ideas were rejected from mathematics. They could easily end up in paradoxes of the type known from Zeno's paradoxes. A consequence of this was that infinitely small quantities were discarded. Infinitesimal considerations could not be used. Around the year 1600 mathematicians, however, were looking for new methods that could make it possible to deal with tangent, area and volume problems more directly. These problems often had a physical and astronomical origin. The work with these problems gave suggestions and direction to mathematical methods, and complicated mathematics was created to solve them. Mathematics got ignition towards a new dynamic way of thinking.

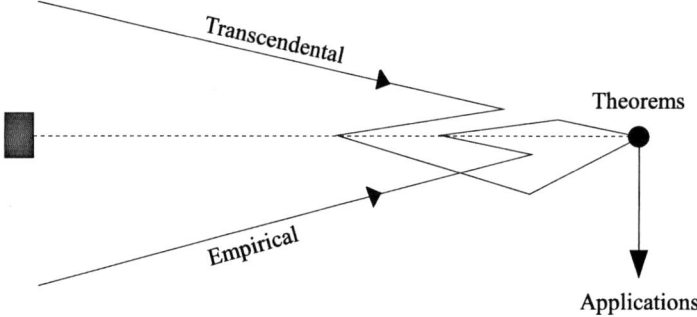

Fig. 6. Context of discovery.

Most mathematicians at this time believed, for religious reasons, that there existed a close isomorphism (structural equality) between the outer world and mathematics. They realized that there were obscurities in the mathematical methods they used. But they were risking venturing far on uncertain mathematical ground because the methods gave correct physical results. Mathematics and physics were so closely linked that the strength of physics supported the weakness of mathematics. This creative factor may be suitably labeled the *empirical* factor. A well-known example here is Newton's theory of limits ("primary and ultimate ratio") that are retrieved from physical empiricism.

But mathematicians also introduced concepts of no definite physical meaning. This we may call the *transcendental* factor, which therefore consists of concepts outside the area of experience. An example here is the concept of indivisibles. It pops up several times in history, for example by a Jewish philosopher, with several of the scholastics in the Middle Ages, with Leonardo da Vinci, Kepler and so on. Leibniz' concept 'infinitesimal' also has its background in a transcendental idealism. The concept 'infinite' was also used, and to think in infinite processes was allowed. It has been proposed that the Greeks' rejection of the 'actual infinite,' especially such as expressed by Aristotle, was one of the principal reasons why they did not manage to unite arithmetic and geometry. This was about introducing a concept that the mathematicians saw with their 'spiritual eye.' The boldness in creating new concepts has much of its explanation in philosophy and religion, and has implied that large parts of mathematics in our time have been described as *"The Science of the Infinite,"* as Hermann Weyl has expressed it. [Weyl 1950]

Even if the old understanding of mathematics as the truth about nature has faded in our days, mathematics still proves to be surprisingly useful in the study of nature. Fields such as group theory, non-Euclidean geometry, and statistical theories appear to be of key importance to understanding the physical world round us.

Conclusions

The first part of an answer to our quest for the origin of Western science must be with the Greeks. They gave the Europeans the right kind of rational thinking. The triumph of the Greek philosophy was that it operated with a rational notion of the Universe. According to the Greek view, the Universe is ordered and based on mathematical principles and ideas. Structure and order were considered to be essential for the understanding of the Universe, and mathematics was the key to this abstract harmony. In this way the human intellect could comprehend the universe. This later on also became the 'mental tool' in modern science.

But the Greek culture alone did not give us the scientific breakthrough. They became in a way 'too theoretical.' Science for them was a part of philosophy. They put too much stress on reaching the truth by metaphysical and rational analysis of the universe. The Greek position was that truth came from man's intellect, and not from the outer, physical world. This implied that their great philosophers were the actual authority. Aristotle was considered to be the greatest among the Greek authorities, and science was based on his thinking more than on observation of the outer world.

The Greek thinking was, however, transferred via the Arab culture to Europe in the Middle Ages. Here we also encounter the analogy where the Universe was likened to a clockwork. The historian Lynn White Jr. writes that:

> "… regularity, mathematically predictable relationships, facts quantitatively measurable, were looming larger in men's picture of the universe. And the great clock, partly because its inexorability was so playfully masked, its mechanism so humanized by its whimsicalities, furnished the picture. It is in the works of the great ecclesiastic and mathematician Nicholas Oresmus, who died in 1382 as Bishop of Lisieux, that we first find the metaphor of the universe as a vast mechanical clock created and set running by God so that 'all the wheels move as harmoniously as possible.' It was a notion with a future; eventually the metaphor became a metaphysics." [White, jr. 1962, p.125.]

This relation must further on be seen in connection with the spiritual climate that was born in Europe with the Renaissance in the South and the Reformation in the North. In this epoch, religion was an important element in cultural life. What people were thinking about God had a strong influence on their concept of nature, and thereafter had effects on their methods to explore nature. In the 16th and 17th century a new worldview was born.

The mathematician Alfred N. Whitehead was a century ago working together with Bertrand Russell on a large philosophical work supposed to give philosophy the same firm basis as science. They intended to reach this goal by using the mathematical science as model. While Russell through his whole life expressed a negative attitude towards a religious worldview, Whitehead changed his understanding of religion. Whitehead insisted that there were convincing evidence that Christianity instead of having been a hindrance for the development of scientific thinking, rather was one of the necessary prerequisites for the modern technological-scientific investigation of nature. Without the Christian conception of the world, created with order and meaning by a divine rational intelligence, science and its interpretation of existence would not have taken place. Whitehead expresses it like this:

> "When we compare this tone of thought in Europe with the attitude of other civilizations when left to themselves, there seems but one source for its origin. It must come from the medieval insistence on the rationality of God, ..." [Whitehead 1926, p. 15]

In other words, because the first scientists believed that the Universe was created by a sensible God, they were not surprised to discover that by the use of reason, it was possible to find some truths of nature and the Universe upon observations and experiments. Men like Kepler, Galileo, Cavalieri, Pascal, Barrow and Newton were all deeply religious and saw the Universe as a design from God's hand. All these pioneers may only be properly understood on the background of the theology where they had their roots. The Bible was not considered a textbook in physics, but it was understood as forming a basic framework within which science itself could be performed. The esthetical qualities of the equations describing the laws of nature and their optimal initial conditions provided the deepest and ultimate guarantee and explanation of a divine design of the universe as taught in the Bible.

According to Whitehead, Jewish-Christian theology should be conceived as the *"the mother of science"* who gave us *"the faith in the possibility of science"* [Whitehead 1926, p. 16]. An understanding of the laws in the material world should also contribute to bettering mankind's daily life. Of course, religion was not the only element that made modern science. We have mentioned inheritance from the Greeks, and social, economical and political factors also played a significant role. But Christianity has been one of the creative and sustaining components. Albert Einstein also underlined the important religious element related to science when stating:

> "Science without religion is lame, religion without science is blind." [Einstein 1950, p.27]

The classic Greek thinking was, as we have seen, subjected to the rational record. But the new worldview that was born in Europe made all scientific activity subjected to the record that could be made from the observations - even if they at first did not seem to be rational at all. Problems were complicated, but solvable because the objective reality existed and was rational and mathematical. In this way two great philosophical trends were united in Europe: Greek philosophy and Jewish-Christian theology. The late R. Hooykaas, who was professor of the History of Science, states:

> "For the building materials of Science (logic, mathematics, the beginning of a rational interpretation of the world) we have to look to the Greeks; but the vitamins indispensable for a healthy growth came from the biblical concept of creation." [Hooykaas 1972, p.85]

Therefore, we must not understand the rise of modern science as a change from faith towards science, or from religion towards criticism, or from an authoritarian view towards a liberation of man's curiosity, or from superstition towards exact measurement. Such presentations are often given both in literature and in lectures. They are, nevertheless, obviously mistaken.

The new science was developed precisely on the basis of what Genesis in the Bible states about reality - namely that the universe is not governed by a lot of fragmented, mythical or magical forces, but instead of a causal relationship. Matter itself is not inhabited by a soul, but it is functioning on the basis of laws that man is capable of comprehending. The world is real, and is discernible in a manner that it is possible for man to grasp intellectually. The unique historic period which we have discussed above is therefore a good example of a positive interaction and linking between science and religion. Within this period of time there were few or no disputes between religion and science. It was rather like a quiet alliance with mutual connections. In the catholic countries the relations were somewhat more upset, but nothing like a regular strife between religion and science.

Often Christianity has been criticized as being restrictive on scientific thinking. Individual representatives from the church have without doubt done stupid things toward scientists, but this constitutes only a small part of the total picture. With the above analysis I have tried to present the true interaction between Christian faith and science that took place in our culture during the 17th century. Faith obviously had a fertilizing and promoting influence on science. The church as such may not be said to represent some type of front against new discoveries and ideas. Problems primarily arose when new theories were advocated as ultimate and final truths, or when the Scriptures were (mis)used to legitimate what was discovered. When the researchers had a sober and undogmatic attitude to their ideas, they had little or nothing to fear from the church. Many church leaders also were active in promoting open minds and forwarding scientific thinking.

Science never developed as a proper and satisfactory study of reality in non-Christian cultures. Neither did it develop in the worshipping of Saints of the Middle Ages, where most of the focus was on how man could go to heaven and less on our existence here and now.

Today, of course, a person may be a clever scientist, no matter what his religion is. Science works with nature out there, and not only with nature as it is apparent in my mind. So a Buddhist is during his research exposed to the same objective reality as the Christian is. The question is, however, whether or not a non-Christian worldview could have produced science as we now know it. The evidence from history suggests that the answer is that non-Christian worldviews are unlikely to have been able to give rise to anything like science, even though the scientific method by now is accepted and adopted in most cultures around the world.

The general pattern that we are facing is an intellectual breakthrough, which took place because of the inner dynamics of some very special scientific, religious, cultural and social relations. Every one of these ingredients played its role, and without one of the elements the events might have happened quite differently. The splitting of the mind in faith and science of our day may lead us into a cold and technical world. In my opinion, it is very likely that we'll be unable to manage our inventions rightly and to understand creation properly, until we again can see material reality in its correct relations to the transcendental realities. Science still has much to gain by 'honoring its father and its mother.'

References

Berlinski, D. *A Tour of the Calculus.* Mandarin Paperbacks, 1996.

Brewster, D. *Memoirs of the life, writings, and discoveries of Sir Isaac Newton.* New York, Johnson Reprint Corp., 1965.

Brooke, John H. *Science and Religion: Some Historical Perspectives.* Cambridge University Press,1991.

Boyer, C.B. *A History of Mathematics*, New York, 1968.

Brynhildsen, Aa. *Johannes Kepler*, Oslo, 1976.

Burtt, E.A. *The Metaphysical Foundation of Physical Science.*1924.

Butterfield, H. *The Origins of Modern Science.* London, 1957.

Caspar, M. and Dyck, W. von *Johannes Kepler in seinen Briefen.* Munich and Berlin, 1930.

Caspar, M. *Johannes Kepler*, London, 1959.

Cohen. *Isaac Newton's Papers and Letters on Natural Philosophy.* Cambridge, 1958.

Drake, Stillman. *Discoveries and opinions of Galileo.* New York, Doubleday & Company, 1957.

Einstein, A. *Out of my later years.* New York, Philosophical Library, 1950.

Einstein, A. and Infeld, L. *The Evolution of Physics.* Cambridge, 1938.

Galilei, G. *Dialogues concerning two new sciences*, New York, 1954.

Galilei, G. *Dialogue concerning two chief World Systems*, 1970.

Henry, John. *The Scientific Revolution and the Origins of Modern Science.* Studies in European History. Macmillian Press Ltd, 1997.

Holton, G. *The Thematic Origins of Science.* Cambridge, Mass, 1973.

Hooykaas, R. *Religion and the Rise of Modern Science.* Edinburgh and London, 1972.

Kepler, J. *Neue Astronomie.* Übersetzt und Eingeleitet von Max Caspar, 1929.

Kline, M. *Mathematies: A Cultural Approach.* New York, 1962.

Kline, M. *Mathematical Thought from Ancient to Modern Times*. New York, 1972.

Koestler, A. *The Sleepwalkers. A History of Man's Changing Vision of the Universe*. New York, 1959.

Kozhamthadam, J. *The Discovery of Kepler's Laws : The Interaction of Science, Philosophy, and Religion.* University of Notre Dame Press, 1995.

Kristiansen, R.E. *Naturvitenskap og kristen tro: fellesskap og brytninger.* Origo no. 40 and 42, 1993.

Kuhn, T.S. *The Structure of Scientific Revolutions*. Chicago and London, 2.ed., 1970.

Lindberg, D. and Numbers, R. (Eds.) *God and nature. Historical Essays on the Encounter Between Christianity and Science.* Los Angeles and Berkeley, 1986.

Merton, Robert K. and Trenn, Thaddeus J. (Eds.) *Genesis and development of a scientific fact.* University of Chicago Press, 1979.

Middelmann, U. and Wilder-Smith, A.E. *Naturvitenskapens grunnlag og begrensning* (Norwegian). University in Trondheim, 1979.

Needham, J. *The Grand Titration. Science and Society in East and West.* London, 1969.

Newton, I. *Principia Mathematica.* A Revision of Motte's Translation, by Cajori. California, 1946.

Polkinghorne, J. *Scientists as Theologians*. London, 1996.

Royal Society. *Newton Tercentenary Celebrations*. Cambridge University Press, 1947.

Schaeffer, F.A. *How Should we then Live? The Rise and Decline of Western Thought and Culture*. New Jersey, 1976.

Suppe, F.(ed.) *The Structure of Scientific Theories*. University of Illinois, 1974.

Thorvaldsen, S. *Opprinnelsen til den matematiske analyse*. Norwegian treatise in mathematics, University in Trondheim, 1979.

Thorvaldsen, S. *Keplers vei til planetlovene* (in Norwegian). Nordisk matematisk tidsskrift, no. 2, 1983, page 49-58.

Weyl, H. *Axiomatic versus constructive procedures in mathematics*, The Mathematical Intelligencer 7 (4), 1985, p. 10-17.

Wilder, R.L. *Evolution of Mathematical Concepts*. John Wiley and Sons, 1968.

White Jr., L. *Mediaeval Technology and Social Change*. Oxford, 1962.

White Jr., L. *Science and the Sense of Self: The Medieval Background of a Modern Confrontation*. Dædalus, Journal of the American Academy of Arts and Sciences, spring 1978, page 47-59.

Whitehead, A.N. *Science and Modern World*. Cambridge, 1926.

Reading for the Creator's Discourse: Speech Acts and Transcendence in Genesis 1-3

NICOLAI WINTHER-NIELSEN

"....to speak is not, as such, to express one's inner self but to take up a normative stance in the public domain. The myth dies hard that to read a text for authorial discourse is to enter the dark world of the author's psyche. It's nothing of the sort. It is to read to discover what assertings, what promisings, what requestings, what commandings, are rightly to be ascribed to the author on the ground of her having set them down." (Wolterstorff 1995:93).

Abstract

How we can read and communicate with a Divine discourser is the focal issue of several highly interesting contemporary approaches. First, the more 'classical' theological and textlinguistic approaches of Aksel Valen-Sendstad, John Sailhamer, and others reaffirm the revealed Biblical ontology in new and interesting ways. Second, the philosopher of religions, Nicholas Wolterstorff, exploits modern insights of speech act theory to reflect on how God is discoursing through Scripture. Third, speech acts also play a central role in a brand-new approach to interactional hermeneutics proposed by Kevin Vanhoozer. All these contemporary approaches are applied and discussed and then exploited in a reading of Genesis 1-3 informed by linguistic pragmatics and discourse studies.

1. On God, Creation and the reading of texts

Correlating lofty themes like time, reality and transcendence inevitably calls for and even stimulates new and fresh approaches in various areas of scientific research. There are no easy ways to tie a transcendent God outside time and space into the reality of the spatial and temporal world we personally know. We are facing the perennial question of how finite human beings can know and talk about a real transcendent God.

Creation has always been at centre of this intellectual debate. Jewish-Christian believers confess that a transcendent God created our real world at the beginning of time, while modern popular and secular scientific wisdom often simply puts this belief aside in advance. What follows is no attempt to challenge the current scientific creeds, but rather an attempt to ask some other equally valid questions.

As a theologian and linguist I will suggest that Genesis chapters 1-3 invite us to consider the language-philosophical issue of how to communicate on authors and other kinds of creators of language, especially on the Creator whom we hear speaking as the Transcendent in the early pages of the Hebrew Scriptures. This God communicates orally and in a written mode which is incorporated in the Hebrew Scriptures, and eventually in the Christian canon. In the beginning of Genesis he speaks his enlightening utterance 'let there be light' (1:3). The Creator of the universe illuminates his own being as a speaking and acting God who crowns his work by creating man, whom he endows with the capacity of speech. As creation is known virtually only in Jewish-Christian belief we are actually also asking how language and communication is defined within this particular tradition.

The fresh questions on the contemporary scene are numerous and potentially very fruitful. What do we do when we read for the discourse of a transcendent Creator? Can he speak? What does it mean to create speech? What do creative speakers/writers do in doing what they do? In what sense can the Creator of the Hebrew Scriptures serve as model for any other creative speakers? And conversely, can our reflection on our own speaking help us to understand the Creator? Last, but not least, how does the Creator's language fare in our postmodern world?

The discussion here will focus on how a few selected contemporary proposals have set out the ontological reality of Divine discourse in terms of theology and text-linguistics, speech act theory, and communicative interaction. I will present the following contemporary thinkers and their key stance on three issues:

(i) Language and Biblical texts as revealed ontology in the work of Aksel Valen-Sendstad (1996) and John Sailhamer (1995);
(ii) Language as spoken by a Divine speaker in the reflections of the philosopher of religions, Nicholas Wolterstorff (1995);
(iii) Language as usage in interpersonal communication between God and humans in the hermeneutics of Kevin Vanhoozer (1998).

My personal background in linguistic pragmatics will become apparent in the way I relate these proposals to the early pages of Genesis.[1]

To summarize, then, the goal is to spell out what it means to read a text for its Creator's discourse in the sense of what is *being done* in speech or words (Wolterstorff 1995:37). Or, *how can text and talk in doing something, function as utterances of a transcendent Being*. The key solution is to read for the discourser's publicly revealed stance, as suggested by the opening quote from Nicholas Wolterstorff (1995:93).

---

[1] On language use, see among others Mey (1993), Schiffrin (1994), and Clark (1996), and in relation to fact and fiction in Hebrew narrative, Winther-Nielsen (2002).

2. *In the beginning God created the heavens and the earth* and the language in Gen 1:1: The theological and text-linguistic ontologies of Valen Sendstad (1996) and Sailhamer (1995)

The opening phrases of the Bible present a new world being shaped by a divine Being who determines the parameters for all future natural reference. The Hebrew Scriptures' unique collection of literature links God and the creation of the universe into a universal ontology where the One, in the challenging language of Isaiah 45:18-21, is the only true and reliably speaking God.

The opening Biblical statement of creation clearly diverges from a number of other alternative stories on the origin of reality. The most prominent version of the Ancient Near East opens as follows:

> "When on high no name was given to heaven, Nor below was the netherworld called by name, Primeval Apsu was their progenitor, And matrix-Tiamat was she who bore them all. They were mingling their waters....." *Epic of Creation* [*Enuma Eslish*] 1.1-5 (tr. Foster 1997:391).

It tells about the revolt of the petty gods and the final victory of exalted Marduk of Babylon. As usual in the Ancient Near East this mythical story is a conservative preservation of the structure of society. The religion of the city state and of the later kingdoms and empires were formed to secure the power of kings and priests and to guarantee the continuation of conditions which had evolved in daily human life in the ancient world.

A different story became increasingly popular by the end of the last century when positivistic scientists united with philosophers of religion to create a new account of the evolution of the species. The Darwinian story was eventually told somewhat along the following lines: 'In the beginning there was nothing at all; out of nothing something eventually had to explode and bring some matter into being which could then change endlessly for billions of years to produce the reality we know.' This naturalistic and rationalistic story about cosmic forces creating itself has by and large captured the imagination of modern man and helped him to dispense with theism and creation. Modern man has managed to adjust to a world view based on survival of the fittest in a cruel process towards more perfect forms of life. This impersonal modern story has given rise to ideas of materialistic, scientific and political progress in exploitation, war and even genocide.

The story of modernity is now slowly demasking as postmodern man attempts to tell a new and different story of postmodernity. He can now listen to deconstruction of (others') authoritarian and suppressive stories. Derrida, in *Writing and Difference* (1978), has subverted metaphysics and transcendence by creating a meaningless play of language and interpretation. Exploiting Biblical imagery and stabbing the knife of deconstruction deep into the open scars of modernity, he heralds that prophets are gone and poets must now take over, the point being that the poet does not *"receive his speech and his law from God"* (1978:67). Furthermore: *"Between the fragments of the broken Tablets the poem grows ... The necessity of commentary, like poetic necessity, is the very form of exiled speech. In the beginning is hermeneutics."* (Ibid).

In the new belief of latter-day deconstructivists, we are back into empty space before language was part of creation. The new semiotics of postmodernism severs the connection between text and reality and places the phantasies of interpretation in its place. It is all hermeneutics and of late it has become a point of debate whether we, in the final analysis, can understand texts at all (Vanhoozer 1998:19).

The three major historically and culturally determined stories of origin are thus the conservative stories of antiquity, the mutational explanations of modern positivism and the poetical destruction of interpretation in postmodernism. Over against these stories, the Jewish-Christian story is remarkably impartial and timeless, devoid of conservatism, rationalism, or irrationalism. It confronts former and current beliefs with a story of monotheism, universal creation, and hymnic speech. This introduction to the Bible *"declares the metaphysical assumption, that is, a present transcendent*

Creator-God, that acts as the philosophical cornerstone of the entire biblical revelation." (Mathews 1996:22).

The story in early Genesis is often reinterpreted in a mythical or even evolutionary mode, but there are also serious attempts today to reflect on the biblical texts on the basis of the extant biblical texts. Two recent approaches may illustrate how language and transcendence may be combined within the framework of theology and text-linguistics.

The new voice in systematic theology is sounded by the Danish-Norwegian professor Aksel Valen-Sendstad, who has formulated his new approach in a mature statement in his non-translated Norwegian work *The Foundations of Belief* which in *"reality-theoretical conformity with the Holy Scriptures"* restates *"the ontology of the revelation"* (1996:72).[2]

Valen-Sendstad's ontological analysis of the reality which is presupposed in the books of the Bible clearly differs from any intellectual reflection inspired by the presuppositions of autonomous philosophy (76).[3] Valen-Sendstad fundamentally agrees with the postmodern demasking of modernity but formulates a completely different alternative by focusing on an understanding which is true to the reality revealed in the Christian Bible and in that sense is 'objective'. This new statement of Christian beliefs dares to be both profoundly 'antiquarian' in adhering to the Bible, and profoundly contemporary in addressing issues of our time on the basis on an ontology of revelation.

---

[2] In some ways Valen-Sendstad presents a confessional Lutheran version of the program launched by Carl F. Henry (1976-83) to reflect theologically on the speaking of God.

[3] Valen-Sendstad emphasizes the otherness of Christian beliefs as did Karl Barth, but without reinterpreting Christianity on the basis of Kant's anti-metaphysical critiques of reason and understanding and its spin-off in historical-critical reinterpretation of the Bible for the last 200 years (1996:96 n. 208).

Valen-Sendstad suggests how we can share the view of reality represented by the authors of the Bible and Christian authors like Augustine and Luther. He formulates a *"Biblical language-ontology"* by focusing on three important basic principles (102-104 and in more detail 115-214):

(a) The Biblical view of reality is that God *"gives knowledge about himself and communicates with human beings in verbal language"*; this is always a *Verbum externum* coming from outside to man.[4] It reflects how man is created in the image of God, especially in his ability to communicate and enter into communion (*leve i fællesskab*).[5]

(b) The religious language of the Bible must be understood in terms of the incarnated Word, Christ, the Son of God, as unfolded in John 1.

The word of revelation must be interpreted against its historical context and background related to time, space and persons in history, and communicated in meaningful contemporary language.

The kernel in Valen-Sendstad's ontology is thus the Creator's divinity and his speech, Christ as the Word, and the contemporary communication of the Scriptures. Reality is fundamentally interpreted in terms of God's word in creation (1993:223), and the language and story of Genesis 1-3 forms the backbone in his theological reflection on religious language. Divine

---

[4] God is completely outside and *"beyond (transcendent) in relation to ... 'human-autonomous' perception, rationality and cognition (erkendelse, fornuft og forstand) ... What and how God is can not be told and expressed without revelation"* (Valen-Sendstad 1993:224).

[5] Thus especially: *"Communion between God and man is constituted by what is verbal-linguistic, and is being conceptualized analogously to fellowship and communication among men (Samfundet mellom Gud og mennesket konstitueres ved det verbal-språklige og er tenkt analogt til samfund og kommunikasjon mellom mennesker)"* (Valen-Sendstad 1996:102). This communication is always related to creationhood so that word is correlated with doing and with reality.

discourse is the *Verbum creans* and *conservans*, the word of God which creates reality, cosmos, and man, and upholds it as revealed in Genesis 1 and 2 (1996:140). There is the same ontological intra-structure in the speech of God and man following Gen 1:3 etc, so that human language derives from divine language: *"language is in and with God"* (1996:118), God gave it to man at creation, but did not create it only then.

A second kind of approach also breaks away from modern rational readings of the Bible, but instead of taking its point of departure in a systematic theology of revelation it is influenced by a contemporary understanding of texts. One of the best proponents of this new approach is the theologian John Sailhamer (1995:200-201) who formulates a canonical approach to studying the theology of the Old Testament on the basis of text-theoretical and text-linguistic notions, and whose work on the Pentateuch combines literary and linguistic analysis (1992).

Sailhamer's main point is that the narrative texts of the Old Testament render a realistic description of the real world through a textual world (1995:45).[6] To read Scripture is to be an observer of the deeds of God in history in the same way as experiencing reality in a theatre or watching a movie made for an audience (38-39). Meaning is communicated to this observer through the events and persons presented in the stories of Scripture. A reader only experiences a representation of the real world and this world is therefore only true and reliable in the same sense as a photograph: it pictures a real existing object without being this object in actual reality.

The obvious theological implication of Sailhamer's approach is therefore that we can depend totally on the reality represented by the narrators in their *mimesis* (46). The locus of God's revelation is nothing but the narration in the Biblical writings which can never be supplanted by another story like a history of salvations or some hypothetical history of Israel (56).

---

[6]The real world is represented in language itself which imitates the real world (Sailhamer 1995:49-50).

A text-linguistic approach can explain several details in the narration of Genesis 1:1-3. The opening clause of Genesis functions in a unique double role of both narrating an event and locating it in brand-new time with space to come, and this is reflected in the word order *In the beginning God created* (Winther-Nielsen 1992). The grandiose creation of the universe described through the word-pair *the heavens and the earth* is then followed by a story-initial description of the original state of the newly created earth. By these means the story from the start focuses on the earth as a suitable place of habitation (Sailhamer 1992:28-29, 82, 86).[7]

The grandiose literary structure is noted in most informed studies (see figure 1). The account has two panels, the first series describing a process of separation until the dry land appears, the second series a process of ordering and embellishing with higher forms of life. There is also a clear synonymous parallelism between the types of action both beginning in light and ending in life.

Day	Creation of		Day	Creation of	
1	Light	1:3-5	4	Luminaries	14-19
2	Water/Heaven	6-8	5	Animals Water/Heaven	20-23
3a	Sea/Land	9-10	6a	Animals Land	24-25
3b	Plants	11-13	6b	Man	26-31
			7	God's rest	2:1-3

Fig. 1: The structure of the creation days in Gen 1:1-2.3

Linguistic analysis can underpin this structure by observations based on the initial clause of Gen 1:2. Tsumura (1989:41-43 *et passim*) has argued convincingly from Ancient Near Eastern texts and Biblical contexts that it should be rendered *the earth was unproductive and uninhabited* rather usual traditional translations like *formless void* (NRSV). These two terms anticipate the amazing structure of the creation account which in a first

---

[7]Sailhamer (1992:85) interprets the unproductive and uninhabited state of the earth as being shrouded in darkness and covered by water. Soon in v 11-12 and 29 it turns out that seed is even more important (Mathews 1996:57-58).

sequence of events describes how the earth is prepared for bringing forth the plant life described in 1:11-13 and in a second sequence narrates how the earth brings forth the movable animals on land described in 1:24-25 and how God as a culmination creates man in 1:26-27. These three creative acts on days three and six are singled out by double divine speech. The first series of three days reports how the earth became productive when plants sprawled from the earth and the second series of three days how the earth was inhabited by animal and man became its ruler. Both series solve what was announced as missing right from the start in v. 2.

There has been several important text-linguistic studies of Genesis 1-3. Andersen (1994) explores the effects of explicit vs. implicit reference to nominals in cross-clausal relationships and observes how the divine name is used in 26 out of 31 clauses in spite of being unnecessary for disambiguation except for a case like 12b where the reference to God follows a different subject in v 12a (1994:107). The effect of mentioning the name of God in a, for Hebrew, quite uncharacteristic way is that actions are singled out as independent and noticeable events. Andersen (1994:108) uses clusters marked by explicit subjects to analyse the component segments of Genesis 2, while Kempf (1993:373-374 and 1996:43-44) segments Genesis 2-3 into episodes determined by distinctions from discourse grammar.[8]

Text-linguistics can also clarify how Genesis 1 differs from other text types using language like *By the word of the Lord the Heavens were created, all their multitude by a breath from his mouth* (Psalms 33:6). The Genesis narrator informs of creation as part of his introduction to the history of Israel in Genesis (Sailhamer 1995:48). He represents it as a realistic past of a real world now gone forever, but in the language of everyday communication in writing and conversation. This narration clearly differs from the poetic version which has rhythm and parallelism and creates other expectations of expression and experience.

---

[8]For the toledoth-structure in 2:4 see now the survey in Mathews (1996:25-41). On a more literary division of Genesis 2-3, see Wenham (1987:50).

Both these approaches, the theological and the text-linguistic, renew the classical heritage of theology predating rationalism and modernity. It can be argued that Christian beliefs in a postmodern age may have to circumvent modernism to renew reformational and early exegetical stances. It is at least clear that both these contemporary approaches can contribute to a reconsideration of creation in terms of theology and text. However, both approaches are just two clear cases among other possible attempts to renew the 'classical' solutions by improving our understanding of the canonical texts and their view of the world. Current reflection beyond theology and linguistics can also improve on our understanding of the use of language in Bible and its relation to reality and the world, as we will show in the areas of philosophy and hermeneutics.

3. "*God said: 'Let there be light'*" and divine speech acts in the context of Gen 1:3: The language philosophical reflections of Wolterstorff (1995)

So far, we have seen more classical solutions emphasizing theology and text-linguistics. In the work of the Yale philosopher of religions, Nicholas Wolterstorff (1995), we find new reflections on Divine speech and Divine actions through language.

In the beginning of the creation account, we observe how the text shifts from narrative to a direct quote of the Creator uttering the famous words *Let there be light* (Gen 1:3) as the first of ten divine utterances in the account of Genesis 1 and the first instance of the *Verbum transcendente* (Valen-Sendstad 1996:134).[9] Hebrew thought therefore consistently presupposes the

---

[9]The *Verbum transcendente* is discussed in detail in Valen-Sendstad (1996:310). It is pre-existent like God (183), and God creates by this word (141, 143, cf. 121, 154, 200). This understanding of the word determines statements of trinitarian theology (239) and human anthropology (301-315).

existence of a totally transcendent God who speaks an immanent and completely appreciable Hebrew language accompanying his creative action. We therefore have to ask with Wolterstorff (1995:11) how God can be counted as a member of the group of language speakers when he is spirit (John 4:24) and has no tongue, nor a mouth in any literal sense of the word.

Wolterstorff's point of departure is what Augustine experienced back in 386 AD (1-8). One day he was told about Antony, the founder of the Egyptian monastic movement, who in the Coptic church had heard Jesus' story about a young rich man read aloud and heard God commanding himself by the words *"If you wish to be complete, go and sell your possessions and give to the poor, and you will have treasure in heaven; and come, follow me."* (Matt 19,21). Greatly impressed by the story Augustine himself the next day heard a girl in a neighbouring house singing *Tolle lege. Tolle lege: `Take and read. Take and read'* and took this highly unsual and unexpected utterance as God commanding him to read from his book with the letters of Saint Paul. His eyes caught the words of Romans 13:13-14: *Let us behave properly as in the day, not in carousing and drunkenness, not in sexual promiscuity and sensuality, not in strife and jealousy. But put on the Lord Jesus Christ, and make no provision for the flesh in regard to its lusts* and immediately he heard them as God's direct discourse to him through reading, stating that the creator of the heavens and the earth now commanded him to stay away from the lusts of the flesh.

The crucial lesson learned by Augustine was that God may speak through a word that is spoken aloud in a church or read in a book as well as through ordinary words of human beings. Wolterstorff suggests that this can be explained quite well on the basis of the theory of speech acts proposed by the language philosopher James Austin in his famous posthumous collection felicitously entitled *How to do things with words* (1962).[10]

The central tenet of speech act theory in Austin's proposal is that language is not only used in order to inform on content matter, because some statements

---

[10]Key figures like Austin, Searle, Morris, and Grice are conveniently presented in Schiffrin (1994:49-96, 190-231).

are part of the doing of an action (1962:5). He captured this difference in distinguishing between declarative *constatives* and the *performatives* of marriage ceremonies, naming of ships, bequeathing by a will, and betting. Austin realized that the right words should be used and the right circumstances should hold to allow for a performative interpretation (13).[11] An utterance is a saying with sense and reference in its predicating and referring expressions (technically, the propositions as *locutionary acts),* but it is also a doing or acting by performing an intended function as when an imperative is perceived as directing someone to perform a certain thing (the *illocutionary force*). This force of an utterance should not be confused with the actual obedient response to an imperative in action (the *perlocutionary force*). The crucial distinction is between saying something in *locution* and doing something in saying this by *illocution* (1962:108).[12]

locutionary acts	to utter or write words
illocutionary acts	to perform actions by means of uttering words
perlocutionary acts	achieving an intended response by the hearer

As speakers we perform *illocutionary acts* when we try to get our hearers to understand what we mean, while affecting and changing their lives is something completely different. We can illustrate this by the famous case of Augustine. God commanded him to open a book which is an *illocutionary act,* and in doing so God did not communicate something new to him, but rather used an already known and revealed *locution,* whose propositional content is available in Romans, and when Augustine personally heeded the force of these words they also performed a *perlocutionary act.*

Later on, Austin's student Searle (1969) reworked and refined the theory by proposing new crucial distinctions between content, force and effect defining linguistic communication as performance of speech acts (1969:16). Austin

---

[11] Appointing require that the person has this authority (Austin 1962:34), while betting misfires if it is not taken on (36-37). All utterances only hold under the appropriate felicity conditions (46-47, 136-137)

[12] Wolterstorff (1995:13) follows Austin, while Searle (1969:24) developed his own terms.

(1962:109ff) had proposed a classification of speech acts, but Searle (1977) also refined the taxonomy to explain how speakers get hearers to believe what they assert or comply with their requests, answer their questions, and follow their advice. They can make future offers or promises and express their own inner feelings, and they can perform something directly through language as when they say *I baptize you* or *I sentence you*. Refining and reshaping Austin's taxonomy he posited a finite classifiable number of 5 speech act types (see figure based on the discussion in 1977:34-38).[13]

The work of Austin and Searle has shown that linguistic expressions are only in effect with the right participants under the right circumstances, i.e., if they meet the right contextual conditions (as specified in *felicity* or *appropriateness conditions*). The goal of language use (its *illocutionary point*) is to communicate a publicly intended effect by committing a speaker and getting a listener to do something (Clark 1996:134-135).

Type	Point of utterance	Key examples
Statement	get H to *believe* X	Assertion, prediction, confession, denial
Directive	get H to *do*	Request action (command) or information (question)
Commissive	commit S to *future action*	Promise, offer (conditional promise)
Expressive	S *expresses feeling*	Thank, apologize, congratulate, greet
Declarative	*do in saying*	Institutional act to change/determine state of affairs

Fig. 2.   Searle's five Speech Act types (H=Hearer; S=Speaker)

Speech act theory was applied to Genesis 1 already by Evans (1963) and developed by White (1991) for literary and structural analysis. The recent work of Wagner (1997) follows the classical notions of Austin and Searle

---

[13] In current research many of the problems of Searle's scheme are exposed, e.g., that some acts belong to several types, context is mainly cognitive and speaker focused, interaction is undeveloped. However, almost all language researchers will grant that it is a useful gross classification (thus recently Clark 1996:136).

much closer and covers much more data in Hebrew. Wolterstorff applies the theory in order to distinguish between revelation and divine speech (20-21).[14] In revelation God uncovers information that has so far been hidden and unknown, but in communicating his words God must always be doing an act and what is communicated will both depend on the understanding of the reader (32-33) and on the normative stance assumed by the speaker (35).

Wolterstorff also brings sociolinguistic insights into play.[15] If we distinguish between different discourse modes we can understand how two different agents can speak at the same time, as when a secretary is authorized to speak in the name of an employer in *deputized discourse* (42-46), or when one person simply uses and identifies with the formulations and even the aims of someone else in *appropriated discourse* (51-52).[16] Discourse mode even helps Wolterstorff to reflect on different functions in story telling (53-54).

---

[14] In the famous case of Abraham offering Isaac in Genesis 22 God commands something whose meaning differs radically from the linguistic content (Wolterstorff 1995:22). Speech action also clarifies how it is possible that a new audience may hear God say something different through the same locution (54-56). He uses this theory to reject Riceour's understanding of revelation as text rather than divine speech (58-63, 130-131) and supplants the text-structuralist approach with an *"authorial-discourse interpretation"*. The new concept of divine speech also counters Derrida's attack on the transcendent and signified (153-170).

[15] For the following note especially Clark (1996:4--21) and for Hebrew, Winther-Nielsen (*2002*).

[16] Wolterstorff (53-55) uses *appropriated discourse* to explain how the whole Bible can form a single work even if it is a composite of many individual works. Along these lines Vanhoozer (1998:349) reflects on the Christian canon as an overlaying, or supervening, genre which has the *illocutionary force* to confess faith and testify to Christ. Canonical intent then derives from divine authorship: *"the canon represents divinely appropriated human discourse; taken together, the various books of the Bible constitute the Word of God."*

One person may report on an event in order to assert that this is what happened, while another person may use the same story to illustrate basic human conditions.

These reflections on the pragmatic aspects of divine speaking can also unlock some peculiar features in the account of creation in Genesis 1. It is remarkable that God is quoted in every act of creation, so that the information about light being put on is preceded by the direct quote *let there be light* (1:3). Intuitively we probably tend to classify this divine speech act as a case of God uttering words that perform something instantly just by being spoken. However, it is hardly a Declarative like *I (hereby) baptize you*, or a performative formula (Austin 1962:61-62). Searle (1979:18) explicitly points out that Declaratives rely on a certain position of a speaker and hearer within an institution, and this is not the case with the Creator's words in Gen 1:3 nor with a case like the naming of *day* and *night* in v 5. When God called light 'day' and darkness 'night' he certainly did not bring them into existence, because both were present already i v 2 and 3.[17] In nine out of ten cases, the Divine utterances are not Declaratives, and the sole and very significant exception is that an explicit performative diction is used when God officially tells man that *I hereby give you all plants* (v 29). This is a Divine doing enabling man instantly for his special task of ruling the earth (Grünwald 1989).

Furthermore, the popular notion of a semi-magical effectiveness of divine utterances is not necessarily presupposed in the story of Genesis 1. It is not literally stated that the light was effected by the uttering of the words, but rather that in succession to this utterance the light *was* present there as a

---

[17]Naming only highlights some particular feature in the existing state of affairs by conventional linguistic means. This is also the case among Hebrews who fare far better than their reputation for magic (see Thiselton 1992:292-293). The example of Gen 25:22-26 is quite typical: when Rebecca observed the struggle between her unborn twins and saw the younger grasping the heels of the elder at birth. Believing that events are being shaped by God she captured this sign in naming him Jacob.

reality and by pragmatic implication certainly caused by an act of God. Nor is this utterance shaped in the characteristic performative form of first person present, e.g. *I hereby put light into existence/switch on the light*, but in the form of the wish *Let there be light* which is a jussive in Hebrew.[18]

Another argument against the magical interpretation derives from the form of the highly structured literary account in Genesis 1. It has a very clear common pattern in the way that Genesis 1 presents ten divine utterances concerning eight creative acts described through sets of seven elements of which at least 5 are formulaic (note Roman numbers below in figure 3 based on Wenham 1987:6-7). They all occur within striking patterns: among 10 divine utterances are 8 utterances of *Let there be* etc. for 8 creative acts, but there are only 7 instances of each of the other elements distributed on only 6 creation days.

Form elements: Day	1	2	3a	3b	4	5	6a	6b
Introduction: *God said*	3	6	9	11	14	20f, 22	24	26, 28f
Utterance: *Let there be* etc	3	6	9	11	14		24	26
Execution: *And it happened*	3	7	9	11	15		24	30
Activity	3	7		12	16	21	25	27
Evaluation: *And God saw...*	4			12	18	21	25	31
Naming	5 (2x)	8	10 (2x)			22		28
Closure: *It was evening...*	5	8	10	13	19	23		31 (2.2)

Fig.3. The structure and form elements in Genesis 1,1-2,3 (Wenham)

Yet, this amazing structure also brings out some peculiar variations in the description of the creative work, which characterizes creation as divine accomplishments without instant actions, as the utterances spoken by the Creator do not coincide with the production of the objects. In v 6 it is

---

[18] Note most recently Wagner's (1997:100-121) work on explicit performatives in 1st person *qatal* form.

explicitly stated that God wishes a firmament and only afterwards makes it. In v 11 God utters the wish *Let the earth put forth vegetation...* and the narrator confirms *And it was so*, yet God only made it happen when *the earth produced* them which is a very far cry from a direct performative act. The same goes for the luminaries which are only mentioned as being placed in specific functions (v 14-19).[19] The beasts of sea and air are expressly said to have been created by God (v 21), but in this case God only wishes *Let the waters bring forth swarms of living creatures, and let birds fly above the earth across the dome of the sky* (v 20). God even wishes the earth to produce beasts on land just like the plants (v 24 and 11-12), even if this of course still implies that God created them (v 25).[20]

Genesis 1 culminates in four powerful divine words on the sixth day and two final addresses of man. Until this point God has created everything according to its kind and with reproductive means (v 11-12, 21, 23), but man is created as an individual man and woman (v 26-28). Here the utterance *Let us make* in v 26 is clearly separated by a summarizing statement of the creation of man in v 27 as against the detail of 2:7 and 22 which shatters the basis for instantaneous creation by word in case of the highest form of creation.

---

[19] Sailhamer (1992:28,92-93) observes from careful linguistic analysis that the light of Gen 1:3-5 came from the sun created in 1:1, and the luminaries were only given a particular function as calendars in 1:14-19. It is not obvious that the light of 1:3 emerged from God, while the real luminaries were only created on day 4 as still maintained by Mathews (1996:145) and many others.

[20] Due to unfamiliarity with speech act theory, Sailhamer (1992:90) chooses the solution that the divine word *per se* created (i.e., that creation occurred by *God said...*), while the following report of creation just functions as "a reader-oriented comment." Andersen (1998:195) accepts a performative interpretation of the words, but views this case as only a border case.

Finally, it is a fair implication of the account that our capacity for speech derives from the discoursing Creator who made us in his own likeness.[21]

This example also proves that, contrary to common opinion, the Creator's utterances should not be interpreted as commands or orders neither in form nor in function. God does, of course, not command non-existing man to be created. And even if one might argue that God issued commands to the light, firmament, water, earth and luminaries, it is very difficult to imagine how the water and air in 1:20 could be commanded to produce fish and flies and v 21 maintains that God created all these creatures. This is not contradicted by the poet who says that *He spoke and it happened* (Psalm 33:9), because this only underpins the tight relation between word and action without specifying the particular illocutionary act.[22]

Another even less likely option in terms of the structure and language of the story is that God utters an Expressive speech act which would mean that his intention is stated as a personal wish, but who would he address with this kind of speech act, and on whom would he depend to have him/them create what he wanted? The Divine plural form of exhortation in *Let us make* (1:26) need not be Expressive if the context instead supports an interpersonal appeal to start some extraordinary significant work.

Wagner (1997:27) in his extensive research on speech acts in Hebrew notes that the Divine speech acts are rarely of the explicit performative type with *hereby* but rather primary performative utterings which can be classified as Commissives. This means that divine speech generally is an announcement of what God promises to do at some point in the future, but because God commits himself to a specific future action it is only natural that the

---

[21] See Valen-Sendstad (1996:309-311), and note the statements on the word in creation (129, 170-171). All the statements are thoroughly personal (Sailhamer 1992:94-95).

[22] The Hebrew word for *commanded* in Psalm 33:9 should in the view of our account of Genesis 1 be translated *he announced it*, i.e. told it in advance, and so it happened.

execution often appears to occur instantaneously (157-158). Nevertheless Wagner interprets the Divine words in Genesis 1 as a unique case of words creating what they say in a religious-mythical world of imagination (160).

However, in view of the fact that the account does not identify the pre-announcing Divine utterance with the subsequent Divine act there is no reason to assume that Genesis 1 belongs to some special mythical world of magic words. In each case the divine word opens a new section and introduces a new creative act before the following creative act. If this is also interpreted as a Commissive, it means that God for every day at its beginning solemnly announces what he is now committing himself to make. The Commissive alternative would require a larger part played by indirectness: by saying *Let there be* God actually means *I now want to do*.

Whether Commissive, Expressive or even Directive, it is at least quite clear that the narrator wants us to listen to these utterances from God in order to understand that God now assumes a public stance as the performer of the acts of creation. The discussion can also show how a detailed discussion of speech acts may actually enrich our understanding of the real world events presupposed in the narrative.

Wolterstorff (1995:208) only once deals with the Divine speech in creation. Discussing the nature of poetry he reflects on how the word of man can mediate God's speech when men are speaking about God or to God. In order to explain how God can possibly appropriate the speech of men in reflection, praise or prayer he suggest that we should try to grasp the main point of the words and sharply distinguish them from *"the author's particular way of making or developing that point"* (209). Wolterstorff's key is to let diction depend on man, but point to God as it is clear from his discussion of Psalm 93 (209-210):

> The LORD is king, he is robed in majesty; the LORD is robed, he is girded with strength. He has established the world; it shall never be moved;

> Your throne is established from of old; you are from everlasting.
> (Ps 93:1-2).

The psalmist here praises God's power, majesty and strength by examples in which a geocentric cosmology pictures the unchanging nature of God. Granted that the earth moves around the sun by Divine arrangement God can hardly communicate the point to us that the earth is immovable. The rhetorical purpose is rather to maintain that God says he wants to be praised for his strength and eternity.[23]

A further significant aspect of the work of Wolterstorff is to understand the implication of the narrative mode of speaking in the discourse in Genesis 1-3. On historical and socio-cultural terms we can only conjecture that these events somehow were told among people long before the times of Abraham and then narrated among his descendants until the times of Moses, when they according to the Hebrew Scriptures were recorded, but it is impossible to reconstruct any details in this process. Nevertheless, they must have told it in order to recount what were believed to be real events of the past, and at the times of Moses/the narrator these events were narrated in order to illuminate

---

[23] I.e., *"We attribute the main point to God, and discard the psalmist's particular way of making the point as of purely human significance"* (Wolterstorff 1995:210). Mathews helpfully clarifies that "scientific discovery adds to our sensibilities in the hermeneutics of a literal versus a nonliteral interpretation" (1996:108). Andersen (1998:194,196) seems both to accept Woltertorff's distinction between God's point versus the diction of the human author, yet he does not share Wolterstorff's aim to hear God discoursing in all of the Scriptures. He argues that God does not speak when humans are the speakers, e.g., when the Snake speaks it is not God who is speaking. I will maintain with Wolterstorff that the discourse about the Snake speaking is still very much God discoursing. I agree with Andersen that revelation is dialogic, or as I will maintain, is communicative, but this does not rule out the appropriation of the words of the human speakers, and in this sense of course does not rule out the ontology of revelation fundamental to the theology of Valen-Sendstad.

contemporary issues for a newly formed people of Israel immigrating to Cana'an.[24] Among the great themes are also the basic human issues of marriage (2:24), suffering (3:14-19), origin of sin (3:1) and certainty of death (3:19).

This discourse would be meaningful to the contemporaries of Moses and a host of later audiences. In Israel's monotheistic, world-view contemporary mythical and polytheistic thought about gods in combat appears to have been exchanged for a religious ideology of an all-powerful Creator and a creature suffering the consequences of his disobedience in relation to God, nature and fellow human beings. This narrator knows that evil already by now is deeply entrenched in the heart of Cain (4:7), and he is convinced that only through the blessings of a woman's giving birth will there eventually be hope (1:28; 3:15; 4:1,26).

Thiselton (1992:573) has called this the pragmatic effect of narrative. An account like Genesis 1 draws the reader into a description which is not solely an objective rendition of the actual process of creation, but also a reminding of the reader of his own creationhood and his responsibility towards all other creatures (566). The account of creation in other words *counts as* a description of a certain role and status for man. Thiselton points out how the narrative authorizes the plants as food (v 29), evaluates the world as good and perfect (v 31), and commands man to be fruitful and rule the earth (v 28).

When we continue to read for this Creator's discourse at an even higher level in the context of the Christian Scriptures we understand that his divine word accomplishes his errand (Isaiah 55:11). In the prologue of the gospel of John we grasp that Jesus the Son of God was the eternal Word revealed at creation (1:1) and the true interpreter of the living God (1:18). We also read how Saint Paul in 2 Chorinthians 4:6 applies the grand story of Genesis in its fullness: *"For God, who said, 'Light shall shine out of darkness,' is the One*

---

[24]See Mathews (1996:24, 51-53). He defends mosaic authorship (76-83 and 109-111), as does Wenham (1987:xli) by arguing from within the documentary hypothesis.

who has shone in our hearts to give the Light of the knowledge of the glory of God in the face of Christ."

God here ultimately speaks through words of Paul using the words of the narrator of Genesis who has God talking on the light coming into existence, and God can speak to us about Christ through these words of the Hebrew Scriptures as they are applied in the New Testament. The God who spoke about what he wanted to do and then did is the same God who has acted in what is now being spoken about Christ. These are some of the far reaching implications of the powerful notions of speech act theory when illuminating divine speech in text and talk.

4. God summoned Man: "Where are you?" and interaction in Gen 3:8ff: The communicative hermeneutics of Vanhoozer (1998)

Exploring the nature of the Creator's discourse in revelationary text and in divine talk by no means exhausts the deeper dimensions of God communicating through Scripture, because God also interacts with human beings in conversation.

In Genesis 1-3 this only happens after the fall when God in person intervenes to conduct a thorough interrogation against the trespassers in the garden, summoning man into interaction by the initial question of *"Where are you?"* (Gen 3:8). This first face-to-face conversation occurs in a world which we can barely imagine today outside the garden, yet the kind of interaction is similar to later forms of less direct contact through angels, dreams or visions.

The first conversation between God and man has a bearing on the communicative interaction in the written mode of the Scriptures. Discussing philosophy, literary theory, theories of communication, and Christian dogmatics, Kevin J. Vanhoozer (1998) argues that a proper understanding of the use of language in communication and interaction in everyday situations can help us understand how we get into communication and communion with God when reading the Bible.

Vanhoozer acknowledges his debt to Augustine's *credo ut intelligam,* 'I believe in order to understand' (1998:30), and even coins the phrase *lego ut intelligam* 'I read in order to understand' (32). Another remarkable way to put this is his advice to obey the Golden Rule to treat others - texts, persons, God - with love and respect. What counts is to read Scripture carefully for its historical, aesthetic, and ideological dimensions and look for what is really there: language, literary features, models of reality, and a value system (404-405).

Communication is tied into creation when Vanhoozer accepts the view of Platinga that there is a divine design in language offering man an ability to relate to his Creator, other people and discourse in order to obtain personal knowledge (205). How language serves as a means of communion and communication can also be illustrated by how God gives Adam information on which trees to eat or not (2:16-17) and has Adam himself relate to his own world through naming of the animals in v 19-20. The final touch is how Adam out of overwhelming love and joy encounters the rib of his life and in praise declares that *This at last is bone of my bones and flesh of my flesh; this one shall be called Woman, for out of Man this one was taken.* (v 23).

Transcendence in a very broad and fundamental sense has a central place in this new hermeneutics and according to Vanhoozer even pertains to a concept of the author with important theological implications:

> "both the "death" and the "resurrection" of the author depend on our ability to conceive of God as a communicative agent. The metaphysics of authorship is related, I submit, to the doctrine of creation and to the *imago Dei.* Human authorship, that is, is grounded in God's ability to communicate himself through the acts of Incarnation and revelation" (1998:26).

This central thesis also concerns the way a reader has the obligation to respond to *"an other that calls us to respond"* (368).[25]

Language is understood in terms of linguistic pragmatics and its use in a textual or situational context. In this regard the proposal resembles Wolterstorff's (1995:183) effort to explain interpretation as an act aiming at exploring what words count as in a specific situation and which act the speaker intended.[26] The new proposal is also deeply rooted in speech act philosophy in the standard version proposed by Searle and to some degree in the universal pragmatics of Habermas (1998:207-218). Vanhoozer formulates an intersubjective and objective understanding of language which explicates the roles of the author, text and reader.[27] The key terms and issues are summarized in the follow sets and definitions (25-29 *et passim*).

---

[25] Note furthermore Vanhoozer (1998:381, 394) and his transcendent-pragmatic rules on p. 401.

[26] The essence of discourse lies in what counts as what and the goals of interpretation is to discover how the *"discourser takes up a normative stance in the public domain by way of performing some publicly perceptible action"* (Wolterstorff 1995:83).

[27] Vanhoozer advocates a hermeneutic realism which assumes that there is an intended meaning of authors out there and it is realized through the text. It is possible to obtain a sufficiently true knowledge of the form and content of the communicative act. Text can also be defined in speech act categories as a communicative act with a content (*locution*), a force (*illocution*), and a goal (*perlocution*), summarized in the definition that text is *"a communicative act of a communicative agent fixed by writing"* (1998:221).

Topic	Discipline	Set of questions and pragmatic aspects
Author intention	metaphysics	Can meaning be communicated? The doing of an author as a communicative agent.
knowledge of text	epistemology	How can literary knowledge be obtained? Text as a communicative act.
reader responsibility	ethics	Is there a responsible way to obtain literary knowledge? Reforming of a reader through communicative ethics and effects.

Following Vanhoozer we are able to explain how we can read for the Creator's discourse from a hermeneutic perspective. As friendly readers we ought to crave for knowledge of the God who made the universe and understand the intended communicative message of the author who created the universe of the text. The preconditions for communication constitute the fundamental axis in this proposal. The speaker and writer are central to the proposal because any hearer or reader in interaction will expect that he really means what she says. In conversations the speaker can adjust his message to the actual hearer and her expectations and preunderstanding.[28] Whenever something misfires, the hearer even has the opportunity to cooperate with the speaker in order to negotiate the final result of what they agree on by redirecting or clarifying the conversation.

Written communication of course is more indirect and less fluid, yet it plays by the same communicative rules when a writer formulates his train of thought in a way which will allow a reader to grasp her intention as clearly and effectively as possible.[29] We communicate daily amazingly well in

---

[28]The many meanings and contexts of language call for *"authorial-discourse interpreters"* (Vanhoozer 1998:199) and we rely on *"our beliefs as to which plan of action for saying something he probably implemented."* Similarly Sailhamer (1992:10-11).

[29]The author has already determined the semantic content and the communicative purpose, but he can not assure the appropriate application of the full meaning.

conversing and reading, and often when we misunderstand or even respond negatively to a text or a conversational partner the fault is ours and not the interlocutor's.

Our role as readers is to bring our whole intellectual and cultural luggage and then engage with the text as a message completely different from ourselves. Preunderstanding can not be avoided and is even necessary as long as an interpreter keeps a distance to his own cultural horizon before merging the horizons of the text and the interpreter (Carson 1996:120). He changes in his meeting with the text and can then reread the text anew.

Rethinking the communicative process in this way need not lead to a vicious circle with presuppositions inevitably determining the horizon of the text, but can equally well develop into a hermeneutical spiral with knowledge constantly growing as the preunderstanding of the reader and the otherness in the message of the text are adjusted to each other in a reciprocal relation, so that the horizon of the reader is broadened rather than fused into the text (Pratt 1990:37-38). The reader creates a new application of the text in his own life, and in this sense is even reading for himself as a creator who is reshaping the language of an Other. His application can only be genuine as long as he relates to the already given meaning and message, because otherwise he is immune to communication and only capable of relating to himself and his own personal views and tradition.[30]

A reader of the Bible will be involved in what is best characterized as an authority-dialogue (Pratt 1990:32). Normal communication depends on

---

The biblical narrator has to choose a strategy to achieve his goals and he must adjust his message to the needs of his audience by figuring out in advance what questions might be put to the text (Sailhamer 1995:46-48).

[30]Reformation theology had to distinguish between Scripture and tradition as two completely different frames of reference. No Christian can cut himself off from tradition which may even support understanding (Carson 1996:127), yet the reformation would never have occurred without a fundamental attack on tradition (129).

whether we communicate with nobles, peers, or paupers, and the social status and power always influences the style and tone of discourse. In the Scriptures we meet an absolutely authoritative message according to the literature's inherent presuppositions. A reader will have to refrain from his personal expectations and leave his cultural and social background in order to enter into dialogue with the authoritative text which far transcends the reader's own personal and cultural horizon. The conditions of the dialogue are that he is communicating with the final word of the absolute God. This stance is very prominent in the communicative model of Wisdom literature when Proverbs 2 addresses the hearer as a son who is admonished to treasure the words of wisdom (v 1-2), to cry out for more understanding looking purposefully for it (v 3-4) and to fear Lord and know God (v 5). This way the speech acts fulfil their *perlocutionary* function.

The pragmatic teacher-pupil model of communication in Proverbs is also presented in the first account of conversation in Genesis 3 in the story about how communication and communion gradually dissolved after 'the fall of Man.'[31] It all began with a hermeneutical chaos when the Snake, one of the created animals in the garden, proved more clever than the other animals and played the role of a *master of suspicion* deconstruing the word in the beginning in a deadly hermeneutical game.[32] The Snake's seduction (3:1-5) and the fall and its consequences (v 6-7) is followed by God's interrogation (v 8-13) and judgment (v 14-19). Almost everything is conversation but gradually God shifts into monologue and verdictive divine Declarative.

The sly Snake opens the conversation with the inquisitive question *"Did God say, 'You shall not eat from any tree in the garden'?"* (v 1). He uses the less intimate divine name *God* rather than *Lord God* elsewhere in Gen 2-3, and

---

[31]On the importance of dialogue in this context, see Andersen (1994:110)

[32]Note how the creature gradually evolves into something beyond common snakes (Sailhamer 1992:103 and 109; Valen-Sendstad 1996:142, 188, 345-346).

questions the first instruction communicated by God in 2:16-17.[33] The woman accepts the language game on the Snake's conditions and corrects his mistakes by explaining that *"We may eat of the fruit of the trees in the garden; but God said, 'You shall not eat of the fruit of the tree that is in the middle of the garden...'"* (v 2-3). But she also interprets and all on her own adds *"...nor shall you touch it, or you shall die"* (v 3b), perhaps being just a bit discontent with the annoying prohibition and forgetting the gracious offer of virtually all fruit which preceded God's command in 2:16-17. And after all, she only knew about the command through hearsay from Adam.

In the next round of conversation the Snake makes his bid for power and flatly rejects the threat of death by saying *"You will not die"* (v 4).[34] He creates a counter-image of a jealous God who by threat of death intimidates his poor ignorant creatures, because he can not otherwise face the opposition from Man: *"God knows that when you eat of it your eyes will be opened, and you will be like God, knowing good and evil"* (v 5). The Woman buys into the Snake's new image of God and eats of the forbidden fruit, and when she offers her Man he gladly eats (v 6). And indeed, their eyes are opened, but their sight is weird, and they gradually split apart from God and each other. They are ashamed of their original innocence in nakedness (Sailhamer 1992:103), and they are now only able to compensate with poor sewn fig leaves (Wenham 1987:76), while hiding before the presence of an all-knowing God. Their knowledge of good and evil is no longer on the good terms intended by God while learning to appropriate his good instructions on what is good and bad.

Communion with God is gone, and now the interrogation proves that communication is also lost by perverted sinners misusing language in revolt

---

[33] The attack is to have man break the law (Valen-Sendstad 1996:314) or an external word (185-186) by confusing language (118); similarly Sailhamer (1992:101 and 104), Kempf (1993:354-355, 374).

[34] The Hebrew in Gen 3:4 is perhaps best translated *It is certainly not the case: "you shall die"* as a downright denial of 2:17 and this would account for the unusual word order negation-infinitive.absolute-verb (Wenham 1987:73-74).

against God and fellow (Wo)man.[35] The initial call of God *"Where are you?"* (v 9) is a cry to make Man stand up to his crime by using a question as a Directive and thus similar to our familiar utterance *"Can you pass me the salt?"* A question can even be interpreted as Commissive in the right circumstances, e.g., *"Can I help you?"* or *"Are you lost?"* said by a local to a driver in a car with out of state plates. If this pragmatic implicature was intended in the context it would imply that God asks for Man's whereabouts rather than outright condemning him and thus in spite of everything proves his care by not letting Man stay in his miserable hiding.

The underlying pragmatic implications of initial divine Directive or perhaps even Commissive is clearly addressed by Adam who does not explain where he is or how nice his trip into the trees were, but rather volunteers to account for his own fear, loneliness and detachment by his *"I heard the sound of you in the garden, and I was afraid, because I was naked; and I hid myself."* (v 10). So much for the knowledge obtained on the conditions given by the Snake and for being like God! The sly Adam only mentions that he hid, not why he did so, but this strategy does not work on a transcendent and all-knowing God who simply responds with the crucial issue of how it could go wrong: *"Who told you that you were naked?"* (v 11). The Omniscient knows that the Sly One must have influenced Man's new religious thinking when he detests an original perfect state of intimacy with his rib and his Creator. Adam is now so thoroughly demasked that his only resort is to launch a self-destructive counter-attack on both the Woman and God: *"The woman whom you gave to be with me, she gave me fruit from the tree, and I ate."* (v 12).

From now on God interrogates the Woman who does at least not lie (v 13) and then renders his verdict on the two culprits (v 14-19). It gives God the opportunity to offer his Commissive promise in v 15 that there will be no end to the continuing battle between descendants of Snakes and women, yet one future descendant of the Woman will some time totally crush the head of the old Snake. This is the real climax of the story (Kempf 1993: 358, 371-372).

---

[35] Andersen (1994:109, 111) observes the pragmatic features evolving from v6 onwards.

Part of the ongoing battle between the seed of the Snake and descendants of the Woman will from now on be on hermeneutics and the sincerity of promises. Language outside the garden will function in a world of trespassers and death where language can easily misfire when deconstructed in differences and deference. Vanhoozer's concept of communicative interaction as the clue to hermeneutics may thus provide one of the best paths through the current hermeneutic mess and provide the key to the challenge of postmodernism which severs interpretation from reality right from the very beginning of the world and reality.

Genesis 3 exemplifies how much of the narration of the Hebrew Scriptures consists of conversation with God or fellow human beings. This everyday language of interaction can be misused, but can also serve as a vehicle of knowledge of the transcendent God and his word. In this way, conversation and interaction serves as the ideal model of modern man's responsible listening to what God is doing as he is reading for the Creator's discourse and overhears how the Creator is conversing with his ancestral fellow Man, doing things with his divine words.

Creation in doing by saying

The new trends in the fields of theology, speech act philosophy, and communicative hermeneutics in various ways unravel how a Creator God and creative authors are acting right from the very beginning of the Hebrew Scriptures.

It has been argued here at length that linguistic knowledge is essential both in understanding the language of the Bible and in interacting with discourse in reading and interpreting. One major key to a reorientation presents itself in modern studies of speech acts in the wake of the work of Austin and Searle and contemporary studies of discourse, language use and communication. The notion of how creative authors do things by what they say or write is a fundamental one in the current scientific situation.

The argument presented here is that a proper understanding of language will be at center stage in any true understanding of the transcendent God of the Biblical creation story. The relation between language and transcendence has been discussed in terms of an ontology resting on theology and on text-linguistics and the new avenues in philosophy of religions and hermeneutics has been brought to the forefront in order to explain how text, speech and conversation in Genesis 1-3 function to connect a transcendent God with the world and reality. Especially the most recent work of Vanhoozer clearly suggests that text and talk can be anchored in reality and intentional communication by a divine speaker and human interlocutors from the beginning of the universe.

Our reading of the story narrated in the early chapters of Genesis only scratches the surface of the communicative evidence of the Hebrew Scriptures and could easily be argued at greater length and in broader sweep both inside and outside the Bible. What is missing is a stronger input from discourse studies, pragmatics and linguistics as well as cognitive and social sciences. Yet the current discourse, which we are about to end, has hopefully shown how creative language can communicate on the Creator and how language can bring us into communion and communication with the transcendent God when we read for his discourse.

References

Andersen, Francis I. *Salience, Implicature, Ambiguity, and Redundancy in Clause-Clause Relationships in biblical Hebrew.* In Robert D. Bergen, ed, *Biblical Hebrew and Discourse Linguistics.* Dallas: Summer Institute of Linguistics. 1994.

Andersen, Svend. Kan Bibelen være Guds ord? Et sprogfilosofisk problem hos Sløk og Wolterstorff. *Dansk Teologisk Tidsskrift.* 61:177-198, 1998.

Austin, J. L. *How to Do Things with Words* (The William James Lectures, Harvard 1955, edited by J. O. Urmson and Marina Sbisà). Oxford: Oxford UP, 1962.

Carson, Donald A. *The Gagging of God: Christianity Confronts Pluralism.* Grand Rapids: Zondervan, 1996.

Clark, Herbert. *Using language.* Cambridge: CUP, 1996.

Derrida, Jacques. *Writing and Difference.* Tr. Alan Bass. Chicago: University of Chicago Press, 1978.

Foster, Benjamin R, translator. *The Epic of Creation.* In William W. Hallo and K. Lawson Younger, Jr, eds, *The Context of Scripture, vol. 1*, 390-402. Leiden: Brill, 1997.

Grünwald, Klaus. Wozu wir essen. Überlegungen zu Genesis 1,29-30a. *Biblische Notizen* 49:25-38, 1989.

Henry, Carl F. *God, Revelation and Authority.* 6 volumes. Waco: Word, 1976-1983.

Kempf, Stephen. Genesis 3:14-19: climax of the discourse? *Journal of Translation and Textlingusitics.* 6(4):354-77, 1993.

— Introducing the Garden of Eden: The Structure and Function of Genesis 2:4b-7. *Journal of Translation and Textlingusitics.* 7(4):33-53, 1996.

Mathews, Kenneth A. *Genesis 1-11:26.* The New American Commentary. Broadman and Holman, 1996.

Mey, Jacob. *Pragmatics.* Oxford: Blackwell, 1993.

Pratt, Richard L. *He Gave Us Stories: The Bible Student's Guide to Interpreting Old Testament Narratives.* Brentwood, TN: Wohlgemut & Hyatt, 1990.

Sailhamer, John H. *The Pentateuch as Narrative: A Biblical-Theological Commentary.* Zondervan: Grand Rapids, 1992.

— *Introduction to Old Testament Theology: a Canonical Approach.* Grand Rapids: Zondervan, 1995.

Schiffrin, Deborah. *Approaches to Discourse.* Oxford UK and Cambridge USA: Blackwell, 1994.

Searle, John R. *Speech Acts.* Cambridge: Cambridge University Press, 1969.

— A classification of illocutionary acts. 1977. In Andy Rogers et al, eds, *Proceedings of the Texas Conference on Performatives, Presuppositions, and Implicatures*, 27-45. Washington, DC: Center for Applied Linguistics June 29, 1999

— *Expression and meaning.* Cambridge: Cambridge University Press, 1979.

Thiselton, Anthony C. *New Horizons in Hermeneutics: The Theory and Practice of Transforming Biblical Reading*. London: Harper Collins, 1992.

Tsumura, David Toshio. *The earth and the waters in Genesis 1 and 2. A linguistic investigation*. Journal for the Study of the Old Testatment Suppl Ser 83. Sheffield: Sheffield Academic Press, 1989.

Valen-Sendstad, Aksel. *Religionsfilosofi. En indføring i forholdet mellem filosofisk og teologisk virkelighedsforståelse*. Århus: Kolon, 1993.

— *Troens fundamenter: Dogmatiske hovedspørsmål i lys av bibelsk ontologi*. Århus: Kolon, 1996.

Vanhoozer, Kevin. *Is there a meaning in this text?: the Bible, the reader, and the morality of literary knowledge*. Grand Rapids: Zondervan, 1998.

Wagner, Andreas. *Sprechakte und Sprechaktanalyse im Alten Testament: Untersuchungen im biblischen Hebräisch an der Nahstelle zwischen Handlungsebene und Grammatik* (BZAW 253). Berlin/New York: de Gruyter, 1997.

Wenham, Gordon. *Genesis 1-15* (Word Biblical Commentary). Waco: Word, 1987.

Winther-Nielsen, Nicolai. *'In the beginning' of Biblical Hebrew Discourse: Genesis 1:1 and the Fronted Time Expression*. In: Hwang, Shin Ja J. og William R. Merrifield, eds. *Language in Context: Essays for Robert E. Longacre*, 67-80. Dallas: Summer Institute of Linguistics and the University of Texas at Arlington Publications in Linguistics 107, 1992.

— *Fact, Fiction and Language Use: Can Modern Pragmatics improve on Halpern's Case for History in Judges?* In: V. Philips Long, Baker, David W. and Wenham, Gordon J. eds. Windows into Old Testament History: Evidence, Argument, and the Crisis of "Biblical Israel". Grand Rapids: Eerdmans.p. 44-81, 2002.

White, H.C. *Narrative and Discourse in the Book of Genesis*. Cambridge: Cambridge University Press, 1991.

Wolterstorff, Nicholas. *Divine Discourse: Philosophical Reflections on the Claim that God Speaks*. Cambridge: Cambridge University Press, 1995.

Acknowledgements

I would like to thank my colleagues in Århus for valuable input on this work, and especially my colleague Aksel Valen-Sendstad. The manuscript was checked by Ulrik Petersen for language use and by Hans-Ole Bækgaard for theological content.

God, Time & Creation: An Essay in Metaphysics

MOGENS WEGENER

Allein Metaphysik führt uns in den dialektischen Versuchen der reinen Vernunft .. auf Grenzen; und die transscendentalen Ideen .. dienen dazu .. solche zu bestimmen.

Wenn wir mit dem Verbot, alle transscendenten Urteile der reinen Vernunft zu vermeiden, das damit dem Anschein nach streitende Gebot bis zu Begriffen, die ausserhalb dem Felde des immanenten (empirischen) Gebrauchs liegen, hinauszugehen, verknüpfen - [sic(k)!] - : so werden wir inne, dass beide zusammen bestehen können, aber nur gerade auf der Grenze alles erlaubten Vernunftgebrauchs.

Wir halten uns aber auf diese Grenze, wenn wir unser Urteil bloss auf das Verhältnis einschränken, welches die Welt zu einem Wesen haben mag, dessen Begriff selbst ausser aller Erkensnis liegt, deren wir innerhalb der Welt fähig sind.

Denn alsdann eignen wir dem höchsten Wesen keine von den Eigenschaften an sich selbst zu, durch die wir uns Gegenstände der Erfahrung denken, und vermeiden dadurch den dogmatischen Anthropomorphismus; wir legen sie aber dennoch dem Verhältnis desselben zur Welt bei und erlauben uns einen symbolischen Anthropomorphismus, der in der Tat nur die Sprache und nicht das Objekt selbst angeht.

So kann uns nichts hindern, von diesem Wesen eine Kausalität durch Vernunft in Ansehung der Welt zu prädizieren und so zum Theismus überzuschreiten.

Der unseren schwachen Begriffen angemessene Ausdruck wird sein, das wir uns die Welt so denken, als ob sie von einer höchsten Vernunft ihrem Dasein und innere Bestimmung nach abstamme.

Immanuel Kant: Prolegomena zu einer jeden künftigen Metaphysik die als Wissenschaft wird auftreten können, 1783 - III, §§57-8

1. FIDES QUAERENS INTELLECTUM

According to Kierkegaard, the great Danish philosopher, proofs of God are either superfluous, or inconsistent. For either there is a God, or there is no God: *tertium non datur* - but if God is, all proof is superfluous, and if He is not, no proof can possibly be consistent! Hence the few hopeful minds engaged in proving God are fools who should not hope for fame; rather than wasting their time by yielding to vain speculation they should concern themselves with the basic facts of existence in a serious struggle for authenticity. Kierkegaard's disdain of speculation was only matched by his disregard of science, and he readily admitted his only interest to be the Augustinian 'God and the soul.' He nevertheless conceded that a proof of God might be reasonable and even useful if it was designed expressly for the following purpose, namely to explain the Idea of God. Unfortunately, he forgot or ignored that this, precisely, was the aim of St. Anselm: his proof was an intellectual inquiry into the foundations of faith.

The so-called ontological proof of Anselm - which should rather be called dialectical - is designed to prove that the plain proclamation of atheism is either irrelevant or inconsistent. The first point to be grasped is that it is not an affirmative syllogism, but a *reductio* directed *ad hominem*, namely against the atheist. The argument derives its very force from the vigour invested by the disbeliever in declaring his own position, so when the atheist is silenced, the theist stops arguing. The second point to be realized is that the premises of the argument is provided by the atheist himself, partly a) by the distinction between reality and illusion entailed by his candid claim that the Idea of God does not refer to anything real although it pretends to, partly b) by the denunciation of the merely illusive, as compared to the real, implied by his enlightened refusal to worship an illusion. The third point to be grasped is that the atheistic repudiation of a divine being applies to any of kind deity, therefore also to God as confessed by the faithful believer who pronounces him to be that than which no greater can be conceived. This is not meant as a definition, however, but as a description; the infinite cannot be defined. The crucial question is, does the Idea thus described refer to anything real?

Now Anselm proceeds as follows: Anything thought of, e.g. the Idea of God, has being in thought, *esse in intellectu*; the distinction between reality and illusion is next expressed as the difference between that which has being both in thought and in itself, *esse in intellectu et in* re, and that which has being in thought only, but not in itself, *esse in intellectu solo*. For the Idea of God to refer or to be real, therefore, is to have being in itself as well as in thought, whereas for the Idea of God not to refer or to be illusive is to have being in thought only, and not in itself. The atheist then claims the Idea of God to be an illusion, nothing but a projection of the human mind, wholly unworthy of religious worship. However, by doing so, and by including that nature than which nothing greater can be thought, he betrays himself to be nothing but a fool, or a numskull, entirely unworthy of intellectual respect. The core of the proof is that what can be denied can also be thought of, hence the atheist by denying the reality of the Idea of God does think of what he denies: but this shows him to think that than which nothing greater can be thought as that than which something greater can be thought, which is a flat inconsistency. Anselm then concludes one of two: either the atheist simply contradicts himself, or he does not know what he is talking about. In any case he shows himself to be a fool.

2. METAPHYSICS: SCIENTIA SUI GENERIS

The importance of Anselm's dialectical proof of God is not that it clarifies the connotation or conceptual content of the Idea of God, for in fact it has none: the significance of the argument is that it specifies the function of the Idea of God. It is impossible for us, as finite and limited natures, to grasp the infinite Godhead, but the function of the Anselmian formula is to show the path to transcendence. This it does by refusing to accept anything as Divine to which another is superior. In that way the proof becomes an instance of *via negativa*, not of *via affirmativa*: the Divine is determined indirectly by the denial of everything which is not Divine. Apart from the fact that it is God's *esse* which is at issue, not His *existentia*, there is no question of inferring the existence of God from "his" essence, or nature. Neither is there any question of using existence, or being, as a special kind of predicate.

All this may be distinctive of the Cartesian approach, but not of the Anselmian one. These facts immunize the proof of Anselm not only to the objections of Aquinas, but also to those of Kant.

It therefore seems as if - in spite of Kant - we possess at least one sample of authentic metaphysics derived from pure reason: atheism seduces us into absurdity. In this way the basic experience of existentialism is affirmed by formal reasoning. So the only safe way to avoid God is to avoid speaking, and even thinking, of God; the faithful can argue successfully against the atheist, but not against the agnostic. Now the agnostic will probably not want to dispute the possibility of metaphysics, and we shall therefore allow ourselves to neglect his awkward position at present. Instead we shall here defend the position that Metaphysics is a *scientia sui generis* - namely the science of pure transcendence - as extracted from the proof of Anselm. Rejecting the classical distinction between analytical and synthetical propositions, we further hold pure logics and mathematics to be practical instruments of reason. As mere techniques they need a minimal interpretation involving basic elements of experience whenever some formal item is to be changed into a genuine proposition. Such a minimal interpretation suspends the distinction above in a way that renders it possible to regard the same theoretical proposition from one point of view as being analytical, and from another point of view as being synthetical. The ram which Kant used to break down the fortifications of classical metaphysics is thereby turned against the central pillar of his own transcendental criticism.

The word 'meta-physics' (gr.: *ta meta ta physika*) was assigned to the First Philosophy of Aristotle by accidence because some librarian placed these rolls on his bookshelves after the rolls with the Physics of Aristotle, but in the course of time popular etymology has transferred a deeper meaning to the term. As we shall take the word in the sense of 'that which transcends physics,' we shall stick to the etymology, only trying to fill it with a new and clearer meaning. Although our new metaphysics - collected from pure reason as its source - appears to be purely theoretical, it is not wholly devoid of empirical elements; this follows from the impossibility of separating analytical and synthetical propositions. Pure transcendence being its sole object, this object is evidently superior not only to all other objects it is possible to conceive of, but also to all conceivable values. It thereby provides us with a unique standard of our assessments and judgments. Still under development it promises to open up new vistas towards unknown horizons. For the present, however, we shall content ourselves by pointing out how this new metaphysics deals with some traditional problems posed by the philosophy of physical science.

In which sense, then, does metaphysics transcend physics as the science of nature? As stated by Galileo, the aim of physics is *'to measure what can be measured and to make that measurable which cannot as yet be measured;'* physics thus focuses on what is measurable, striving to reduce quality to quantity whenever possible. Now an act of measurement involves the comparison of an entry with a standard; in this way physics fulfils the rule of reason laid down by the philosophy of Plato. As stated by Plato, reason (*dianoia*) depends on proportion (*analogia*) in making an inference from three known components to a fourth which is as yet unknown (the dialectical underpinning of this rule is given in his famous parable of the line). What is infinite, however, cannot enter as the component of a definite proportion: pure infinity, as constituted by pure transcendence, is therefore incommensurable. Now this way of reasoning enables us to embrace the idea of André Mercier: Metaphysics is a science *sui generis* having the Incommensurable as its proper object. Our only disagreement is minor and derives from the fact that I am somewhat more reluctant than he to accept that this object can be properly referred to as a "being". In line with the Platonic tradition of Christian philosophy, I prefer to speak of the Infinite Godhead as transcending all Being, in the sense of being its Creator. Hence I shall distinguish between 'being' as a noun and 'being' as a verb (or copula); moreover, I shall explicitly renounce metaphysics interpreted as ontology (the doctrine of being).

What metaphysics can properly do is merely to "point" towards a certain direction. Although irrefutable, the "being" of a Godhead transcending the categories of reason cannot be sustained as more than a hypothesis - all reference to it is hyperbolic. This pure transcendence, nevertheless, involves a demarcation of limits to reason, limits that may not be transgressed by smartness illegitimately feigning authority. Hence the principal thesis of my paper is that a new metaphysics, conceived as an intellectual discipline investigating that which transcends both science and nature, is possible and legitimate to the purpose of evaluating the pretensions of physics and refuting the improper claims of a philosophy, misinterpreting scientific results by exploiting such insights far beyond the proper limits of reason and experience. This obligation to criticism, however, does not restrain our new metaphysics from inquiring into the possible origin of time and world in a Divine Act of Creation. On the contrary: if it is at all conceivable that the universe as we know it can have originated from Divine Creation, it must be mandatory to our new metaphysics to investigate the rational implications to science of this assumption. The Idea of Divine Creation is meta-physical in the sense of transcending physics, and the very fact that it can be denied shows that it cannot be devoid of meaning; for the very same reason, the possibility of atheism indirectly affirms the Idea of God. Atheists seldom realize that they jeopardize their position by denying God, but in fact, the only consistent position of the infidel is agnosticism. Such agnosticism, however, is detrimental to the pursuit of science.

Before we present the consequences of the Idea of Creation to physics and cosmology we shall give some few hints regarding its consequences to metaphysics. Without implying God to be "being as such" (Aristotle), nor a very special kind of being, like "the most perfect being" (Descartes), or "the most real being" (Kant), we shall characterize "him" as: Creator, that is: the Source and Origin of everything else. In accordance with our reasoning hitherto we shall further characterize the pure Act of Creation as that act by which the Godhead transcends all nature or existence. Let us define the world, or universe, as 'the totality of everything existing'.

It is immediately evident that a universe in which nothing happens cannot be a real universe. What happens we shall call events, and events take place in time. For this reason we take Time to be the basic feature of any possible, or conceivable, universe. Now, if a universe is to be a Cosmos, and not a mere chaos, it must display features which make it possible to discern one event from another, and the succession of events anywhere in the universe must appear to be governed by laws. The infinite set of possible worlds, or universes, must therefore contain subsets of worlds of which each one is an equivalence class governed by the same set of laws, the members of a given equivalence class being discernible by their various contents. Of course only one world is real, this follows from its definition as a totality. There is no need to suppose the infinity of other conceivable worlds to be real, not even "virtually real": possible worlds are nothing but conceptual constructions. The actual world is temporal - not given all at once but from instant to instant, as a succession - and what successively differentiates it from all other possible worlds is that these other worlds, relative to some now, are mere unactualized futures. But how is "our" actual world realized as the only "real" one from among all possibles?

According to Plato it is impossible that something can come from nothing: we must therefore search for a cause to the becoming of everything which becomes. Causal relations do not relate things directly, but indirectly, by means of events; hence the concept of an event, but not that of a thing, is relevant to causal relationship. The causal relationship is distinguished by an asymmetry, entailed by the asymmetry of time, which gives rise to three questions hinting at three very different formulations of the causal principle: a) is it necessary that every event be regarded as the effect of some cause which is temporally prior? - or: b) is it necessary that every event be regarded as the cause of some effect which is temporally posterior? - or: c) both? While the first kind of necessity is tacitly presupposed by the scientific explanation of events, the second is tacitly presupposed by the scientific prediction of events. Clearly, God as that than which nothing greater can be thought cannot be thought to be effected by a prior cause, hence, if God be a cause 'He' must be the primary cause.

But is the concept of cause as sketched above compatible with a first cause? A first cause can only be conceived in relation to a first event but, granted a first event, is this event to be imagined as the first cause or as the first effect? The difficulty is that our three questions implicitly assume a causal relation to be a horizontal relation between entries, which are on a par. What we need in order to explain the relationship between God and his creation as a causal one is, by contrast, a vertical relation between entries which are not on a par - a relation depicting God as transcending both time and world in one act. Such a kind of causal relationship seems to be unique, and *sui generis*.

3. CREATION: THE WELL-SPRING OF TIME

Much of traditional Christian theology describes God not only as first cause, *prima causa*, but also as pure act, *actus purus*. This, for instance, is the case with Aquinas. In the famous BBC-discussion between F. Copleston and B. Russell concerning the cosmological proof of God, father Copleston recalled "the third way" of St. Thomas; what is at issue here is not as much the concept of cause as that of contingency: The continued existence of a contingent universe depends entirely on its Divine Creator. This seems to presuppose that all causal series of the universe can be conceived in their entirety as one simultaneous whole, but their temporality prevents that. However, it is still possible that the world may depend on its Creator in the sense that it is being kept in existence by God successively, that is, from instant to instant.

The famous doctrine that *Conservatio est Creatio* goes to the core of 'the five ways', and is the essence of what has been called "the existentialistic sway" of Thomism. The thesis of the contingency of the universe can be defended on the supposition that the world is preserved from instant to instant by God. For this to be possible it is not necessary that all causal series of the world can be conceived in their entirety as one unique simultaneous whole, and neither is it necessary that the entire world course in time can be surveyed from an initial to a terminal event. The point is that the idea of contingency can be accorded a clear and distinct meaning on the condition that the Universe is upheld as a *totum simul* from instant to instant in the sense that Time and Life is continuously being bestowed upon it as a creative Flow which emanates from the Future, becomes manifest in the Present, and expires in the Past.

God's Act of Creation might be a unique event buried in an inscrutable past; but it may also be interpreted in accordance with the contingency of the present as the preservation of *nunc stans*, a standing Now, in the midst of the river of time. That a Now is standing is a sign of Divine Creation; the result, being the effect of Divine Creation as its first cause, is *nunc fluens*, the contents that flows through the Now. But the notion of time in flow is ambiguous. What is the direction of such flow? Mediated by the present, does it point from past to future or from future to past? The relativization implied by the question is legitimate, and the solution is easy. Whereas the emergence of reality is followed by an increase of factual contents pointing from past to future, the extinction of possibility points in the opposite direction from future to past. Now, which sense is deeper than the other? The Biblical answer is that God, by creating the Future, is the Wellspring of Time, and therefore Time, which is Possibility and Grace, flows from the Future to the Past. I am very grateful to prof. André Mercier for having pointed this out to me.

Thus time flows; but as we cannot ascribe a velocity to this flow we shall not follow Bergson in giving the concept of duration a fundamental status. But there is another problem: Granted that the universe is time-in-flux, an absolute or universal time should be definable; however, this is incompatible with the standard interpretation of Einstein's relativity theory. So we are faced with the fact that if God has once created - or is still creating - the universe, then our universe must be contingent in a manner which presupposes the definability of an all-embracing simultaneity, and this is in blatant conflict with Einsteinian standard relativity. And, conversely, if Einsteinian standard relativity is true, then the universe cannot be contingent, which shows that the universe cannot depend on creation, hence cannot be created by God.

The upshot of all this is that, if we want to vindicate our new metaphysics, we have to face the challenge of physics as represented by Einsteinian relativity. Now the application of the General Relativity Theory (GR) to cosmology leads to a very general metric, the so-called Robertson-Walker Metric (RWM), common to all models of the universe structured according to the principle of cosmic isotropy. Despite the incompatibility of absolute simultaneity with the standard space-time interpretation of relativity, all RW-models of the universe allow of a cosmic time. All we need in order to demonstrate that the universe is contingent, hence that it may be preserved in existence by God, is to prove the definability of cosmic time. To begin with we thus merely have to bring this cosmic time to the fore by insisting that the universe, if created, must conform to the principle of cosmic isotropy.

Indeed, at present an overwhelming evidence fortunately shows this to be the case. Hence creation is compatible with the facts.

This is not yet a formal proof of God: the world may be contingent and yet not be created. But if the world is clearly contingent, the need of an explanation will be acute, and then only an agnostic who does not defend even the *ex nihilo nihil fit* may readily renounce. In this case we can claim to possess an informal proof of God. But the proof can be strengthened to necessity if the onus of proof is transferred to the atheist. The point is that he has to choose one of two: The universe, being contingent, either forms a self-preserving and self-explaining mechanism - i.e., a *perpetuum mobile* - or it does not. Now if, insisting on rationality, he does not wish to ascribe divine properties to the universe itself, it seems fair to ask him to prove that it is in the least a *perpetuum mobile*. The atheist, however, will never be able to satisfy such a demand.

In fact, lots of evidence show that the universe is not - cannot be - a *perpetuum mobile*. No closed physical system, being part of the universe, can be a *perpetuum mobile*, and if the universe itself forms a closed system, it cannot be a *perpetuum mobile*. But a *perpetuum mobile* which is not a closed system is a contradiction in terms. Therefore an open universe, being no *perpetuum mobile*, is obviously a contingent one. We conclude that the universe, be it open or not, cannot be a *perpetuum mobile*. But a universe which is not a *perpetuum mobile* is not self-preserving and lacks all explanation. Now the universe is open in at least 3 senses of this word: 1) it is open towards the past; 2) it is not wholly determined; 3) it is open towards the future. The validity of all scientific knowledge is necessarily conjectural and provisional, and what science can offer is merely to draw up possibilities in the form of world-models.

It can never be decided by final proof whether the universe had a first instant or not; the same holds for the question whether there will be a last instant or not - and the same even holds for the question as to which laws are valid in our universe, if any laws are valid in it at all. Now the universe is open towards the past in the sense that it is possible it had a first instant, and it is possible that this first instant was given to it by Divine Creation.

Further, the universe is indeterministic in the sense that even if it be determined by laws how the future follows from the past, quantum physics has demonstrated the laws to be probabilistic. Finally, the universe is open towards the future in the sense that its fate depends on whether a future is given to it or not. The ultimate question, at any instant, is whether the universe is going have a future at all!

These arguments are decisive; the only conceivable objection to them seems to be that, after all, it might be impossible to define an absolute simultaneity valid for the entire universe. In that case it would not make sense to speak of a common future of the universe and the notion of contingency would not make sense either. But this objection has already been dealt with.

If the universe is subject to the principle of universal isotropy, a cosmic time will be definable. Hence the only way left of jeopardizing the notion of absolute simultaneity is to assume that the universe, after all, is not subject to the principle of cosmic isotropy. Apart from the fact that such an hypothesis is in obvious conflict with current observation, it also amounts to the ad hoc introduction of a basic element of irrationality into cosmological science.

Why do physicists so often prefer to construe the universe as a *perpetuum mobile*? Why do philosophers invent all sorts of irrationalities in order to avoid the Idea of Creation? The claim of Grübaum and others, that the standard conservation laws suffice to ensure the continued temporal existence of the universe, involves a major misinterpretation of science.

In fact, conservation laws, teaching us everything about the conservation of quantities in time, have absolutely nothing to tell us concerning an eventual suspension of time. A law of conservation is a formal guarantee that a certain quantity will neither increase nor decrease: this presupposes that there be a quantity at all! Thus, what a conservation law states is that if the universe continues to exist, if this present instant has a successor, then the total energy of any well-defined physical system will not deviate from its present value but remain constant.

It should further be noticed that if the law of the conservation of energy is to be tested then it will be necessary to specify the physical system by referring to its volume. The limits of a certain volume will be unspecifiable if there be no cosmic time to rely on, and if the spatial limits of the system in question are unspecifiable, the assumption of conservation threatens to degenerate into a pure tautology, a mere repetition of the *ex nihilo nihil fit*, which is indeed not a physical principle but rather a metaphysical principle. This also shows that the regularly uttered qualms against the assumption of a continued creation of matter are nothing but inarticulate grumbling. What kind of argument can demonstrate that the proper volume over which the energy is to be integrated must necessarily be measured by coordinate distance, and not by proper distance? The imputation of deficiency to the idea of continued creation is itself invalid.

We will now try to demonstrate the fruitfulness of our new metaphysics by showing how it makes use of arguments derived from considerations of symmetry. In the first instance it should be realized that the definability of a universal time depends on whether the universe displays some elementary properties of symmetry: a cosmic time is definable only in case the universe possesses the symmetry of cosmic isotropy. The Christian, accepting the universe to be created by whom-than-which-no-greater-can-be-thought, will naturally take the universe to be everywhere isotropic. A universe created by a perfect Creator will be as perfect as possible, and faith in Divine Creation naturally leads to ideas of universal symmetry and to hypotheses tending to assimilate the created universe to its Divine Creator.

By contrast, the atheist who is eager to discard creation can only feel safe if it can be proved that the universe will never run out and needs no explanation for its origin. It therefore seems probable that atheism in general will show predilection for inventing models of the universe that suffer from all possible kinds of anomalies. History offers ample evidence that this is precisely the case: most scientists hold time to be illusory, just as they brand creationism as vain speculation, and the list of absurdities proposed in the name of science is tediously long: rotating universes, irregular universes, oscillating universes, universes with imaginary time, etc. My conclusion will be surprising only to those unfamiliar with the facts of history: there is a secret alliance between the rationality of good science and the Christian faith in God as Creator! As Whitehead said: *"Faith in the possibility of science, generated antecedently to the development of modern scientific theory, is an unconscious derivative from medieval theology."*

God, as the incommensurable being, necessarily transcends all kinds of symmetry. There are nevertheless good reasons for assuming that Creation, in the sense of a progressive formal differentiation of the universe as a created manifold of things, takes place in accordance with the successive introduction and suspension of symmetries of lesser and lesser generality. The most fundamental symmetry of the universe is that which makes its structure definable in terms of a universal class of equivalent so-called fundamental particles, and this symmetry precisely correlates the very concept of structure to that of an all-embracing, universal time. Hence, in a very fundamental sense, simultaneity - and not causality - is the cement of the universe. In fact, everything in cosmology may be said to depend on the idea of universal time.

Assuming all fundamental particles to carry observers supplied with identical clocks, that is, clocks based on the same mechanisms and controlled by atoms of the same type, their equivalence can be interpreted in the usual relativistic way. The condition of speaking of laws being invariant to the translation of data between different observers is that their clocks be adjusted by means of unique radar-signals distinguished by delays depending on the distances traversed, and that equivalent observers by definition assign the same velocity to such signals. Now the first, and decisive, breaking of symmetry is associated with the imposition of a layer of so-called accidental particles, particles not perfectly equivalent to those of the universal set. As shown in the *Kinematic Relativity* (KR) of Milne, local deviations from universal symmetry lead to spontaneous accelerations which approximate the classical law of gravitation!

This fact encourages us to suggest a new program of physical science which diverges from that of Einstein by not having as its purpose to reduce time to space and gravitation to inertia but - on the contrary - to derive space from time, and to explain gravitation by inertia. The program, which is inspired by Milne, is at variance with all attempts to geometrize physics. Instead, it proposes to solve the basic problems of cosmology in the 'kinematic' way by taking as its paradigm neither SR, nor GR, but Milne's KR which, as pointed out by J.Merleau-Ponty, is *"a Leibnizian monadology translated into mathematics"*. What counts in favour of Milne is that his program (in contrast also, e.g., to that of Whitehead which is a mere 'half-way house') incorporates the relationalist and conventionalist philosophy of the great mathematician and physicist Poincaré who, before Einstein, discovered the Lorentz Group and SR.

The central issue, separating the relativist tradition culminating in Poincaré from the mediumist tradition culminating in Lorentz, is reducible to this basic question: Is the existence of a universal substratum defined by the mass-distribution of the class of all fundamental particles, granted that such a class exists, to be regarded as mere coincidence, a brute fact of nature, or is it the manifestation of some law? This question presents us with a choice between a pure theory of strong relativity and a theory of weak relativity based on the aether-hypothesis (a consequence of the latter would be that the relativity principle is valid for fundamental particles only).

In another place I have shown how it is possible to develop a new tense logic allowing for the creation not only of reality but even of truth. My general conclusion is that it is indeed possible to construct a new philosophy of time, reality, and transcendence, namely as a synthesis which plausibly assumes the character of a metaphysics of God, Time & Creation.

REFERENCES

St Anselm, *Proslogion*, Oxford, 1965.
Aristotle, *Metaphysics*, esp.1006a.
Bondi, H. *Cosmology*, Cambridge, 1962.
Duffy, M. C. & Wegener,M. (eds.) *Recent Advances in Relativity Theory.*
    Vol.1: Formal Interpretations. Vol.2: Material Interpretations.
      Hadronic Press, Florida (Institute for Basic Research) - forthcoming.

Grünbaum, A. *The Pseudo-Problem of Creation in Physical Cosmology*, in: J. Leslie, ed.: Physical Cosmology and Philosophy, Macmillan/Collier, 1990.

Kierkegaard, S. *Philosophical Fragments,* 1844.

Lucas, J. R. *The Open Future*, in: Flood & Lockwood, eds.: *The Nature of Time*, Blackwell, 1986.

Lucas, J. R. *A Century of Time*, cf. http://users.ox.ac.uk/~jrlucas/century9.html

Merleau-Ponty, J. *Cosmologie du XXme siecle*, Gallimard, 1965.

Milne, E.A. *Kinematic Relativity*, Oxford, 1949.

North, J. *The Measure of the Universe*, Oxford, 1965.

Phipps, T. E. *Heretical Verities*, Class. Non-Fict. Lib., Urbana IL.1986.

Poincaré, H. *The Value of Science*, Dover Books, 1906.

Prokhovnik, S.J. *The Logic of Special Relativity*, Cambridge, 1967.

St.Thomas Aquinas. *Selected Writings*, Random House, NY, 1945.

Wegener, M. *Time and Harmony in the Philosophy of Leibniz*, in: L'Art, la Science & la Metaphysique (to André Mercier), P. Lang, Bern, 1994.

Wegener, M. *The Radar-Technique as a Theoretical Device*, Physics Essays 8, 1995.

Wegener, M. *A Classical Alternative to SR*, Physics Essays 8, 1995.

Wegener, M. *A-Priorism in Poincaré, Eddington & Milne*, in: Philosophia Scientiae 1 (cahiers spécial 1) - ACERHP, Nancy 1996 (Entretiens 1994 de l'Académie Internationale de Philosophie des Sciences)

Wegener, M. *Ideas of Cosmology. A Philosopher's Synthesis*, Late PIRT-Proceedings 1996, Physical Interpretations of Relativity Theory, (Biennial Conferences sponsored by British Society for the Philosophy of Science).

Wegener, M. & Øhrstrøm, P. *A New Tempo-Modal Logic for Emerging Truth*, in: Faye & alies: *Perspectives on Time*, Kluwer 1996 (Boston Studies Phil.Sc.,vol.189) (cf. the kind acknowledgment by Lucas in ref.8 above)

Whitrow, G.J. *What is Time?,* Thames & Hudson 1971/Penguin.

Whitrow, G.J. *The Natural Philosophy of Time*, Oxford, 1980

Relativity and the 'Elimination' of Absolute Time

WILLIAM LANE CRAIG

Abstract

It is often asserted today that Relativity Theory (RT), particularly the Special Theory (SR), served to eliminate Newton's concept of absolute time. Such an attitude, however, fails to understand either the metaphysical foundations of Newton's absolute time or the defective epistemological underpinnings of Einstein's theory.

Newton's absolute time, as distinguished by him from relative time, was 'absolute' in a number of senses, but the sense relevant for this paper is that it was metaphysical time, whereas relative time was physical. Metaphysical or 'true' time holds independently of physical events. Physical time, by contrast, is the time kept by our clocks when we endeavor to measure as accurately as possible the 'true' time, which is metaphysical.

Modern secular scientists and philosophers often fail to appreciate how central a rôle Newton's theism played in his conception of absolute time. For Newton absolute time is rooted in the eternal being of God. If God exists, we may ascribe 'reality' to everlasting duration and to 'true', or absolute, time. By tying physical time to 'frames of reference' RT radically revised Newton's concept of physical time. But in the absence of any critique of Newton's theism, his concept of absolute time remains untouched.

The illusion that RT had eliminated Newton's absolute time is due to the positivistic epistemological foundations of Einstein's theory. This was inspired by Ernst Mach's radical sensationalism, which was thoroughly verificationist and operationalist. Similarly, Einstein's method of clock synchronization by light signals simply assumes that because absolute time and space cannot be empirically established they are not real. Einstein's theory did not eliminate absolute simultaneity; it merely re-defined simultaneity along verificationist lines.

But Machian positivism is now nearly universally rejected in the philosophy of science. Accordingly, the achievement of Einstein's RT should be understood to lie not in the elimination of Newton's absolute time, but in the relativization of physical, measured time. But if we with Newton wish to adopt a metaphysic of theism, how then is Relativity Theory to be understood? Poincaré provided us the clue in his hypothesis of 'une intelligence infinie' who would classify all events in his time, even as we class in our time the little we see.

In God's experience of absolute time there would be an absolute 'now' wholly independent of physical events. He would know all events in the universe, which coincide with the 'now' of metaphysical time. But if there is a class of absolutely simultaneous events it follows:

1) that the standard interpretation of RT is wrong,
2) that the Lorentz-Poincaré interpretation of the theory must be adopted,
3) that there is a privileged foliation of space-time which yields a cosmic time coinciding with the 'true' time of God.

1. INTRODUCTION

Nicholas Lash recently remarked that in the 'dialogue' between science and theology, it is the former which has been doing most of the talking.[36] Well, today I intend to talk back.

As a theologian and philosopher, I am committed to the enunciation of a synoptic world-view which takes into account the theories and discoveries of modern science. In return, I believe that a theological perspective will also serve to shed surprising light on certain theoretical problems of modern physics. The conceptions of time and becoming are a case in point.

Most physicists and philosophers of science tend to agree with Wolfgang Rindler that, with the construction of RT, Einstein took a step *"that would completely destroy the classical concept of time"*[37]. Many also contend that, along with universal time and absolute simultaneity, temporal becoming and an objective 'now' also go by the board. I believe such judgments to be mistaken and to be predicated partly upon a deficient understanding of the metaphysical, particularly theistic, foundations of the classical concept of time, and partly upon a defective epistemological approach to these problems.

2. NEWTON ON ABSOLUTE VERSUS RELATIVE TIME

In the Scholium to his definitions in the Principia, Newton drew a distinction between what he called 'absolute time' and 'relative time'. Newton's much misunderstood and greatly vilified distinction deserves careful consideration. In order to overcome 'common prejudices' concerning time, space, place and motion, Newton distinguished between 'absolute and relative, true and

---

[36] In Russell, Stoeger & Coyne, eds.,1988: *Physics, Philosophy, and Theology*, Vatican Obs.

[37] In: *Am.Jour.Phys.*38,1970,1112.

apparent, mathematical and common'. As regards time he asserted: *"Absolute, true, and mathematical time, of itself, and from its own nature, flows equably without relation to anything external, and by another name is called duration. Relative, apparent, and common time, is some sensible and external (whether accurate or unequable) measure of duration by the means of motion, which is commonly used instead of true time; such as an hour, a day, a month, a year."*[38]

An obvious feature of this distinction is the independence of absolute time from the relative measures thereof. Absolute time, or simple duration, exists regardless of the sensible and external measurements, which we try to make of it. In other words, clock time may, or may not, be identical to true time. As J. R. Lucas succinctly puts it, *"time is not what the clocks say, but what they are trying to tell"*[39]. If we reject Newton's distinction, the statement that two time intervals are isochronous can only be conventionally true. Without absolute time, the notion of clock synchrony is jeopardized and the unity of time becomes an empty assumption.

Newton's distinction, as thus far considered, concerns only the 'absolute-measured' distinction, according to which true time is distinct from measured time. But as is well-known, Newton also conceived of time as absolute in a more profound sense, namely that it exists independently of any physical objects whatsoever. Usually this is interpreted to mean that time would exist even if nothing else existed. Hence, even in an otherwise empty world the abstract flow of absolute time would permeate the abstract structure of absolute space.

But here we must be careful. Modern secular scholars tend frequently to forget how ardent a theist Newton was and how central a rôle his theism played in his metaphysical outlook. Noting that Newton assumed God to be temporal, and thus time to be everlasting, David Griffin observes that *"Most commentators have ignored Newton's heterodox theology, and his talk of*

---

[38] Sir Isaac Newton's *'Mathematical Principles of Natural Philosophy'* (I.6), A. Motte, trl., Univ.Cal.Pr.1966.

[39] In: *A Treatise of Time and Space*, Methuen 1973, p.64.

'absolute time' has been generally misunderstood to mean that time is not in any sense a relation and hence can exist apart from actual events"[40]. In fact, Newton made quite clear that absolute time and space are constituted by the divine attributes of eternity and omnipresence: *"He is eternal and infinite ..; that is, his duration reaches from eternity to eternity; his presence from infinity to infinity ... He is not eternity and infinity, but eternal and infinite; he is not duration or space, but he endures and is present. He endures forever, and is every-where present; and, by existing always and everywhere, he constitutes duration and space. Since every particle of space is always and every indivisible moment of duration is everywhere, certainly the Maker and Lord of all things cannot be never and nowhere."*[41]

Because God is eternal there is an everlasting duration, and because He is omnipresent there is an infinite space. So absolute time and space are relational in that they are contingent upon the existence of God. Newtonian time is thus not absolute in the sense of 'non-relational'. With respect to physical time, what Newton did not realize, nor could he even suspect, is that physical time is not only relative, but also relativistic, and that the approximation of relative, physical time to absolute, metaphysical time depends not only upon the regularity of one's clock, but also upon its motion. Unless a clock were at absolute rest, it would not accurately register the passage of metaphysical time. Moving clocks run slow. This truth, unknown to Newton, but intimated by Larmor and Lorentz in the concept of 'local time', was grasped by Einstein.

Where Newton fell short, then, was not in his analysis of metaphysical time, but in his incomplete understanding of physical time. He assumed too readily that an ideal clock would give an accurate measure of metaphysical time independently of its motion. If confronted with relativistic evidence, Newton would no doubt have welcomed this correction and seen therein no threat at

---

[40] In: *Physics and the Ultimate Significance of Time*, St.Univ.NY Pr.1986, pp. 6-7.

[41] Sir Isaac Newton's *'Mathematical Principles of Natural Philosophy'* (II.545), A. Motte, trl., Univ.Cal.Pr.1966.

all to his doctrine of absolute time. As Lucas emphasizes: *"The relativity that Newton rejected is not the relativity that Einstein propounded; and although the Special Theory of Relativity has shown Newton to be wrong in some respects ... it has not shown that time is relative in Newton's sense and merely some numerical measure of process."*[42]

In short, relativity corrects Newton's concept of physical time, but not his concept of metaphysical time. Should relations of absolute simultaneity not obtain in physical time, they still do in metaphysical time, and God knows which events occur simultaneously regardless of physical reference frames. God's time is the foundation of becoming; God knows the absolute 'now' of metaphysical time. But what relativity theory did, in effect, was simply to remove God from the picture and to substitute in His place a finite observer. Thus, according to Holton: *"RT ... shifted the focus of space-time from the sensorium of Newton's God to the sensorium of Einstein's abstract Gedanken-experimenter ... the final secularization of physics"*[43]

Of course, as we all know, there is a great deal of antipathy in modern physics and the philosophy of science toward metaphysical ideas of time and space, since they are not testable. But Newton would have been singularly unimpressed with this equation between physical testability and non-existence. His grounds for metaphysical space and time were not physical, but philosophical or, more precisely, theological. Epistemological objections fail to worry Newton since, as Lucas puts it: *"He is thinking of an omniscient, omnipresent Deity whose characteristic relation with things and with space is expressed in the imperative mood."*[44]

Modern physical theories, being silent on this issue, say nothing against the existence of such a God, nor against the metaphysical time constituted by His eternity.

---

[42] In: *A Treatise of Time and Space*, Methuen 1973, p.90.

[43] In: *Thematic Origins of Scientific Thought. Kepler to Einstein*, Harvard Univ. Pr. 1973, p.171

[44] ibid.p.143.

3. THE 'DESTRUCTION' OF NEWTONIAN TIME

By the latter part of the nineteenth century, physicists had already realized that there must be something fundamentally wrong with Newton's analysis of physical time and space. The failure to detect the earth's motion through the aether, which constituted physical space and which was assumed to be at rest with regard to metaphysical space, prompted a crisis in physics. This crisis ultimately compelled Lorentz and Poincaré to abandon the classical so-called Galileo transformation equations in favour of the new relativistic ones named after Lorentz.

In so doing, they had already sounded the death knell of Newtonian physics, for they had relativized the sensible measures of metaphysical time and space in ways undreamed of by Newton. But they did so without abandoning the notion that there really is a true time and a true space, even if these remain undetectable to us. Einstein interrupted this research program with a radically different approach. Basic to Einstein's approach was his denial of absolute space and his re-definition of simultaneity, which led him to deny the absolute status of time as well. What Einstein did, in effect, was to shave away Newton's metaphysical time and space and along with them the aether, thus leaving behind only their sensible measures, so that physical time and physical space were the only ones to be considered real.

What justification did Einstein have for so radical a proposal? How did he know that metaphysical time and space do not exist? The answer, in a word, is: *positivism*. Although one rarely finds this discussed in textbook expositions of the theory, or even in discussions of the foundations of RT, nevertheless historians of science have convincingly shown that at the roots of Einstein's theory lies an epistemological positivism of Machian provenance, which issues in a verificationist analysis of the concepts of time and space.

Mach's philosophy of science was hardcore phenomenalist. In experience we are given various sensations, such as colors, sounds, and pressures, and the aim of scientific theorizing is to construct the simplest possible description of the connections among these. Mach had no use for theoretical entities nor even for entities behind the sensations. Theoretical statements are meaningful only if related directly to sensations. In his *Die Mechanik in ihrer Entwicklung*, which Einstein studied carefully, Mach declared his aim to be *"bluntly anti-metaphysical"*; claiming space and time to be *"well-ordered systems of series of sensations"* on a par with our sensations of colors, sounds, and smells, he denounced Newton's absolute concepts.[45]

In 1905, when Einstein published his paper on the electrodynamics of moving bodies, and for several years to come, Einstein was a self-confessed pupil of Mach; the epistemological analysis of space and time in the opening section of that paper clearly displays this influence. Writing off Mach's rejection of the theory of relativity to the intransigence of old age, Einstein continued to insist that the whole gist of his theory was in conformity with the thinking of Mach. Although his own work on gravitation later on made him come close to a critical rationalism, Einstein in his "Autobiographical Notes" connected his original denial of absolute simultaneity with the critical reasoning of Mach, also mentioning the influence of David Hume.[46]

Turning to the 1905 paper itself[47], we find that Einstein's verificationism is clearly evidenced in his operationalist redefinition of key concepts. Einstein does not even attempt to justify his position; he takes for granted that all judgements in which time plays a rôle must have physical meaning. So he asserts: *"Now we must bear carefully in mind that a mathematical description of this kind has no physical meaning unless we are quite clear as to what we will understand by 'time'."* The meaning of "time" is thereby made to depend upon the meaning of "simultaneity," which is defined in terms of occurrence at the same local clock reading.

In order to "define" a common time for spatially separated clocks, Einstein adopted the convention that the time which light takes to travel from A to B equals the time it takes to travel from B to A. This presupposes that absolute

---

[45] See *The Science of Mechanics* (pp.xxii & 611), McCormack trl., Open Court 1960.

[46] In P.A. Schilpp, ed.,1949: *Albert Einstein, Philosopher-Scientist*, Evanston.

[47] Reprinted in A. Einstein & al., 1952: *The Principle of Relativity*, Dover.

time or space do not exist. Thus time is reduced to physical time (clock readings) and space to physical space (readings of measuring rods), both of which are relativized to local frames. Simultaneity is defined in terms of synchronization by light signals. Due to such operational definitions of time and space, Mach's positivism triumphs. Reality is reduced to what our measurements read. Newton's absolute time and space, which transcend operational definitions, are implied to be mere figments of the imagination.

In Einstein's other early papers on relativity, his verificationist theory of meaning comes even more explicitly to the fore. Concepts which cannot be given an empirical content and assertions which cannot be empirically verified in principle are discarded as meaningless. In his 1907 paper to *Jahrbuch der Radioaktivität und Elektronik*, after stating his operational definitions for time and simultaneity, he writes: *"According to the definition of time given in §1, a specific time has sense only (relative) to a reference frame (in) a particular state of motion."* To refer to the time of an event without also referring to its inertial frame thus has no sense.

In his 1909 piece to *Physikalische Zeitschrift* he muses on the apparent contradiction between the Relativity Principle and Lorentz's conviction that light travels at constant velocity in the aether, commenting: *"The theorem of addition of velocities rests, however, on the arbitrary presupposition that time specifications, as well as statements about the shape of moving bodies, have a meaning independent of the state of motion of the relevant coordinate system. But one is convinced that the introduction of clocks which are at rest relative to the relevant coordinate system is required for a definition of time and the shape of moving bodies."*[48]

In a summary paper entitled "Die Relativitäts-Theorie" and published in 1911, Einstein expresses himself more at length concerning the meaning of statements about time and space.[49] He contends *"We must ... try to so define time that time measurements are possible on the basis of this definition."* He goes on to describe the light signal synchronization procedure, remarking:

---

[48] In: *Phys.Zeitschr.*10, 1909, p.819.

[49] In: *Vierteljahrschr.d.naturforsch.Gesellsch.*Zürich 56, p.7.

"When we have fulfilled this prescription, we have thus attained a time determination from the standpoint of the measuring physicist. The time of an event is, namely, equal to the reading of these clocks regulated by the above prescription which are at the place of the event."

Even subsequent to his development of General Relativity (GR), Einstein continued to consider absolute space and time as meaningless notions. In 1920, for example, he wrote: *"We thus require a definition of simultaneity such that this definition supplies us with the means by which, in the present case, he can decide by experiment whether both lightning strokes occurred simultaneously. As long as this requirement is not satisfied, I allow myself to be deceived as physicist (and of course the same applies if I am not physicist) when I imagine that I am able to attach a meaning to the statement of simultaneity."*[50]

Einstein continued to cling to his rejection of metaphysical time and space, insisting that the claim that two events occur simultaneously is meaningless if an operational definition cannot be given for that concept: *"The only justification for our concepts and system of concepts is that they serve to represent the complex of our experiences; beyond this they have no legitimacy. I am convinced that the philosophers have had a harmful effect upon the progress of scientific thinking in removing certain fundamental concepts from the domain of empiricism, where they are under our control, to the intangible heights of the a priori. For even if it should appear that the universe of ideas cannot be deduced from experience by logical means, but is, in sense, a creation of the human mind, without which no science is possible, nevertheless this universe of ideas is just as little independent of the nature of our experiences as clothes are of the form of the human body. This is particularly true of our concepts of time and space which physicists have been obliged by the facts to bring down from the Olympus of the a priori in order to ... put them in a serviceable condition."*[51]

---

[50] A. Einstein, 1920: *Relativity, the Special and the General Theory*, Methuen.

[51] A. Einstein, 1967 (1922): *The Meaning of Relativity*, Chapman & Hall.

Positivistic philosophers and physicists were quick to recognize in SR a kindred spirit, and they embraced the theory eagerly. Under the influence of positivism and the verificationist criterion of meaning, physicists and philosophers of space and time during the first half of this century openly expressed their abhorrence for what was called "metaphysics." For most thinkers "time" became synonymous with "physical time."

4. THE POSITIVISTIC FOUNDATIONS OF SR

What, then, can be said of SR's elimination of metaphysical time and space? The first thing to be noticed is that the positivism which characterized the historical formulation of SR belongs essentially to the philosophical foundations of the theory. The relativity of length depends upon the relativity of simultaneity, which in turn rests upon Einstein's redefinition of simultaneity in terms of clock synchronization by light signals. But that redefinition assumes necessarily that the time which light takes to travel between two relatively stationary observers A and B is the same from A to B as from B to A. This assumption presupposes that A and B are not both in absolute motion, or in other words that there is neither a metaphysical space nor a privileged rest frame. The only justification for that assumption is that it is empirically impossible to distinguish uniform motion from rest relative to such frame, and if metaphysical space and absolute motion or rest are undetectable empirically, they do not exist (and may even be said to be meaningless). Such an inference is clearly verificationist, and therefore positivistic.

In a clear-sighted analysis of the epistemological foundations of SR, Lawrence Sklar stresses the essential role played by verificationism: *"Certainly the original arguments in favor of the relativistic viewpoint were rife with verificationist presuppositions about meaning, etc. And despite Einstein's later disavowal of the verificationist point of view, no one to my knowledge has provided an adequate account of the foundations of relativity which isn't verificationist in essence."* It would be desirable to do so, muses Sklar, but *"what I don't know is either how to formulate a coherent underpinning for relativity which isn't verificationist to begin with, or how, once begun, to find a natural stopping point for verificationist claims of under-determination and conventionality."*[52]

Untenability and obsolescence of Positivism

But if positivism belongs essentially to the foundations of SR, the next thing to be noted is that positivism has proved to be completely untenable and is now outmoded. The untenability of positivism is so universally acknowledged that it is not necessary to rehearse the objections against it here. Healey observes that "... positivism has come under such sustained attack that opposition to it has become almost orthodoxy in the philosophy of science."[53] Positivism provides absolutely no justification for thinking that Newton erred, e.g., in holding that God exists in a temporal series which transcends our physical measures of it and which may or may not be accurately registered by them. It matters not a whit whether we finite creatures know what time it is in God's metaphysical time: God knows, and that is enough.

Contemporary physics has in any case ignored the constrictions of positivism. When the contemporary student of physics reads the anti-metaphysical polemics of the past generation, he must feel as though he were peering into a different world. For it is now widely recognized that the boundaries of science are impossible to fix with precision, and during the last few decades theoretical physics has become characterized precisely by its metaphysical, speculative character. In various fields such as quantum mechanics, classical cosmology, and quantum cosmology, debates rage over issues which are overtly metaphysical in character.[54] In the essay, "Is Physics

---

[52] In R. Healey, ed., 1981: *Reduction, Time & Reality*, Cambridge (p.141).

[53] ibid., p.vii.

[54] Physics becomes most metaphysical in the budding field of quantum cosmology. Relativistic physicists in the first half of this century exulted in the four-dimensional space-time view of reality which RT had given them - now QC threatens to undo the fabric of their world. In the most famous model, that

at the Threshold of New Stage of Evolution?," Rompe & Treder echo Planck's question of 1908 and answer in the affirmative: *"For several decades physics wächst über sich selbst hinaus (has expanded beyond its own limits)."*[55]

George Gale, surveying some "Metaphysical Perplexities in Comtemporary Physics," contends: *"... we are entering a phase of scientific activity during which the physicist has out-run his philosophical base camp, and, finding himself cut off from conceptual supplies, he is ready and waiting for some relief from his philosophical comrades-in-arms."*[56] Noting that in recent years such "metaphysical conundrums" as *creatio ex nihilo* "have entered the mainstream of scientific discussions," John Barrow remarks: *"Traditional dogmas as to what criteria must be met by a body of ideas for it to qualify as 'science' now seem curiously inappropriate in the face of problems and studies far removed from the human enterprise."*[57]

The inevitable conclusion is that the positivistic, anti-metaphysical view of physics which dominated the first two-thirds of the 20th century is simply outmoded today. With the failure of positivism one is free, especially if one is a theist, to make a distinction between physical time and space (clock and rod measurements) and metaphysical time and space (ontological time and space independent of physical measures thereof). As P.J. Zwart states: *"Only when adopting the positivistic view that time is nothing more than what is measured by a clock could the relativistic theory of time be considered a*

---

of Hartle & Hawking, the position is adopted that time is imaginary (the time coordinate is an imaginary number), that is, if one is to avoid intractable infinities in performing the calculations. But clearly, the notion that our universe exists 'in imaginary time' raises profound metaphysical difficulties.

[55] In Barut, v.d. Merwe & Vigier, eds., 1984: *Quantum, Space & Time - the quest continues*, Cambridge.

[56] G. Gale, 1985, in paper presented at the 36th Ann.Meeting Metaphys.Soc.Am., March 14-16.

[57] J. Barrow, 1988: *The World within the World*, Oxford (pp.2 & vii-viii).

philosophical one."[58] SR is a theory about physical time and space and says nothing about the nature of metaphysical time and space. Questions dealing with the latter are philosophical in nature and must be treated as such. An exclusively physical methodology is simply inadequate to deal with all the problems of time and space.

All too often scientists' failure to draw the above distinction has led them into faulty theological inferences. For example, Paul Davies, observing that if a space-time singularity did occur at the "Big Bang," as predicted by the Friedman models, it will be impossible *"to continue physics, or physical reasoning, through it to an earlier stage of the universe,"*[59] goes on to conclude from this that it is "meaningless" to speak of God's creating the universe, for a cause must precede its effect temporally; but there is no temporal moment before the "Big Bang."[60] Therefore, according to Davies, the "Big Bang" can have no cause. But - leaving aside the faulty premiss that a cause must temporally precede its effect - if we accept the distinction between metaphysical time and physical time, it is quite evident that a beginning of the latter does not imply a beginning of the former. God in metaphysical time could very well have been active prior to the creation of the physical world - perhaps creating angelic realms.

Again the uncertainty involved by quantum geometrodynamics in the time coordinate prior to the Planck time is exploited by T. Banks to draw a marvelous metaphysical inference: *"... as we enter this regime [prior to Planck time] the intuitive concept of time loses all meaning. There is no content in the question of what happened before the big bang, not because the universe becomes singular, but because quantum fluctuations invalidate the notion of 'absolute time'."*[61]

---

[58] In: *Synthese* 24, 1972, p.134.

[59] P. Davies, 1977: *Space and Time in the Modern Universe*, Cambridge (p.160).

[60] P. Davies, 1983: *God and the New Physics*, NY (p.38-39).

[61] In: Nuclear Physics B249, 1985, p.340.

But it is not explained how the indeterminacy of physical time is supposed to invalidate Newton's absolute time, which, since it is based in God's eternity, *"ought to be distinguished from what are only sensible measures thereof."*

Sometimes the metaphysical conclusions professed on basis of the positivistic analysis of time can be quite absurd. For example, appealing to the invariance of quantum field theories under consecutive reversals of time, charge and space (TCP invariance), H. Mehlberg proclaims: *"If all natural laws are time reversed invariant and no irreversible processes occur in the physical universe, then there is no inherent, intrinsically meaningful difference between past and future - just as there is no such difference between 'to the left of' and 'to the right of'. If this is actually the case, then all mankind's major religions which preach a creation of the universe (by a supernatural agency) and imply, accordingly, a differentiation between the past and the future, i.e., an intrinsic difference between both, would have to make an appropriate readjustment of man's major religious and 'creationist' creeds and the scientific findings."*[62]

This solemn and ridiculous pronouncement clearly rests on the identification of God's time with physical time, a reduction which is definitely positivistic in character. So it is evident that the demise of positivism is not at all to be mourned, but that, on the contrary, its lingering shadow has sometimes resulted in quite unjustified and erroneous metaphysical conclusions.

We have thus seen that positivism belongs essentially to the philosophical foundations of SR and that such an epistemological outlook has been justifiably and universally rejected as untenable and obsolete. It is difficult, indeed, to understand how contemporary philosophers and physicists can speak of SR's "forcing" us to abandon the classical concepts of space and time, or of its "destruction" of Newtonian absolute time. L. Sklar concludes: *"The original Einstein papers on special relativity are founded, as is well known, on a verificationist critique of earlier theories ... Now it might be argued that Einstein's verificationism was a misfortune, to be encountered not with rejection of special relativity, but with an acceptance of the theory*

---

[62] In: *The Monist* 53, 1969, p.363.

now to be understood on better epistemological grounds ... But I don't think a position of this kind will work in the present case. I can see no way of rejecting the old aether-compensatory theories, originally invoked to explain the Michelson-Morley results, without invoking a verificationist critique of some kind or other. And I know of no way to defend the move to a relativized notion of simultaneity, so essential to special relativity, without first offering a critique, in the same vein as Einstein's, of the pre-relativistic absolutist notion, and then continuing to observe that even the relativistic replacement for this older notion is itself, insofar as it outruns the 'hard data' of experiment, infected with a high degree of conventionality."[63]

5. GOD AND PHYSICAL TIME

The Independence of God's Time

We have seen that, for Newton, God's eternity and omnipresence were ontologically foundational for his views of time and space. Unfortunately, in our secular age physicists and philosophers of space and time rarely, if ever, give careful consideration to the difference God's existence makes for our conceptions of time and space. Such indifference was characteristic of Einstein himself. Only after 1930 he began to refer more frequently in his non-scientific writings to religious questions. But he was, as Holton says, *"quite unconcerned with religious matters during the period of his early scientific publications."*[64] Thus, he did not consider the difference theism would make to one's views of time and space.

On the other hand, Poincaré in a fascinating passage in his essay *La mesure du temps* does briefly entertain the hypothesis of *"une intelligence infinie,"* and considers the implications of such a hypothesis. In consciousness, he submits, the temporal order of mental events is clear, but going outside

---

[63] In R. Healey, ed., 1981: *Reduction, Time & Reality*, Cambridge (p.132).

[64] In 1970: *Ernst Mach, Physicist and Philosopher*, Bost.St.Phil.Sc. 6 (p.198).

consciousness we confront various difficulties. One of these concerns how we can apply one and the same measure of time to events which transpire in "different worlds," i.e., to spatially distant events. What does it mean to say that two psychological phenomena in two different consciousnesses occur simultaneously? Or what does it mean to say that a supernova emerged before Columbus observed the isle of Espanola? According to the opinion of Poincaré, *"all these affirmations have by themselves no meaning."* Then he remarks:

> "We should first ask ourselves how one could have had the idea of putting into the same frame so many worlds impenetrable to one another. We should like to represent to ourselves the external universe, and only by so doing could we feel that we understood it. We know we can never attain this representation: our weakness is too great. But at least we desire the ability to conceive an infinite intelligence for which this representation could be possible, sort of great consciousness which should see all, and which should classify all in its time, as we classify, in our time, the little we see. This hypothesis is indeed crude and incomplete, because this supreme intelligence would be only a demigod; infinite in one sense, it would be limited in another, since it would have only an imperfect recollection of the past; it could have no other, since otherwise all recollections would be equally present to it and for it there would be no time. And yet when we speak of time, for all which happens outside of us, do we not unconsciously adopt this hypothesis; do we not put ourselves in the place of this imperfect god; and do not even the atheists put themselves in the place where God would be if he existed? What I have just said shows us, perhaps, why we have tried to put all physical phenomena into the same frame. But that cannot pass for a definition of simultaneity, since this hypothetical intelligence, even if it existed, would be for us impenetrable. It is therefore necessary to seek something else."[65]

---

[65] In his 1982 (1913): *The Foundations of Science* (p.228).

Poincaré suggests that, in considering the notion of simultaneity, we instinctively put ourselves in the place of God, classifying events as past, present or future according to His time. Poincaré does not deny that this perspective would disclose to us true relations of simultaneity. But he rejects the hypothesis as yielding a definition of simultaneity, since we could never know such relations; indeed, such knowledge would remain the exclusive possession of God Himself. But evidently, Poincaré's misgivings are relevant to a definition of simultaneity only if one is presupposing some sort of verificationist theory of meaning, as he undoubtedly was; the fact remains that God knows the absolute simultaneity of events even if we grope in total darkness. Nor need we bother about Poincaré's argument that such an infinite intelligence would be a mere demigod, since it is a *non sequitur* that a being with perfect recollection of the past cannot be temporal: there is no problem with the idea of God's knowing all true past-tense propositions. That such a God would be temporal is clear from the fact that, as events transpire, more and more past tense propositions become true, so the content of His knowledge is constantly changing.[66] So it does not follow that if God is temporal, He cannot have a perfect recollection of the past.

Poincaré's hypothesis suggests that God's present is constitutive of relations of absolute simultaneity. Therefore J.M. Findlay was simply wrong when he claimed that *"... the influence which harmonizes and connects all the world-lines is not God, not any featureless, inert, medium, but that living, active interchange called ... Light, offspring of Heaven firstborn."*[67] The use of light signals to establish clock synchrony is a convention, which finite and ignorant creatures have been obliged to adopt; but the living God, who knows all, is not so dependent.

As M. K. Munitz has correctly pointed out: *"Let us imagine a superhuman observer - a god - who is not bound by the limitations of the maximum velocity of light. Such an observer could survey in a single instant the entire domain of galaxies that have already come into existence. His survey would*

---

[66] For a discussion, see my 1990: *Divine Foreknowledge and Human Freedom*, Leiden.

[67] In: *Review of Metaphysics* 32, 1978-9, pp.6-7.

not have to depend on the finite velocity of light. It would not betray any restriction in information of the kind that results from the delayed time it takes to bring information about the domain of galaxies to an ordinary human observer situated in the universe, and who is therefore bound by the mechanisms and processes of signal transmission. The entire domain of galaxies would be seen instantaneously by this ... superhuman observer. His observational survey of all galaxies would yield what Milne calls a 'world map'."[68]

In God's temporal experience, there is a moment, which is present in metaphysical time, wholly independently of physical clock times. Thus God would know, without any dependence on clock synchronization procedures, or on any physical operations at all, which events were simultaneously present in metaphysical time - and He would know this simply in virtue of His knowing at every such moment the unique set of present-tense

---

[68] In his 1986: *Cosmic Understanding*, Princeton, p.157. Kanitscheider (in: *Kosmologie*, Reclam 1984, p.193) proceeds, *"The theorist ... would like to draw up, as Milne put it, a world map. On it the state of the world at a specific moment of cosmic time is indicated. All points of space on a hypersurface of space-time are at once grasped and physically described. Such a slice through the happening of events corresponds, of course, to no datum of observation, rather it concerns a theoretical construction. Only a hypothetical, spiritual observer, who could visit all points on the hypersurface without any delay, would be able to achieve such an overview and could confirm the statement that does in fact possess the same value at every place."* Kanitscheider explains that we earthbound observers have only a world picture, in which distant parts of the world actually belong to earlier moments of cosmic time. Only an omnipresent, cosmic observer, he concludes, who sees the world *sub specie aeternitatis*, can be in the position to draw up a world map. Here the relevance of cosmic time to the theological doctrine of divine eternity becomes explicit.

propositions true at that moment, without any need of a sensorium or any physical observation of the universe.[69]

Neo-Lorentzian Relativity

The question now is: how does God's metaphysical time relate to our physical time? From what has been said thus far, it seems that God's existence in metaphysical time and His real relation to the world imply that the Lorentz-Poincaré Theory of Relativity is correct after all, for God in the "now" of metaphysical time would know which events in the universe are now being created by Him and are thus absolutely simultaneous with each other and with His "now." This startling conclusion clearly demonstrates that Newton's theistic hypothesis is not some idle speculation, but has important

---

[69] How, then, should we assess Minkowski's oft-repeated claim, that *"henceforth, space by itself, and time by itself, are doomed to fade away into mere shadows, and only a kind of union of the two will preserve an independent reality"*? (in: *The Principle of Relativity*, Dover, p.75). In making such a claim Minkowski forgot Kant's insight that time is a form applicable not only to the external world, but to consciousness as well. Concerning Minkowski space-time, Wenzl cautions: *"From the standpoint of the physicist, it is a thoroughly consistent solution. But the physicist will (doubtless) understand the objection, raised by philosophy, that time is by no means a merely physical matter. Time is, as Kant put it, the form not merely of our outer sense but also of our inner sense ... Should our experiences of successiveness and memory be mere illusion?"* (in: *Albert Einstein: Philosopher-Scientist*, Evanston, pp.587-88). Indeed, time is more fundamental than space, as Lucas has emphasized (in: *Treatise on Time and Space*, Oxford, p.3). For while a series of mental events is a sufficient condition of time, it is not sufficient to constitute space. Since God is incorporeal, He would not be spatial prior to the creation of the universe even though He were temporal. Nor would His omnipresence entail the existence of empty metaphysical space prior to His creation of the physical universe, as Newton believed.

implications for our understanding of how the world is and for assessment of rival scientific theories.

Despite the widespread aversion to a neo-Lorentzian interpretation of Relativity Theory, such antipathy is really quite unjustified. Admitted on all sides to be empirically equivalent to the Einsteinian interpretation, the neo-Lorentzian interpretation is neither ad hoc, nor is it more complicated than its rival.[70] The physical effects it posits are no less real in the Einsteinian version, only there they appear as axiomatic deductions wholly lacking

---

[70] It is often asserted that Einstein's version of the theory is simpler and therefore to be preferred. This is, however, misleading. Though Lorentz's own theory was more complicated than Einstein's, H.E. Ives (*Phil.Mag.* 36,1945,392-401 and *Spec.Sc.Techn.* 2, 1979, 247-55) was able to derive the Lorentz transformation equations from (i) the laws of conservation of energy and momentum and (ii) the laws of transmission of radiant energy. On Ives's achievement, Martin Ruderfer (*Spec.Sc.Techn.* 2, 1979, 243) comments that he succeeded in elevating Lorentz's ad hoc theory to an equal status with SR and did so with the same number of basic assumptions as Einstein, so that his theory has the same beauty: *"The Ives and Einstein interpretations represent two different, but equally valid, views of the same set of observations."* Hence, assertions that Einstein's version is simpler than a neo-Lorentzian theory appear to be incorrect. In any case, as is well-known, one must be very cautious about the connection between the simplicity of a theory and its truth, as opposed to its utility. What right do we have to infer that, if Einstein's version is simpler, it is therefore true, especially in light of the extraordinary metaphysical commitments it entails (no absolute space, no absolute time)? Moreover, that simplicity is achieved by means of conventional definitions, which makes it difficult to regard the theory as being true rather than merely useful or expedient. Besides all this, the fact remains that the theist has good reasons for believing that a neo-Lorentzian interpretation is correct, namely, the existence of God in metaphysical time implies it, so that concerns about which version is simpler become of little moment.

causal explanations (see Appendix). Indeed, its fecundity in opening the question about physical causes seems to be an important advantage of the neo-Lorentzian interpretation.

Of course, one could continue working within the theoretical framework of Einstein's version, being accustomed to so working, thereby retaining the advantage of using a received view of the scientific community, and yet consistently affirm what I have said concerning God, metaphysical time, and physical time, by rejecting a realistic understanding of Einstein's theory. So long as one accords to his theory a purely instrumentalist interpretation, one can employ it on pragmatic grounds without regarding it as even approximately true. But if one is interested in being a scientific realist on matters of time and space, then one ought - at least if one is a theist - to affirm a neo-Lorentzian interpretation.

6. GOD AND COSMIC TIME

A final issue now needs to be engaged, and that is whether we have some idea of what measured time coincides with God's metaphysical time, or in other words, what clock time is the true time? The answer to this question will take us from Special into General Relativity, as we seek to gain cosmic perspective on time. Troubled by the non-equivalence of inertial and non-inertial frames, Einstein endeavored in his GR to enunciate a General Principle of Relativity which would serve to render physically equivalent all inertial and non-inertial frames alike. In his article "The Foundations of General Relativity Theory" (1915), he boasted that his theory *"takes away from space and time the last remnant of physical objectivity."* It was, in effect, intended to be the final destruction of Newton's absolute space and time.

In fact, however, Einstein was only partially successful in achieving his aims. He did not succeed in enunciating a tenable General Principle of Relativity after the pattern of the Special Principle, nor was he able to show the physical equivalence of all reference frames. He did succeed in drafting a revolutionary and complex theory of gravitation, which has been widely hailed as his greatest intellectual achievement. The so-called General Theory of Relativity is thus something of a misnomer: it is really a Theory of Gravitation and not an extension of the Special Theory of Relativity from inertial reference frames to all reference frames.[71]

It might appear, therefore, that GR has nothing more to contribute to the understanding of time than SR. They simply differ over the presence of curvature in space-time; if one adds a condition of flatness to GR, then SR results. But such a conclusion would be hasty, indeed, for GR serves to introduce into relativity theory a cosmic perspective, enabling one to draft cosmological models of the universe governed by the gravitational field equations of GR.

Within the context of such models, the issue of time resurfaces dramatically. Einstein himself proposed the first GR model in a paper of 1917, entitled "Cosmological Considerations on the General Theory of Relativity."[72] This model describes a spatially finite universe which possesses at every time the geometry of the surface of sphere in three dimensions with a constant radius. The model is characterized by the static metric

$$ds^2 = -dt^2 + R^2(dr^2 + sin^2 r\,(d\theta^2 + sin^2\theta\,d\varphi^2))$$

Time, which is now decoupled from space, extends from $-\infty$ to $+\infty$. Hence, space-time takes the form of a four-dimensional cylinder, temporal cross-sections of which are 3-spheres. Kanitscheider draws our attention to the sort of time coordinate which shows up in the metric: *"It represents in a certain sense the restoration of the universal time that was destroyed by SR. In the static world there is a global reference frame, relative to which the whole of cosmic matter finds itself at rest. All cosmological parameters are independent of time. In the rest frame of cosmic matter, space and time are*

---

[71] See M. Friedmann, 1983: *Foundations of Space-Time Theories*, Princeton (pp.204-15). See also H. Bondi, 1979, in F. De Finis, ed.: *Relativity, Quanta, and Cosmology*, NY (pp.179-86).

[72] In: *The Principle of Relativity*, Dover, pp.177-88.

separated. For fundamental observers at rest, all clocks can be synchronized and worldwide simultaneity can be defined."[73] Thus cosmological considerations prompted the idea of a cosmic time measuring the duration of the universe.

Nor was this cosmic time limited to Einstein's static model of the universe. Expansion models, tracing their origin to de Sitter's 1917 model of an empty universe, may also involve a cosmic time. The standard for contemporary expansion models derives from Friedman's 1922 model of an expanding universe characterized by the principles of homogeneity and isotropy. Several features of the cosmic time parameter in the Friedman models merit comment.

First, although one can slice space-time into various spatial hypersurfaces wholly arbitrarily, some space-times have natural symmetries to guide the construction of cosmic time.[74] GR does not itself lay down any formula for dissecting the space-time manifold of points; it has no inherent "layering." Theoretically, then, one may slice it up at one's whim. Nevertheless, certain models of space-time, like the Friedman model, have a dynamical, evolving geometry, i.e., a geometry which is tied to the boundary conditions of homogeneity and isotropy of the cosmological fluid, and in order to ensure a smooth development of such geometry, it is necessary to construct a time parameter based on a preferred foliation of space-time. For example, in 1935, H.P. Robertson and A.G. Walker independently showed that a homogeneous and isotropic universe requires space to be characterized by the constant curvature metric:

$$(dr^2 + r^2(d\theta^2 + \sin^2\theta \, d\varphi^2))/(1 + kr^2/4)^2$$

In the ensuing Robertson-Walker space-time metric, the spatial geometry is dynamic over time:

$$ds^2 = -dt^2 + R(t)^2 (dr^2 + r^2(d\theta^2 + \sin^2\theta \, d\varphi^2))/(1 + kr^2/4)^2$$

---

[73] In: *Kosmologie*, 1984 (p.155). See also G. J. Whitrow, 1980: *The Natural Philosophy of Time*, Oxford (pp.283-84).

[74] See Misner, Thorne & Wheeler, 1973: *Gravitation*, (pp.713-14).

In the Robertson-Walker line element, *t* represents cosmic time, which is detached from space and serves to render space dynamic. The factor *R(t)* determines that all spatial structures of cosmic proportions, for example, a triangle demarcated by three galactic clusters, will either shrink or stretch through the contraction or expansion of space into a similar smaller or larger triangle. The boundary condition of homogeneity precludes other geometrical changes such as shear, which would preserve the area but not the shape of a triangle. The condition of isotropy further precludes that a triangle could be altered in such way as to preserve both its area and shape while nonetheless undergoing rotational change of direction. Thus, in a Friedman universe there are certain natural symmetries related to the dynamic geometry which serve as markers for the foliation of space-time and the assigning of a cosmic time parameter. Of course, there are other cosmological models which do not involve homogeneity and isotropy and so may involve a different cosmic time or lack such a time altogether. Cosmic time is therefore not nomologically necessary, and its actual existence is an empirical question.

Cosmic time is fundamentally parameter time and only secondarily coordinate time. Physical time can be related in two quite different ways to the manifold in which motion is represented. If it is part of that manifold, then it functions as coordinate. If it is external to that manifold, it functions as parameter. In Newton's physics time functioned only as a parameter. Motion in his theory takes place in absolute space and is parameterized by absolute time. Likewise, in Einstein's original formulation of SR relativistic time functions only as a parameter. Einstein rejected the existence of absolute space and a fundamental rest frame in favor of a plurality of relatively moving inertial frames, each of which was characterized by a parameter indicating the proper time for that frame. Nevertheless there was no absolute parameter time, only separate parameter times assigned to their respective inertial frames.

The familiar space-time formulation of SR which is used in virtually all contemporary expositions of the theory, and according to which time is a coordinate of an event in space-time (along with the three spatial coordinates), derives from Minkowski, and not from Einstein. The space-time formalism of Minkowski, in which time is part of the manifold in which motion is represented and so functions as a coordinate, was a wonderful aid to the visualization and comprehension of relativity theory; but Newton's theory can also be cast in terms of a space-time formalism in which time functions as a coordinate of events in space-time.

Thus both theories admit of either a space-time formulation in which space-time is the manifold, or a space-and-time formulation in which the manifold is/are space(s) and time is a parameter. In the space-time formulation, time functions both as a co-ordinate, locating events in the manifold, and as a parameter, recording the lapse of proper time along an observer's inertial trajectory, the difference between the two theories being that in SR parameter time loses the universality it possessed in Newtonian space-time, so that simultaneity becomes relative.

When it comes to GR, it is unclear, according to Kroes, whether the theory could be formulated in terms of space and time rather than of space-time. He observes that differences in coordinate time values generally have no direct physical significance in GR, due to the variable space-time geometry or the gravitational fields which distort the co-ordinate grids laid on them. But insofar as time functions as a parameter in GR it is a more fundamental concept of time, since it does possess direct physical significance. Parameter time can serve as a direct measure of the time elapsed between two events.

Moreover, parameter time is well-suited, according to Kroes, for accommodating the notion of temporal becoming.[75] Whereas there is no

---

[75] In his 1985: *Time, its Rôle and Structure in Physical Theories*, Synthese Libr.179 (p.96), Kroes writes: *"In the space and time formulation of Newtonian physics, the increase of parameter time represents the objective flow of absolute time; for increasing values of parameter time, the distribution of the particles in space will be different, and therefore there is change and becoming with regard to parameter time. However, the same kind of reasoning, applied to parameter time in the space-time formalism of relativity theory, leads to the*

intrinsic difference between past and future in coordinate time, there is a distinction in parameter time. So the "flow" of time could relate to parameter time. Since parameter time in SR is the proper time of each inertial observer and since no inertial frame is preferred, the "flow" of parameter time in SR cannot be universal, but insofar as cosmic time plays a rôle in cosmological models based on GR that universality is restored.

It is thus highly important that cosmic time appears as a fundamental parameter in GR, though it can be used to generate coordinate time as well. As a parameter, time is not part of the space-time manifold but yields an observer-independent measure of the duration of the universe: the lapse of cosmic time is the same for all observers. Further, cosmic time supplies a physical time which is able to accommodate the philosophical notion of temporal becoming.

Finally, the universe contains a privileged class of fundamental observers whose individual planes of simultaneity mutually combine to align with the hypersurface which demarcates the cosmic time.[76] These hypothetical observers are conceived to be moving along with the cosmological fluid so that, although space is expanding and they are therefore mutually receding from each other, each is in fact at rest with respect to space itself.

As time goes on and the expansion of space proceeds, each fundamental observer remains in the same place: his spatial coordinates do not change, although his spatial separation from other fundamental observers steadily increases. Because of this mutual recession, the class of fundamental observers does not serve to define a global inertial frame, technically speaking. But since each one is at rest with respect to space, his plane of simultaneity will coincide locally with the hypersurface of cosmic time. Were he in motion with respect to the cosmological fluid, then his plane of simultaneity would not be orthogonal to the local hypersurface. But in virtue of being at rest, he can be guaranteed that local events which he judges to be

---

conclusion that parameter time has an objective flow (but with the proviso that the flow of parameter time is not universal)."

[76] See S. J. Prokhovnik, 1985: *Light in Einstein's Universe*, Reidel, chs. 4, 5, 6.

simultaneous will lie on the same hypersurface. This has two important implications: first, that the proper time of each fundamental observer will coincide with cosmic time, and second, that all fundamental observers, when properly synchronized, will agree as to what time it is.

It is noteworthy that deviations from this time are purely local effects to be explained due to velocity (SR) or to gravitation (GR). Hence it seems that, on a cosmic scale, we have that universality of time and absolute simultaneity which SR had denied. As Whitrow has stated: *"... in a universe that is characterized by the existence of a cosmic time, relativity is reduced to a local phenomenon, since this time is world-wide and independent of the observer."*[77] Based on a cosmological, rather than a local, perspective,

---

[77] G.J. Whitrow: *The Natural Philosophy of Time*, p.371; cf. p.302. Kanitscheider explains (*Kosmologie*, pp.186-87): *"... with the parameter we can so order all slices through space-time (the homogeneous hypersurfaces) that an unequivocal earlier/later relation can be set up worldwide. Within such a slice $t=t_0$ (in a three-space) the material quantities p and ρ as well as the physical geometry, are everywhere the same. Isotropy moreover implies that a particle of the cosmological fluid traces a worldline that orthogonally intersects the hypersurface of homogeneity. One recognizes that there is here again a privileged reference frame; to an observer at rest relative to the substratum, who swims along with the fluid, the universe has a simple form in material structure and space-time geometry ...The particular form of the motion of matter in this class of models suggests the utilization of a co-moving co-ordinate system, in which a worldwide, absolute simultaneity is defined. This is, however, no contradiction to the STR, since here the universe itself, with its limited possibility of movement, serves as an instrument of synchronization. The special relativistic time dilation, which we are acquainted with through local experiments, still holds as before for clocks moving relatively to the substratum. Nevertheless, the proper times of all observers who are at rest with respect to the flowing (expanding or contracting) substratum can be harmoniously fitted into a cosmic time."*

cosmic time appears to restore those intuitive notions of universal time and absolute simultaneity which SR had abandoned.

The question, then, becomes an empirical one: does cosmic time exist? The answer to that question comes from the evidence for large scale homogeneity and isotropy in the universe. In models like those of Gödel and Ozsvath & Schücking, there is posited a worldwide rotation of the homogeneous substratum, so that the isotropy condition of the Friedman model is violated and the proper times of fundamental observers cannot be fitted together into universal time. However, the observational evidence for cosmic isotropy, particularly for the isotropy of the cosmic microwave background radiation, which has been measured to an accuracy of one part in 10^5, makes it very likely that our actual universe does approximate a Friedman universe.

Reviewing the evidence, Martin Rees concludes: *"The most remarkable outcome of fifty years of observational cosmology has been the realization that the universe is more isotropic and uniform than the pioneer theorists of the 1920's would ever have suspected."*[78] This conclusion is supported by Whitrow: *"Consequently, we have strong evidence that the universe as a whole is predominantly homogeneous and isotropic, and this conclusion ... is a strong argument for the existence of cosmic time."*[79]

In fact, Hawking has demonstrated that existence of stable causality, that is, the absence of any null or time-like closed causal paths, is a necessary and sufficient condition for the existence of a cosmic time.[80] Therefore, far from *"taking away from space and time the last remnant of physical objectivity"*, as Einstein thought at first, GR through its cosmological applications seems to give back what SR had removed.

It is thus my contention that, since the inception of the universe, which also marked the beginning of physical time, this cosmic time coincides with God's metaphysical, absolute time. So it provides the right measure of God's

---

[78] In: *Some Strangeness in Proportion*, Mass. 1980 (p.293).

[79] In: *The Natural Philosophy of Time*, 1980 (p.317).

[80] In: Proc.Roy.Soc.Lond. A308 (pp.433-35).

time and is the true time, in contrast to the multiplicity of local times indicated by clocks in motion relative to the cosmological substratum. Already in 1920 Eddington had hinted at a theological interpretation of cosmic time: *"The world taken as whole has one direction in which it is not curved; that direction gives a kind of absolute time distinct from space. Relativity is reduced to a local phenomenon ... But we have already urged that the relativity theory is not concerned to deny the possibility of an absolute time, but to deny that it is concerned in any experimental knowledge yet found; and it need not perturb us if the conception of absolute time turns up in a new form in a theory of phenomena on a cosmical scale, as to which no experimental knowledge is yet available. Just as each limited observer has his own particular separation of space and time, so a being co-extensive with the world might well have a special separation of space and time natural to him. It is the time for this being that is here dignified by the title 'absolute'."*[81]

A couple of items in this remarkable paragraph deserve comment. First, Eddington interprets SR as imposing merely an epistemic limitation on our temporal notions rather than an ontological limitation on time and space. But as friend and foe alike have emphasized, SR requires metaphysical, not merely epistemological, commitments concerning the non-existence of absolute space and time. If not, one winds up with the Lorentz-Poincaré interpretation of the theory, which is, in truth, the position Eddington is describing.

Second, Eddington deliberately calls cosmic time absolute in view of its independence from space, that is to say, its status as a parameter. Relativistic time is, as Lorentz and Poincaré held, only local time, whereas cosmic time, being non-local, is the true, or universal, time.

Third, although in 1920 there was no empirical evidence for cosmic time, within a few years astronomical evidence confirmed the prediction of the Friedman model of universal expansion and, hence, of cosmic time. The veil of epistemic limitation had been torn away.

---

[81] In: *Space, Time & Gravitation*, Cambr.1920 (p.168).

Finally, this cosmic time would be the time of an omnipresent being, whose reference frame is the hypersurface of homogeneity itself. Is Eddington recalling here Poincaré's *"intelligence infinie,"* who classified everything according to his universal frame of reference, his "world map," just as finite observers classify events according to their local frames? Cosmic time is not merely the "fusion" of all the proper times recorded by the separate fundamental observers, but even more fundamentally as the measure of the duration of the universe, cosmic time also measures the duration of time for a being which is co-extensive with the world. For Eddington, it is the time of this being that deserves to be called "absolute." The theological application is obvious.

Given the existence of cosmic time, it is my contention that the moments of God's metaphysical time - while perhaps not strictly identical with the moments of cosmic time - are nonetheless coincident with them. So we have this hypothesis:

$$\text{God's metaphysical time} \approx \text{the universal time of cosmology}$$

Consider analogously the relation between cosmic time and the proper time of any fundamental observer. These times are not identical, for the former is a parameter attached to three-dimensional hypersurfaces in space-time marked out by natural symmetries, whereas the latter is a parameter designating the proper time along the inertial trajectory of an observer at rest with regard to the cosmological fluid. Nevertheless, as we have already seen, the two times coincide: the clocks of all fundamental observers will, according to our hypothesis, record the same duration as recorded by the universe itself when considered as one unique clock.

Now, similarly, God's metaphysical time may turn out to differ from the cosmic time, since the former is capable of exceeding the latter. Thus metaphysical time could precede physical time (think of God's "counting down" to creation). Nevertheless, since the inception of cosmic time, the moments of God's time might coincide with the moments of cosmic time. Indeed, when we remember that God is causally related to the cosmos, sustaining it in being from instant to instant, then it seems difficult to deny that duration as measured by cosmic time is also the duration of God's activity as a creator. If the duration of the universe, when measured by cosmic time, is fifteen billion years (since the singularity) - is not then the duration of God's creational activity, as measured in metaphysical time, also fifteen billion years?

In God's "now" the universe has (present tense) certain specific and unique properties, for example, a certain radius, a certain density, a certain temperature background, and so forth; but in the cosmic "now" it has all the same properties, and so it is with every successive "now." Is it not obvious, then, that these "nows" coincide and designate one and the same present?

Perhaps we can state this consideration a bit more formally by expressing it by means of the following principle:

P: *For any constantly and non-recurrently changing universe U, and temporal intervals x, y large enough to permit change: if the physical description of U at x is the same as the physical description of U at y, then x and y coincide.*

Given that in metaphysical time there is a temporal interval, or duration, during which a certain physical description of the universe is true, and that in cosmic time there is a similar interval, then it follows from P that those intervals of metaphysical and cosmic time coincide. It seems to me, therefore, that God's time and cosmic time ought naturally to be regarded as coincident since the inception of cosmic time.

Such an affirmation will, however, be typically met with passionate disclamations. Any assimilation of cosmic time with absolute time will probably be vigorously repudiated. Such protestations strike me, however, as being for the most part misconceived. Much of the disagreement seems due simply to the ambiguous term "absolute," compounded by the failure to appreciate the notion of the coincidence of cosmic time with metaphysical time.

For example, it is frequently objected that cosmic time is contingent and reference frame dependent; it therefore cannot be regarded as absolute. Since cosmic time does not exist in all GR based models and depends in any case on the existence of hypersurfaces of homogeneity, it cannot be said to record "absolute" time.

But all that follows from the existence of models lacking cosmic time is that cosmic time coincides with metaphysical time only contingently. Our world is characterized by cosmic time, and its absence in other cosmological models is wholly irrelevant to whether it coincides with God's time in the actual world. In virtue of that coincidence, it is absolute in the sense that it records the true time in this world.

The contingency of cosmic time says nothing against its privileged status in this world; in fact, a relationalist can consistently hold that even metaphysical time exists contingently, for if God had chosen to remain absolutely changeless and had never created a world, there would be no events at all and, hence, not even a metaphysical time. The existence of both metaphysical and cosmic time is thus a contingent fact dependent upon God's will.

The fact that cosmic time is relative to a reference frame is not incompatible with its absoluteness in the above sense. Otherwise one might as well charge that the time of nineteenth century physics was not absolute either, since it was relative to the aether rest frame. The point is that, in both cases, the reference frame in question is privileged, and therefore the time kept with respect to it measures absolute time.

Another way of putting this is to affirm that cosmic time and metaphysical time both concern the same duration, at least since creation, but do so under different definitions. To use an analogy, we might speak of Mrs. Thatcher as "the woman who has properties a, b, c" or, alternatively, as "the wife of the man who has properties a, b, c." Obviously the definitions are not the same; one is relational, while the other is not. Nonetheless, they pick out the same entity under different descriptions.

Similarly, cosmic time and metaphysical time, while radically different in that one is physical and the other is not, pick out the same duration under different names. They thus differ *de dicto*, but they are the same *de re*. Definitionally, cosmic time is not absolute, since it is, after all, a physical time, and so relative to a frame of reference. But in terms of real duration, cosmic time coincides with God's metaphysical time, and so it measures the lapse of metaphysical time. The universal reference frame is, like the aether frame of nineteenth century physics, therefore privileged and so, as Lorentz and Poincaré saw, the time relative to it is true time as opposed to merely local time. Cosmic time can thus be said to be absolute *de re*, if not *de dicto*.

To conclude, we have seen that, when one moves from SR into GR, the application of the latter theory to cosmology yields cosmic time, which is plausibly regarded as being the measured time which coincides with God's time and is therefore the true time.[82]

---

[82] One final point should be made to avert possible misunderstanding. Padgett, in *God, Eternity & the Nature of Time*, 1992 (p.127) intimates that God could not be in cosmic time, or indeed, any measured time, because God would also then have to be spatial as well as temporal. For in order to have cosmic time coordinates, God would also have to have spatial coordinates as well. But my claim is not that God exists in cosmic time as such; rather He exists in metaphysical time as such, but since creation the moments of cosmic time coincide with the moments of metaphysical time. It is in virtue of this coincidence that cosmic time measures God's metaphysical time. God thus exists in metaphysical time *per se*, but He exists in cosmic time *per accidens*. God does not exist in cosmic time because He exists at all points on a three-dimensional hypersurface of space-time, but rather because all the events on a given hypersurface are causally related to God as simultaneous and present. Cosmic time corresponding to that hypersurface is "now" for Him. In virtue of the coincidence of the moments of cosmic time with the moments of His metaphysical time, God can be said to be in cosmic time in the sense that it is true for any instant that "God exists at t and God believes t is now." His omnipresence may be explicated in terms of His being aware of and causally active at every point in space.

7. CONCLUSION

In summary, we have seen that in virtue of God's temporal duration, Newton correctly distinguished between metaphysical time and physical time. Newton's shortcoming lay not in his analysis of metaphysical time, but in his failure to realize that physical time is relativistic. Einstein's SR did nothing to disprove the existence of metaphysical time or absolute simultaneity. Rather his paring away of absolute time was rooted in a positivistic epistemology of Machian provenance and a verificationist philosophy which is philosophically untenable and wholly out of step with contemporary physics and philosophy of science. Moreover, we saw that this positivism belongs essentially to the philosophical foundations of that theory and serves to distinguish it from the Lorentz-Poincaré interpretation of the mathematical core of SR.

The almost universally recognised failure of positivism permits us to adhere rationally to a doctrine of metaphysical time and objective becoming independent of physical measures. Nothing compels us to adopt Einstein's interpretation of either the mathematics of his theory or of the relevant experimental data. If God exists in metaphysical time and temporally causes the successive states of the world, then the "now" of His metaphysical time demarcates a three-dimensional slice of space-time which is equally "now."

This universal frame of reference would thus be privileged, so that events which God knows to be present in it are absolutely simultaneous. What the privileged status of such a frame implies is that a neo-Lorentzian interpretation of SR is correct after all. In this frame absolute length, absolute motion, and absolute simultaneity obtain and are known to God, and rods and clocks in motion relative to it undergo intrinsic contraction and retardation.

Finally, we have seen that in order to discover which physical time corresponds with God's metaphysical time, it is necessary to explore the time concept in GR, which supersedes the restricted concept in SR. That theory, when applied to cosmology, discloses that in a causally well-behaved model there emerges a cosmic time which records the duration of the universe. This cosmic time is plausibly taken to coincide with metaphysical time since creation.

APPENDIX

It is important to realize in comparing the neo-Lorentzian and Einsteinian versions of SR that the FitzGerald-Lorentz contraction and clock retardation, which seem to be such stumbling blocks to some for the acceptance of a neo-Lorentzian theory, are just as much real, physical effects in Einstein's theory as in Lorentz's. Einstein realized right from the start that these effects described in his theory were real, not apparent, and could be shown to be real by various *Gedankenexperimente*. When V. Varicak asserted in 1911 ("Zum Ehrenfestschen Paradoxen," *Phys.Zeitschr.*12,1911,169) that length contraction in Einstein's theory is, in contrast to Lorentz's theory, *"only an apparent, subjective appearance," "psychological, not physical,"* Einstein (*Phys.Zeitschr.*12,1911, 509-10) responded with a *Gedankenexperiment* designed to show that the contraction does not have its roots in the arbitrary establishment of clock synchronization and length measurement procedures. Though examples of this sort are widely known, it seems that not all physicists have assimilated their significance. J.S. Bell (*Speakable and Unspeakable in Quantum Mechanics*, Cambr.Univ.Pr.1987,p.68) recounts an interesting anecdote in this connection. He invites us to imagine three spaceships A, B, C drifting freely in a region of space remote from other matter, without rotation and without relative motion, with B and C equidistant from A. On reception of a signal from A, the motors of B and C are ignited and they gently accelerate. Let ships B and C be similar and have similar acceleration programs. Then, as reckoned by an observer in A, they will have at every moment the same velocity and so remain separated from one another by the same distance. Suppose that a fragile thread is initially tied between B and C, just long enough to span the distance between them. Then, as the rockets speed up, the thread will be Lorentz-contracted and become too short and so must finally break. Having explained the situation, Bell recounts, "This old problem came up for discussion once in the CERN canteen. A distinguished experimental physicist refused to accept that the thread would break, and regarded my assertion, that indeed it would, as a personal misinterpretation of (SR). We decided to appeal to the CERN Theory Division for arbitration, and made a (not very systematic) canvas of opinion in it. There emerged a clear consensus that the thread would not break! Of course many people who give this wrong answer at first get the right answer on further reflection. They usually feel obliged to work out how things look to observers B or C. They find that B, for example, sees C drifting further and further behind, so that a given piece of thread can no longer span the distance. It is only after working this out, and perhaps only with a residual feeling of unease, that such people finally accept a conclusion which is perfectly trivial in terms of A's account of things, including the Fitzgerald contraction. It is my impression that those with a more classical education, knowing something of the reasoning of Larmor, Lorentz, and Poincaré as well as that of Einstein, have stronger and sounder instincts." It is interesting that this very *Gedankenexperiment* is employed by the neo-Lorentzian physicist L. Janossy (Budapest: Akadémiai Kiadó, 1971, pp.28-31) as illustrative of the real Lorentz contraction in connected systems. He points out that if the thread is strong enough, then the entire connected system will suffer a Lorentz-contraction, whereas if the thread is too fragile, then it will break, leaving the entire system uncontracted. Examples such as these could be multiplied to prove that, perhaps contrary to expectation, the Einsteinian interpretation of Relativity Theory involves real, physical length contraction and clock retardation, just as much as does the neo-Lorentzian interpretation. Podlaha concludes, (*Ind.J.Th.Phys.* 25,1975,74-75) "*In the relativity theory, the length contraction and time dilatation in all frames is often viewed as a consequence of a 'perspective of observation', similarly as a rod seems to change its length as observed under different angles ... however, it is seen that the results of relativistic experiments have their origin in the length contraction and time dilation effects which are so real as a change of the length of a rod caused by the change of temperature.*" Hence, it is entirely misconceived to prefer the Einsteinian version of SR to a neo-Lorentzian interpretation out of an aversion to the physical realism involved in the latter's postulate of length contraction and clock retardation.

On the Mind-dependence of Temporal Becoming

WILLIAM LANE CRAIG

The phenomenon of tense is experienced by human beings in a variety of ways which are so evident and so pervasive that the belief in the objective reality of past, present, and future and in the passage of time is a universal feature of human experience. Phenomenological analyses of temporal consciousness carried out by philosophers have emphasized the centrality of what McTaggart called A-determinations to our experience of time. In his classic phenomenology of time consciousness, Edmund Husserl described our experience of time in terms of retentions of the past and protentions of the future, both anchored in the "now." We experience on the one hand a sort of *"flowing away"* (*Ablaufsphänomene*) consisting of the recession of experience from the "now" into the past: *". . . this now apprehension is, as it were, the nucleus of a comet's tail of retentions referring to the earlier now-points of the motion."*[83] But we also protend the future in that we anticipate and live toward that which is to come. The transformation of now-consciousness to consciousness of the past and its replacement by a new now-consciousness, says Husserl, *"is part of the essence of time consciousness."*[84] Thus, our differing attitudes toward the past and future, as

---

[83] Edmund Husserl, *The Phenomenology of Internal Time-Consciousness*, ed. Martin Heidegger, trans. James S. Churchill, with an Introduction by Calvin O. Schrag (Bloomington, Ind.: Indiana University Press, 1964), p. 52. For a discussion of the importance of Husserl's work, see J.N. Findlay, "Husserl's Analysis of the Inner Time-Consciousness," *Monist* 59 (1975): 320, and Peter K. McInerney, *Time and Experience* (Philadelphia: Temple University Press, 1991), esp. chap. 5.

[84] Husserl, *Phenomenology of Time-Consciousness*, p. 86.

well as our apprehension of temporal becoming are constitutive of time consciousness: *"The immanent contents are what they are only so far as during their 'actual' duration they refer ahead to something futural and back to something past ... In each primal phase which primordially constitutes the immanent content we have retentions of the preceding and protentions of the coming phases of precisely this content ... "*[85]

Though Husserl, in line with his phenomenological practice of *epoché*, made no judgement concerning what he called the "objective flow of time" or "world-time" or "real time"[86], he accurately described how we experience the temporal world. Psychologist William Friedman, who has made a career of the study of time consciousness, reports, *"Like [temporal] order and the causal priority principle, the division between past, present, and future so deeply permeates our experience that it is hard to imagine its absence."*[87] We have, he writes, *"an irresistible tendency to believe in a present. Most of us find quite startling the claim of some physicists and philosophers that the present has no special status in the physical world, that there is only a sequence of times, that the past, present, and future are only distinguishable in human consciousness."*[88]

---

[85] Ibid., p. 110.

[86] Ibid., p. 23.

[87] William Friedman, *About Time* (Cambridge, Mass Press, 1990), p. 92.

[88] Ibid., p. 2. The development of time consciousness begins quite early. The main evidence for children's awareness of past, present, and future comes, interestingly, from studies on their use and comprehension of linguistic tense. Two and a half to three year olds already use tense correctly, and spontaneous use of tenses occurs even earlier. At about the same time, an appreciation of the relations of temporal order before and after develops. Even in unfamiliar tasks, children as young as three have demonstrated comprehension of relations of temporal succession and simultaneity. According to Friedman, *"These findings show that young children's experience of temporal order is not just the product of some automatic tendency of memory to record temporal sequences. Instead children as young as three years must understand the meaning of priority,*

As a result, virtually all philosophers of space and time, including B-theorists of time, admit that the view of the common man is that time involves a past, present, and future which are objectively real and that things or events really do come to be and pass away in time. For example, Oaklander grants that *"non-philosophers have never doubted that there is such a phenomenon as temporal flow or passage ..."*[89] Horwich muses that *"The quintessential property of time, it may seem, is the difference between past and future"*[90].

---

posteriority, and simultaneity in some abstract sense" (Ibid., pp. 127-128). Children also display since infancy an ability to estimate the duration of temporal intervals, an ability which certain animals also share. Animals, however, lack a sense of orientation in time, which combines the dynamism of the ever-changing present with temporal relations between time markers. *"... to an extent unique among species we are gifted with the mental processes which allow us to step outside the 'now', the endless succession of stimuli, and to build elaborate models of time: of the fluctuations of nature, the past, present, and future, near time and far time, even the fictitious time of novels and plays"* (Ibid., p. 7). By adulthood, *"not only do we conceive of an ever-changing present with the future vanishing into the past, but our experience is infused with knowledge of conventional time systems and of history, our ability to extrapolate the trajectory of our lives, and to impose order on our memories"* (Ibid., p. 93). *"In our experiential world there is a sharp contrast between memories of the past and plans for the future, and much of our thinking is devoted to determining the current time . . . and considering the relative times of past and future events"* (Ibid., pp. 23). Although very young children have difficulty measuring time and seldom have memories which are intrinsically ordered, still, Friedman reports, before they reach adolescence they operate with a reasonable semblance of Newtonian time (Ibid., p. 100).

[89] L. Nathan Oaklander, *Temporal Relations and Temporal Becoming* (Lanham, Maryland: University Press of America, 1984), p. 1.

[90] Paul Horwich, *Asymmetries in Time* (Cambridge, Mass.: MIT Press, 1987), p. 15.

Coburn confesses, *"If the existence of A-facts is an illusion, it is one of our most stubborn ones."*[91] The depth and pervasiveness of the common-sense belief in A-determinations lead A-theorist Godfrey-Smith to state flatly, *"Anyone who rejects the notions of past, present, and future has got a lot of explaining to do."*[92] Mellor does not deny it: *"the experienced presence of experience, is the crux of the tensed view of time"*, he acknowledges, *"and the tenseless camp must somehow explain it away."*[93]

B-Theorists claim that temporal becoming is not a feature of the world which exists independently of sentient beings. All points in the space-time manifold are on an ontological par, so that in the absence of sentient life there would be no temporal becoming. The B-theorist's claim that temporal becoming is purely mind-dependent is however, attended by a host of difficulties. In the first place, it is not at all clear what is meant by the "mind-dependence of becoming" or similar expressions of the subjectivity of temporal becoming on the part of B-theorists. Such expressions clearly connote that in the absence of sentient observers there would be no such thing as temporal becoming. In the absence of minds, every temporal moment and event simply exists tenselessly; there are no tensed facts; no past, present, or future; nothing comes into existence or happens except in the tenseless sense of existing at certain appointed stations as opposed to others; the space-time

---

[91] Robert C. Coburn, *The Strangeness of the Ordinary: Problems and Issues in Contemporary Metaphysics* (Savage, Maryland: Rowman & Littlefield, 1990), p. 118.

[92] Wm. Godfrey-Smith, critical notice of *Real Time*, by D.H. Mellor, *Australasian Journal of Philosophy* 61 (1983): 109.

[93] D.H. Mellor, *Real Time* (Cambridge: Cambridge University Press, 1981), p. 6. Oaklander concurs, stating that *"it is necessary for the detenser to deal adequately with the experience of temporal becoming"* if the ineliminability of tensed discourse is to be compatible with time's being tenseless (L. Nathan Oaklander, "On the Experience of Tenseless Time", *Journal of Philosophical Research* 18 [1993]: 160).

manifold as a whole exists timelessly *en bloc*, time being simply a tenseless, internal dimension of the manifold; and change is merely the tenseless possession of different properties by things and/or events at their various fixed space-time locations. This much is clear. But what is not clear is how the presence of minds serves to introduce temporal becoming into this picture.

Are we to understand that there actually exists a temporal becoming in the mental realm which is absent from the physical realm? Do mental events, unlike physical events, come to be and pass away? Does the mind-dependence of becoming mean that due to consciousness there exists what would otherwise not exist, temporal becoming, but of a peculiarly mental sort? Or are we rather to understand that temporal becoming is an illusion of consciousness, a chimaera as unreal in the mental realm as in the physical? Is our experience of temporal becoming wholly non-veridical, even our experience of the passage of psychological time? Do mental events exist as tenselessly as physical events, so that becoming is absent from both aspects of reality?

As I say, B-theorists have not been very forthcoming in addressing such questions. But I shall argue that on either account, the B-theory fails to provide a coherent account of temporal becoming.

II

Consider, first, the interpretation that temporal becoming exists in the mental realm, but is absent from physical reality. This alternative at least has the advantage of giving an accurate phenomenology of our temporal consciousness. The becoming of the contents of consciousness is a datum of experience with which any adequate theory of time must make peace. But the idea that temporal becoming characterizes mental events, but not the physical world, can easily be shown to be untenable. It leads, in the first place, to what Capek characterizes as *"an absurd dualism"* of the tenseless physical world and temporal consciousness, *"a dualism of two altogether disparate realms whose correlation becomes completely unintelligible.*"[94] Imagine, for example, a possible world in which only minds exist, say, God and the angels, and that these minds experience temporal becoming of the contents of consciousness. In such a world tense and temporal becoming would be objective features of reality, since no physical realm exists and *ex hypothesi* temporal becoming characterizes the mental realm. If, then, we imagine a similar world except that some of those minds are incarnated in physical bodies, bodies which do not undergo temporal becoming but exist tenselessly, then Capek's intolerable dualism results. The absurdity of such a dualism is heightened if we reflect on the causal relationships supposedly sustained between a mind and its body. The physical states of the body at some time *t* tenselessly induce mental states at *t*, but that time may not be present for the mind and so, as past or future, such states are nonexistent. Conversely, the mind may will to cause a bodily movement now, but the effect is not produced now, but tenselessly - but then the effect exists even when the mind is not now producing it. It seems evident that if mental temporal becoming is real, then the states of physical reality which are even loosely correlated with states of consciousness also undergo temporal becoming.

It is in this light that Frederick Ferré's troupe of objections to Grünbaum's thesis of the mind-dependence of becoming are best understood.[95] Unless Ferré is presupposing the reality of becoming in the mental realm, most of his objections are so misconceived that they are easily refuted. But if we interpret the mind-dependence of becoming to imply temporal becoming of the contents of consciousness, then Ferré's criticisms strike home.[96] Take, for

---

[94] Milic Capek, *The Concepts of Space and Time*, Boston Studies in the Philosophy of Science 22 (Dordrecht: D. Reidel, 1976), p. XLVII.

[95] Frederick Ferré, "Grünbaum on Temporal Becoming: A Critique", *International Philosophical Quarterly* 12 (1972): 426-445; idem, "Grünbaum vs. Dobbs: the Need for Physical Transiency", *British Journal for the Philosophy of Science* 21 (1970): 278-280.

[96] See Ronald C. Hoy, "Becoming and Persons", *Philosophical Studies* 34 (1978): 273-274, who points out that Ferré presupposes a view of persons as

example, what Ferré calls the problem of temporal location. Why do I have the now-awareness of t_2, rather than of, say, t_1? The A-theorist has a ready response: because it really *is* t_2. But for the B-theorist all times are equally existent, so that my being aware of t_2 as present is inexplicable. Lynn Rudder Baker responds that Ferré's objection boils down to the question: why am I now at t_2 rather than at t_1? - and the answer to that question is that that now-awareness is part of the simultaneity class of events at t_2.[97] One's now-awareness associated with t_2 could not be experienced at any time other than at t_2, so of course at t_2 one has the now-awareness associated with t_2, just as at t_1 one has the now-awareness associated with t_1. This response is adequate, however, only on the assumption that all these various now-awarenesses tenselessly exist and do not come to be and pass away. But if there is temporal becoming in the mental realm, then no other now-awarenesses exist except for the present one. But then the question is, why, if all physical events exist tenselessly, am I experiencing just the now-awareness which I have? All Grünbaum can say is that such an awareness is part of the simultaneity class of events occurring at t_n. But that is true of all now-awarenesses at their respective t_i. The question is not, why do I have the now awareness of t_n at t_n, but why do I have the now awareness of t_n *simpliciter*? Why is this one now-awareness privileged? The answer seems to be: because t_n is present; but Grünbaum cannot accept such an explanation. Thus, the B-theory on this interpretation is explanatorily deficient.

Or take Ferré's so-called problem of order in transiency. Nothing in Grünbaum's tenseless universe requires that now-awarenesses be experienced in a particular order. There is no reason why one's consciousness is not filled willy-nilly with now-awarenesses from random points on one's tenselessly existing world-line. Baker's response is that the order of one's now awarenesses is based on the order of the physical brain states correlated with them. Ferré *"overlooks the fact that, on Grünbaum's view, the order of those*

---

enduring entities and finds this incompatible with the tenseless existence of the world.

[97] Lynne Rudder Baker, "Temporal Becoming: The Argument from Physics", *Philosophical Forum* 6 (1975): 230.

mental events which constitute awareness of physical events depends on the order of the physical events which cause them together with the distances and velocities of the influence chains reaching the percipient."[98] This response assumes that there actually exists a tenseless series of now-awarenesses correlated with the tenseless series of brain states; but if there is only one now-awareness that exists, namely, the present one, then it is not at all obvious why the now awarenesses associated with different brain states at random locations on one's world-line should not become successively present. None of the tenselessly existing influence chains, nor the tenselessly conceived relations of *earlier than/later than* among physical events would be violated by this bouncing about of presentness with respect to mental states. But the result would be an incredible dualism; better to say with the A-theorist that physical states associated with nowawarenesses also become and do so in the order specified by the *earlier than/later than* relations.

Or consider Ferré's problem of uni-directional transiency. He observes that the anisotropy of time fails to explain the transiency of temporal becoming; so why does becoming in the mental realm occur uniquely in one direction, rather than in the opposite or both? Baker answers the question in terms of entropic increase and accumulation of memories:

> "The preferred direction of our experience, as well as its order, can be explained solely by reference to the physical world without appeal to an ongoing now. The anisotropic 'is later than' relation can be provided by the increasing entropy in branch systems of the universe. It is a fact that increases of entropy in branch systems generally accompany the production of traces or memories; and thus the direction of entropy increase (i.e., the direction of the 'is later than' relation for physical events) is the same as the direction of increase of stored information. And the direction of entropy increase is toward the future in 'psychological' time … The preferred direction of our experience can thus be accounted for without appeal to a mind-independent 'now'."[99]

---

[98] Ibid., p. 225.

[99] Ibid., pp. 225-226.

It seems to me that the efficacy of this response is moot even if we deny that mental states become,[100] but it is clearly inadequate on the assumption that temporal becoming does characterize the contents of consciousness. For there is no reason that events in the direction of decreasing entropy should not become successively present, even if that should involve a progressive loss of information content on the part of the sentient subject. Such *de facto* physical asymmetries are not sufficient even for time's having a direction.[101] How much less do they determine the direction in which consciousness experiences some tenselessly existing physical state as occurring now! Even if the tenseless, ordinal ordering of events were determined by thermodynamic considerations, that order could be experienced by consciousness in either direction.

This leads to another of Ferré's concerns: the problem of inter-subjectivity. How is it that we all experience the tenseless series of physical events in the same order and direction, if they do not in fact become present in just that way? Why do we share the same now? Baker replies that an event at *t* is the terminus of two causal chains, one issuing in my awareness of it and the other in someone else's awareness of it; since the causes are simultaneous, so are our respective awarenesses. This answer is completely satisfactory on the assumption that mental events do not become. But if there is becoming in the mental realm independently of the tenseless existence of the physical world, there is no reason why there should be a single time order among the community of minds. Each person could have a different A-series of mental states with differing directions. They might on occasion share the same now, only to discover that they have differently ordered pasts - or, their paths through successive now's might never intersect (even if they both on

---

[100] The correlation between higher entropy states and greater memory will not yield a direction to psychological time, since such a correlation is directionally neutral. See also comments by James McGilvray, "A Defense of Physical Becoming," *Erkenntnis* 14 (1979): 281.

[101] See Lawrence Sklar, *Space, Time, and Space-time* (Berkeley: University of California Press, 1976), pp. 352-411.

occasion shared the same tenseless space-time coordinates, since that moment might not ever be experienced by both as present) and so they remain mutually unknown to one another. This is a bizarre picture, but it comes from trying to wed a tenseless physical world to a mental realm in which temporal becoming occurs.

I have probably belabored this point unnecessarily, for it is rather obvious that tense and tenselessness cannot be combined coherently in the way described. It would be as if a modal realist were to espouse the mind-dependence of *being actual* and thereby mean that although the physical universe is actual only relative to a world, our conscious life has actuality *simpliciter*. This is clearly incoherent, and the first interpretation of the mind-dependence of becoming is equally so.

III

But do B-theorists mean to affirm the second interpretation, that there is no becoming of mental states? Such a position flies in the face of our inner experience of temporality. Eddington, who struggled to understand the relationship between thermodynamic irreversibility, the direction of time, and temporal becoming, finally came down squarely on the side of temporal becoming as the true source of the arrow of time on the basis of the phenomenology of time consciousness: *"We have direct insight into "becoming" which sweeps aside all symbolic knowledge as on an inferior plane. If I grasp the notion of existence because I myself exist, I grasp the notion of becoming because I myself become. It is the innermost Ego of all that is and becomes."*[102] In Eddington's view, then, temporal becoming is as obvious as one's own existence; indeed, one perceives one's existence as becoming, not as static being.

---

[102] Sir Arthur Eddington, *The Nature of the Physical World*, with an Introductory Note by Sir Edmund Whittaker, Everyman's Library (London: J.M. Dent & Sons, 1964), pp. 102-103.

Now according to the second interpretation of the mind-dependence of becoming, this fundamental intuition is wholly non-veridical. But then what of our experience of temporal becoming? Grünbaum seems to deny that we do, in fact, experience temporal becoming, allowing us at most our experience of diverse "now's" and the (tenseless) order of events, but not of temporal becoming:

> "Hence it is a matter of fact that the 'Now' shifts in conscious awareness to the extent that there is a diversity of the Now-contents, and it is likewise a fact that the Now-contents are temporally ordered. But since these diverse Now-contents are ordered with respect to the relation 'earlier than' no less than with respect to its converse 'later than', it is a mere *tautology* to say that the Now shifts from earlier to later ... a non-directional or directionally neutral claim of the transiency of the Now and of the temporal order of the various 'Now'-contents does codify factual truths pertaining to psychological (common sense) time."[103]

Here Grünbaum appears to assert that although it is a fact that psychological time does involve an experience of "nowness" and temporal order, it does not involve any experience of becoming or the direction of time. Such an assertion is so obviously false a description of psychological time that it is hard to believe that this is Grünbaum's meaning. In speaking of the psychological phenomenon of melody awareness, Grünbaum recognizes that we do not have merely the succession of states of awareness, but also an instantaneous awareness of succession, which, he says, *"is an essential*

---

[103] Adolf Grünbaum, *Philosophical Problems of Space and Time*, 2d ed. Boston Studies in the Philosophy of Science 12 (Dordrecht: D. Reidel, 1973), pp. 315-316. Peter Geach's argument against the illusory character of temporal becoming based on the incompatibility of present contents of consciousness at best proves a diversity of now-awarenesses (Peter Geach, "Some Problems about Time", in *Logic Matters* [Berkeley: University of California Press, 1972], p. 306), which fact is admitted by Grünbaum, and so is not decisive as an argument for the objective reality of becoming.

ingredient of the meaning of 'now': the now-content, when viewed as such in awareness, includes an awareness of the order of succession of events in which the occurrence of that awareness constitutes a distinguished element."[104] If succession were understood in the A-theoretical sense of becoming, this would be an admirable analysis of now-awareness. But Grünbaum only speaks of the tenseless order of events and does not mean to affirm any experience of becoming. He claims that the transiency of the now arises from the diversity of the now-contents of awareness and the differences among them concerning what is remembered of earlier events.[105] By "arises" he must mean that the transiency of the now just consists in those two facts, for he does not allow any further experience of temporal becoming beyond this. Not only is this a phenomenologically incomplete analysis of time consciousness or psychological time, but it is far from clear how one could not have an experience of temporal becoming in the sense of moments elapsing or events becoming present and then passing away, if there are for a conscious subject a diversity of nowawarenesses and the consciousness of temporal order in which one awareness (the last) is distinguished. For such an awareness of changes in present-tense consciousness engenders the experience of temporal becoming. Moreover, as events or moments become successively present, then past, a direction of time inevitably arises in experience. It thus seems futile to try to avert the inevitable clash with an adequate phenomenology of temporal consciousness by claiming that our experience only involves a diversity of now-contents and an awareness of the order of those contents.

The question, then, is what sense it makes to say that we experience temporal becoming in consciousness but that mental events do not become. The very awareness of a "now" is an awareness of tense, and if we are successively aware of different experiences as present, how is it that there is no mental becoming? Grünbaum himself affirms the presentness of experience when he says such things as: *"presentness or nowness of an event requires conceptual awareness of the presentational immediacy of either the experience of the*

---

[104] Grünbaum, *Philosophical Problems of Space and Time*, p. 325.
[105] Ibid.

event or ... of the experience of another event simultaneous with it."[106] The notion of *"presentational immediacy of experience"* coincides with what D. H. Mellor calls the *"presence of experience,"*[107] but whereas Mellor strives to give some tenseless account of this crucial notion, Grünbaum is strangely silent. All we get is Baker's dismissal of the query, *"Why are events ever characterized as occurring now?"* as a pseudo-question, equally inappropriate to mind-dependence or mind-independence theorists.[108] But since the presentness of experience, affirmed by Grünbaum, lies at the heart of our experience of temporal becoming, it is crucial that the B-theorist offer some account of this notion if he is to explain away temporal becoming, as Mellor recognizes and struggles vainly to do. The A-theorist answers Baker's question straightforwardly in terms of the objectivity of A-determinations and a presentist ontology. Grünbaum's failure to account for our experience of "nowness" or better, presentness, signals a singular weakness in the position that temporal becoming is as absent from the mental as from the physical realm. Grünbaum has not explained away the phenomenological data that mental events become.

Moreover, Grünbaum's own account of the mind-dependence of becoming implies the reality of temporal becoming in the mental realm. Grünbaum explicates the notion of an event's occurring now in terms of its simultaneity with a sentient subject's experiencing the event while being aware that he is

---

[106] Adolf Grünbaum, "The Meaning of Time," in *Basic Issues in the Philosophy of Time*, ed. E. Freeman and W. Sellars (La Salle, Ill: Open Court, 1971), p. 206.

[107] D. H. Mellor, *Real Time* (Cambridge: Cambridge University Press,1981), p. 53. For a critique of Mellor's view, see my "The Presentness of Experience," in *Time, Creation, and World Order*, ed. Mogens Wegener, Aarhus, University of Aarhus Press, pp.107-120

[108] Baker, "Temporal Becoming," pp. 223, 230.

experiencing the event.[109] This characterization is, as Grünbaum came to realize, circular, since the verbs contained in this explication are present-tensed.[110] But he dismissed the circularity as non-vicious because he claimed that he was not trying to provide a tenseless analysis of "nowness," but merely to articulate the mind-dependence of "nowness." But if the characterization is circular, how can it possibly articulate successfully the mind-dependence of becoming? On the contrary, by presupposing the objectivity of tense, does it not rather underline the fact that presentness is not mind-dependent? In order to articulate what it is for some event *e* to be present, Grünbaum has to presuppose that a sentient subject is experiencing (present-tense) *e*. If this is an objective matter of fact, then the presentness of e cannot be merely illusory. McGilvray formulates a tenseless rendition of Grünbaum's conditions for the truth of "*e* is now for M":

a. *E* be an experience of *e*
b. *E* be had by *M*.
c. *M* be conceptually aware that *E* be had by *M* (*C* = this event of conceptual awareness)
d. the content of *C* include an awareness that *E* be coincident with *C*.

But (a-d) as they stand are not sufficient conditions for "*e* is now for M," since (a-d), if ever true, are always true. What, then, would make these conditions sufficient for the truth of "*e* is now for M"? McGilvray answers,

> "There is a simple answer, and it is that C and perhaps E become. This is a legitimate answer, consistent with Grünbaum's account of the 'mind-dependence' of becoming, and it has the advantage of clarifying his cheerful use of present progressives throughout the

---

[109] Adolf Grünbaum, *The Status of Temporal Becoming, Modern Science and Zeno's Paradoxes* (Middletown, Conn.: Wesleyan University Press, 1967), p. 17.

[110] Adolf Grünbaum, "Meaning of Time," rep. in *The Concepts of Space and Time*, ed. Milic Capek, Boston Studies in the Philosophy of Science 22 (Dordrecht: D. Reidel, 1976), pp. 480-81.

argument. Here is where one must look for the sense of tensed as opposed to tenseless occurrence. Moreover, it is difficult to imagine any other way in which to get a sufficient condition for the nowness of C and E; it is apoarent that conditions (a-d), if true at some time, are always true."[111]

Thus, Grünbaum seems forced by his own account of what it is for an event to occur now to regard becoming as real in the mental realm, even if unreal in the physical realm. But then his account of the mind-dependence of becoming lies open to all the objections discussed above.

More fundamentally, it seems to me that the position that the temporal becoming of mental as well as physical events is purely illusory is self-referentially incoherent. The point here, stated simply, is that the very illusion of becoming involves becoming. The German metaphysician Herrmann Lotze, contemplating whether the Principle of Identity entails the unreality of becoming, made this point when he remarked, *"This consideration might lead us to repeat old attempts at a denial of all Becoming, or - since it cannot be denied - to undertake the self-contradictory task of explaining at least the becoming of the appearance of an unreal becoming."*[112] The position of the B-theorist is reminiscent of Buddhist, Parmenidean, and Idealist denials of the reality of temporal becoming and their consigning becoming to the realm of appearance and illusion. The principal difference is that the B-theorist insists that time is real, even though temporal becoming is not - to that extent these temporal illusionists were more consistent than the B-theorist, as I have argued. But never mind; the point remains that for the B-theorist as well as for atemporalist schools of philosophy, temporal becoming is real neither in the physical world nor in the life of the mind, but is somehow wholly illusory. But then the B-theory labors under the same incoherence as all temporal illusionist theories,

---

[111] McGilvray, "Defense of Physical Becoming," p. 293.

[112] Hermann Lotze, *Metaphysic*, 2 vols., 2d ed., ed. Bernard Bosanquet (Oxford: Clarendon Press, 1887), 1: 105. See also John Laird, *Theism and Cosmology* (London: George Allen & Unwin, 1940), pp. 145-146.

namely, that an illusion or appearance of becoming involves becoming, so that becoming cannot be mere illusion or appearance. A Buddhist philosopher can consistently deny the reality of space and spatial objects and hold these to be mere illusions of the mind, for an illusion of spatiality does not entail spatiality, one's thoughts and perceptions not being spatial in nature. But an illusion of temporal becoming, by contrast, is itself an experience in which becoming plays a part. We can conceive of a person accepting tenselessly and with no experience of becoming the putatively false proposition "Temporal becoming is real," and such a one would be genuinely deceived about the reality of becoming. But such a person would not experience the illusion or appearance of becoming. We do. And therein lies the inescapable difficulty for the B-theorist.

To make the same point in a different way, imagine a state of consciousness existing at a particular position in McTaggart's atemporal C-series.[113] How could the illusion of temporal becoming - as opposed to merely false belief - possibly arise in such a static consciousness? How could a C-series person experience the appearance of temporal becoming? The B-theorist may protest that the C-series is atemporal, whereas the B-series is temporal. But on the B-theoretical account, the only difference between them is that the irreflexive, transitive, and asymmetric relations which order the terms of the two series are in the one case *included in/inclusive of* and in the other *earlier than/later than*; moreover, on the B-theory the latter relations are so emasculated as to make the difference between earlier and later merely conventional, and time isotropic and directionless. So whence the illusion of becoming?

---

[113] McTaggart's view was that the B-series is derivable from the combination of the A-series with a C-series, which is a timelessly ordered series based on an atemporal ordering relation like the relation *greater than* ordering the natural numbers. The conjunction of A-determinations with the C-series renders its members earlier/later than one another (J. M. E. McTaggart, "The Unreality of Time", *Mind* 17 [1908]: 463).

To say that there is an illusion of becoming just is to say that things become in consciousness, though not in reality. Becoming in consciousness is thus undeniable and, hence, the denial of becoming self-referentially absurd.

IV

In summary, then, the B-theoretical denial of the reality of temporal becoming cannot be sustained in the light of our experience. If the B-theorist concedes that becoming is real in the realm of consciousness, then he is saddled with a metaphysical dichotomy between the external, physical world and the inner life of the mind which is intolerable. Such a bifurcation of reality leads to intractable problems concerning the temporal location of the now, the order of transiency, the direction of becoming, and the intersubjectivity of the "now". On the other hand, if the B-theorist regards even mental becoming as unreal, he flies in the face of our most deeply-seated experiences of temporal becoming and the presentness of experience. Moreover, it seems that he actually needs to affirm temporal becoming in consciousness in order to explain the mind-dependence of physical becoming. Finally, the B-theorist's position is self-referentially incoherent, since the posited illusory experience of becoming entails becoming. It therefore seems that the common experience of mankind with respect to temporality is not to be dismissed: the world becomes.

Christian ethics in a secular world

SØREN HOLM

Abstract

When my field of research and teaching, the field that is now called 'bioethics', was emerging in the late 1960s and early 1970, many of the most prominent figures in the field where Christian theologians, or committed Christian lay persons [Walters 1985]. If we look at the field today, this has changed. There are still Christian voices, but they are no longer in the mainstream, but are seen as being on the fringes of the field.

Some have seen this as a consequence of the increased secularization of our society. Whereas you could expect to be understood if you talked a Christian language, and referred to Christian values 30 years ago, this is arguably no longer the case today.

The present paper will look at the different roles Christian ethics can play in a secular society, and will argue that many of these roles are both necessary and valid roles for a true Christian ethics.

Secular and multicultural

It is very obvious that we in the Northern part of Europe live in societies where most people have lost any living connection with Christianity and the Christian churches. People may attend church on special occasions (baptism, marriage, funeral, Christmas etc.) and they may have vague religious beliefs, including some taken from the repository of Christian beliefs, but they are not Christian in a sense that would be recognised by the mainstream Christian churches (think for instance of the fairly widespread belief in re-incarnation).

This means that certain kinds of traditional Christian arguments are now unlikely to get a hearing or even to be understood. This is true for arguments of the type "…but the Bible says that…", but it also holds for a range of other arguments that make explicit reference to their Christian origin.

In the USA we have the even more paradoxical situation that although the country has one of the largest proportions of practicing Christians in the population of any industrialised country, it also has a constitution demanding a separation between church and state. In modern American jurisprudence this has been interpreted as entailing that an argument for the legal regulation of a certain activity can be dismissed summarily if the argument has a religious underpinning. Some, most notably Ronald Dworkin in his book "Life's Dominion" have even argued that the mere fact that there is no commonly accepted non-religious underpinning for a certain argument, should entail that it be labelled as religious and therefore ruled out of court [Dworkin 1993]. Dworkin, for instance, applies this to rule arguments based on an intrinsic value of human life out of court, since there is no commonly accepted secular argument for the intrinsic value of human life. That the American congress, despite the separation between church and state, has a congressional chaplain is just one of the many inconsistencies in American public life.

The situation is further complicated in most countries by a publicly stated commitment to multiculturalism and tolerance. In its crudest form, those putting forward this commitment admonish us to show respect towards all cultures and all cultural practices. In this crude form, multiculturalism is obviously an inconsistent moral and/or political principle. If I after careful consideration believe some practice or some specific prohibition to be seriously wrong (for instance because it harms certain types of people), then I cannot at the same time say that I respect the right of those who perform the practice or enforce the prohibition to do it. And if respecting a practice does not minimally entail allowing it, then it is hard to see that "respect" is more than a nice word to be paraded at special occasions. We could try to claim that we do respect a given culture, even in cases where we prohibit some of the central manifestations of this culture, but this seems to rob "respect" of all significant content.

Even if the crude form of multiculturalism is obviously flawed, there is a more sophisticated form which is much more plausible. The sophisticated multiculturalist will admit that we don't have to respect all cultural practices, that there are practices which should be prohibited, but he or she will then go on to say that, in order to prohibit a practice, it must either be the case that it is wrong, even seen from within the value system of the culture in which it occurs, or it must be extremely damaging to some weak and vulnerable group in that culture. The sophisticated multiculturalist will thus maintain that we have no right to interfere in other peoples' culture, unless we are absolutely sure that what we are doing is not simply imposing our own values on them.

The multiculturalist has to face a further difficult problem in trying to implement a multiculturalist policy, since there seems to be no neutral way of defining a culture. Cultures are, by definition, not natural classes to be discovered, they are complex human artefacts. The class of cultures thus has extremely fuzzy borders. If we recognise certain sub-cultures, like for instance a gay sub-culture, then it seems plausible to claim that we should also recognise (and respect) the Mafia sub-culture or the biker sub-culture. The Mafia sub-culture is, for instance, one that persons are often born into, it has a very strong value system, members of the sub-culture will often claim it as their primary allegiance, and it has substantial coherence over time and place.

Thus multiculturalism suffers from its own very complex set of problems as a moral or political theory, but the official acceptance of multiculturalist ideals adds to the problems of a Christian ethics trying to influence the non-Christian segments of society. In one way, multiculturalism initially seems to be a good opportunity for Christian ethics, since the principle of respect straightforwardly entails that Christian points of view should also be given respect in public debates. In the long run, multiculturalism is, however, problematic because it de-legitimises any attempt to speak to people outside of one's own culture. At least if what one is saying contains any criticism of the "outsiders," their views, or their practices. A Christian discourse will almost by necessity contain an explicit or implicit critique of outsiders, since part of the Christian message often is that both insiders and outsiders need to reform their ethics

The basic choice of contemporary Christian ethics

In an increasingly secular and avowedly multicultural society, a contemporary Christian ethics is faced with the basic choice of whether it will still try to speak broadly to society, or whether it will limit itself to speaking to those within the Christian community. This is not an exclusive choice on conceptual grounds, but given the present social situation outlined above it may well be an exclusive choice seen from a pragmatic point of view, since the form of argument and communication which can be effective is likely to be very different with respect to the two distinct audiences.

If this is a realistic diagnosis of the situation, it raises one immediate problem, because Christianity undoubtedly puts forward a claim to be universal in its teachings, both with regard to how one should live, and with regard to more specific religious issues. This seems to indicate that a Christian ethics can never give up its aim of speaking to all people, and still be fully Christian. The latter may be true, and I personally believe it to be true, but it is not inconsistent with claiming that when a person puts forward ethical views he or she should consider whether the form these views are given, and the arguments used to back them, are going to be understandable and relevant for the intended audience. A commitment to speak to the world does not in itself tell us how this is to be done.

Before we are in a position to discuss the different ways in which a Christian ethics can be communicated, it is, however, necessary to discuss a certain argument, which claims that Christian ethics and all other kinds of ethics cannot be understood or communicated in philosophical terms. This argument is put forward by Søren Kierkegaard under the pseudonym of Johannes Climacus in *Philosophical Fragments* and *Concluding Unscientific Postscript to the Philosophical Fragments*. In its modern form it is clearly stated by Stephen Mulhall:

> "We can therefore conclude that ethical truth cannot be properly understood or communicated in objective terms; and from that it follows not only that anyone who attempts to communicate such truths in such terms thereby manifests her misunderstanding of what she is communicating, but also, and more importantly, that she thereby manifests her own failure to live up to – to live – that truth. For insofar as she claims to accept that ethical vision, she takes on the obligation to ensure that her life as a whole reflects or embodies it; but if she chooses to communicate that vision in a form which not only implies that her interlocutor's relation to it should be exclusively cognitive but also determines her own relation to it as impersonal and epistemic, then her communicative act at once fails to convey that its topic is a subjective existential possibility, and itself amounts to a failure to actualize that possibility." [Mulhall et.al. 1994, p. 33]

What is claimed is thus that what should be communicated in a true communication of any ethics is not a propositional content, but a whole ethical way of life. Even if somebody understands all the arguments, accepts all the conclusions, and changes all his or her behaviour, this would still not be a successful outcome, unless his or her motivational structure and way of life were also changed, and such change cannot be brought about by cognitive understanding, but only by choice. If this argument is sound, then any attempt to communicate the Christian ethical message in cognitive and/or non-religious terms would be immediately disqualified.

There are, however, two potential flaws in the argument. First, it seems to rely on a conception of ethics where I as an individual am always in a position to find out what action my way of life requires, and in those situations where this is not the case I cannot be helped by discussing the situation with other people, even in cases where these other people share my way of life. Second, the argument requires the premise that ways of life are so radically separate that there is no cognitive or non-cognitive overlap between them. If there is overlap between ways of life, then it will in some cases be possible for one person to show (cognitively) to somebody with another way of life, that his or her way of really requires that he or she acts differently.

The sceptical argument is thus only sound if we accept two fairly dubious premises.

Speaking to the world

A Christian ethics has very definite things to say about how we ought to live our lives, whether or not we are Christians. Christian ethicists may differ extremely widely in their views about exactly how we should live, but they all agree that the main part of Christian ethics is an ethics for all people and not only for Christians[114]. In communicating these ethical views to a secular world, there seems to be four different kinds of role or voice a Christian ethicist can adopt:

1. The disguised Christian ethicist
2. The Christian values-ethicist
3. The apologetic Christian ethicist
4. The ethical prophet

The disguised Christian ethicist puts forward arguments which are neither explicitly nor implicitly based on any kind of religious foundations, and he or she usually writes in a style which is indistinguishable from the average non-Christian ethicist. The conclusions that are argued for are, however,

---

[114] There are Christian ethicists who deny this, and see Christian ethics as something solely for Christians, but this seems to be very difficult to reconcile with the general universalist claims of Christianity.

conclusions which are compatible with the conclusions the Christian ethicist reaches when he or she reasons on Christian grounds. This may initially seem as a very deceptive form of writing in ethics, but if it is really deception then it is a deception that is widely practised in applied ethics. If one looks at the abortion debate in the 1960s and 1970s it is now fairly easy to see, in retrospect, that a lot of the argumentation produced by both sides of the debate was not really argumentation leading to a specific conclusion (whether it be for or against the legalisation of abortion), it was argumentation where the desired conclusion was known in advance, and the arguments where produced and the premises chosen from that point of view, even though in the writing this was often hidden. In defence of this way of writing Christian ethics, it can also be pointed out that one of the most effective methods of philosophical argument is to accept your opponents premises (for the sake of the argument, as philosophers like to say) and show that they actually support your conclusions.

The reasons behind adopting the role of the disguised Christian ethicist are manifold, but the main reason is probably a belief that if you want to speak to people outside the Christian community, you will have to speak to them on their terms, and perhaps more importantly, you will have to speak to them in a way which does not allow them immediately to say "Oh, but this is a Christian argument, so we don't need to look carefully at what it is saying."

The main problem with the role as disguised Christian ethicist is, however, that as Christians we know certain things to be good or right, for which it is very hard to find secular, non-Christian arguments. Despite the repeated pronouncements of the Roman-Catholic magisterium that the existence of God can be proven, a conclusive and compelling proof has not been forthcoming [Curran 1970], and the same situation exists for a number of the central tenets of Christian ethics. There does not, for instance, seem to be a compelling proof for the proposition that all human beings have intrinsic value, although there are of course arguments for the proposition. The Christian ethicist who exclusively works inside the role of disguised Christian ethicist is therefore only able to deal with part of Christian ethics, and if all Christian ethicists adopted that role, some parts of Christian ethics would be completely lacking in the public debate in our societies.

A very extreme version of the position that there are narrow limits to what ethical propositions can be defended in a secular world is held by the American bioethicist H. Tristram Engelhardt. In the preface to the second edition of his influential "The Foundations of Bioethics," he writes:

> "If one wants more than secular reason can disclose – and one should want more – then one should join a religion and be careful to choose the right one. Canonical moral content will not be found outside of a particular moral narrative, a view from somewhere. Here the reader deserves to know that I indeed experience and acknowledge the immense cleft between what secular philosophical reasoning can provide and what I know in the fullness of my own narrative to be true. I indeed affirm the canonical, concrete moral narrative, but realize it cannot be given by reason, only by grace. I am, after all, a born-again Texan Orthodox Catholic, a convert by choice and conviction, through grace and in repentance for sins innumerable (including a first edition upon which much improvement was needed). My moral perspective does not lack content. I am of the firm conviction that, save for God's mercy, those who willfully engage in much that a peaceable fully secular state will permit (e.g., euthanasia and direct abortion on demand) stand in danger of hell's eternal fires. As a Texan, I puzzle whether these are kindled with mesquite, live oak, or trash cedar. Being schooled in theology, I know that this is a question to be answered only on the Last Day by the Almighty. Though I acknowledge that there is no secular moral authority that can be justified in general secular terms to forbid the sale of heroin, the availability of direct abortion, the marketing of for-profit euthanatization services, or the provision of commercial surrogacy, I firmly hold none of the endeavours to be good. These are great moral evils. But their evil cannot be grasped in purely secular terms. To be pro-choice in general secular terms is to understand God's tragic relationship to Eden. To be free is to be free to choose very wrongly." [Engelhardt 1996, p. xi]

On Engelhardt's fairly pessimistic analysis of the situation, the Christian ethicist who wants to speak to the world must therefore either divorce his or her Christian and secular sides, or must adopt the prophetic role described below.

It is also evident that the disguised Christian ethicist must implicitly accept an, at least partly, meliorist view of the relationship between the Christian and the world. For the role of disguised Christian ethicist to be meaningful, it must be the case that it is not meaningless to try to effect a change for the better in the present world. If one believes that Christians should withdraw as far as possible from the world, and that the only contact should be evangelistic, then the role adopted by the disguised Christian ethicist is seriously misguided.

In the ethical literature it is also possible to find people occupying the reverse role of the disguised Christian ethicist, that is, the role of disguised secular ethicist. There are ethicists whose arguments initially look as if they are based in a Christian understanding, but where further study reveals that the arguments and conclusions are basically secular in nature, and that the invocations of Christianity are inessential to the argument.

The second possible role for the Christian ethicist is the role as 'Christian values-ethicist'. This was the role that was adopted by many of the Christians who were prominent in the early phases of the development of modern bioethics, and it is the role adopted by most of the well known Christian participants in the current public debate. The Christian values ethicist puts forward explicitly Christian arguments and writes in an explicitly Christian way, but the arguments are never the less claimed to be relevant and valid even outside the Christian community. This feat is accomplished by drawing on the idea that what is important in Christian ethics is not primarily certain specific rules laid down in the Bible or certain specific sayings of Jesus or the apostles, but instead one or more underlying values which can be discovered by careful deliberation on the biblical testimony, by careful attention to the life of actual Christian communities, or by a number of other methods. These values are believed to be Christian in the sense that they are developed from Christian sources and foundational for the Christian ethical message, but they are at the same time claimed to be universal because they are necessary for human wellbeing, flourishing, peaceful co-existence etc.. Examples of such values could be agapeic love, the importance of covenant relationships, the importance of liberation, or solidarity with the poor.

After having done the exegetical work necessary to discover these underlying Christian values, the Christian ethicist can then begin 1) to explain why they are relevant in a secular context, and 2) to apply them in ethical argument. The reader will thus be fully aware that what he is reading is Christian ethics, but he will be invited to follow the argument for a bit, and hopefully discover that it is relevant for him, even if he is not a Christian. This strategy for communication may well work, because even if many countries are now fairly secular, the Christian heritage is still a major cultural influence and the values may well be both recognisable and acceptable to many people. The Christian values ethicist thus, to some extent, exploits our common Christian cultural heritage.

There are, however, a number of problems with the approach taken by the Christian values ethicist.

First, there is a theological problem in the assumption that the ethical message of the Christian faith can be summed up in one or a few values. This theological problem is caused by two factors. 1) The Biblical testimony is diverse, and among Biblical scholars there are wide disagreements about what parts of the Bible should be taken as kerygmatic. The optimism felt around the middle of this century concerning the possibility of developing a univocal Biblical ethics, even in the face of the results of scriptural criticism, has waned considerably [Siker 1997]. 2) There is no *a priori* reason to believe that the Christian ethical message is simple and formulable in a few values.

Second, the Christian values ethicist is affected by the same problem as the disguised Christian ethicist that there may be parts of Christian ethics that are not derivable in any straightforward way from the postulated basic Christian values. In some cases it will be necessary to put additional Christian premises in the arguments. This is not a problem for the person who believes that the values are all there is, because such a person will not claim that there is any part of Christian ethics outside the values, but it will be a problem for the ethicist who uses the values approach mainly as a strategy for communication.

The apologetic role is the third role a Christian ethicist can adopt. The writings of the apologetic ethicist are partly Christian, partly secular. The strategy adopted is to explain what ethical conclusions follow from a Christian point of view, and then show that the same conclusions follow from acceptable secular premises. The apologetic ethicist thus tries to put forward the whole Christian ethical message, and to show how it can be supported on purely secular grounds. This role thus has many similarities with the role as disguised Christian ethicist, but it has one main advantage, since the explicit Christian nature of the communication makes it possible to point out exactly when and how secular arguments have to be abandoned and Christian arguments have to be brought in. The main problem with this role has already been mentioned above in the discussion of the disguised Christian ethicist. It is often difficult to find the secular arguments to support all aspects of Christian ethics, and this may entice some to use questionable forms of argument in order to reach the desired conclusion.

The fourth and final possible role for a Christian ethics wishing to speak to the world is the prophetic role. A prophetic Christian ethics desires to speak to the world in order to portray a better way of living (i.e. the Christian), and to show how this contrasts with the way people live in the world. A prophetic Christian ethics is interested in communicating with the world, but not in order to convince and persuade by the weight of argument. The aim is to create repentance and conversion. What is important here is the display of the right way of living and the right ethical judgements in order to give people a choice. Just like the Old Testament prophets, a modern prophetic ethics may speak of both wrongdoing and judgement and of redemption.

The main strength of the prophetic role is at the same time its main weakness. There is no compromise in views or arguments, and all parts of the Christian ethics can be enunciated fully and clearly. The price which is paid is, however, that the message will only be truly heard and appropriated by those who decide to accept Christian beliefs.

Speaking to Christians

A Christian ethics wishing to speak to Christians does not meet the same problems as a Christian ethics trying to speak to the secular world, but there are other problems that again lead to a number of different possible roles.

One main problem is that most Christians have fairly definite ideas about what a Christian ethics has to say. Every church has its own tradition, and part of that tradition is an implicit list of Christian dos and don'ts. In some churches this list also has an official written version. Being and becoming a Christian involves a socialization to Christian values and Christian behaviour, and this socialization may not involve large degrees of reflection on the tradition which is being internalised.

The Christian ethicist therefore sometimes has to argue that acts that are traditionally seen as prohibited are in fact morally innocuous or perhaps even commendable, or to argue the reverse that acts which the tradition accepts or supports are really ethically problematic. In this role as renewer of the tradition, a Christian ethicist will in some cases come into conflict with the "guardians of the tradition," but this may be a necessary conflict if the tradition is to develop.

Another difference between talking to the world and talking to Christians is that, whereas it is probably counterproductive to give very detailed advice about what is the right thing to do, when one is communicating with the secular world, there is a need for such concrete advice among Christians. Christian doctors, for instance, often want to know exactly what they should do in end-of-life situations. Is it acceptable to stop treatment, is active euthanasia ever acceptable etc. Whether a Christian ethics can (or should even attempt to) fulfil this advisory role depends on the view one holds on the relationship between the individual believer and God.

A Christian ethicist talking to Christians thus has three possible roles to choose from:

1. The renewer of tradition
2. The advisory role
3. The ethical prophet

The first two of these roles have been outlined above, and the last prophetic role is parallel to the prophetic role of a Christian ethics speaking to the world. We know from the Bible, and from church history, that even the community of believers may go so far astray that they need to hear a prophetic voice.

Conclusion

In this paper I have tried to identify a number of different roles that a Christian ethics can assume in the modern secular world. But can something be said about which of those roles are appropriate and which are not?

As will be evident from the discussion above, none of the roles are completely without problems. Which role one should adopt will thus depend on a balancing between the advantages and the disadvantages of the different roles. The most difficult part of this balancing is probably deciding how successful the various strategies for speaking to the world are. I must admit that I don't have any evidence to illuminate this question. The question also points to a difficult underlying question, namely "what is the measure of success in this context?" Is success getting persons to change their ethical views towards views in conformity with Christian views, or does success require at least a number of persons to become Christian. It is very likely that the different roles would fare very differently on the success scale, depending on what criterion of success is chosen.

References

Walters, L. *Religion and the Renaissance of Medical Ethics in the United States. 1965-75.* In: Shelp EE. (ed.): *Theology and Bioethics – Exploring the Foundations and Frontiers.* Dordrecht: D. Reidel Publishing Company, 1985. (pp. 3-16)

Dworkin, R. *Life's Dominion.* New York: Alfred A. Knopf, 1993.

Mulhall, S. *Faith & Reason.* London: Duckworth, 1994.

Curran, C.E. *A New Look at Christian Morality.* Notre Dame: Fides Publishers, 1970. (Ch. 3 *Absolute Norms in Moral Theology,* pp. 72-123)

Engelhardt, H.T. *The Foundations of Bioethics.* (2nd Ed.). Oxford: Oxford University Press, 1996.

Siker, J.S. *Scripture and Ethics.* Oxford: Oxford University Press, 1997.

Truth, Time and Mythos in Cicero, St. Paul and St. Jerome

An Essay in the Relation between a Rhetorical and an Early Christian Conception of Truth and Communication

PER HASLE

> "But even from the point of view of a secular historian of ideas, the Christian and Catholic system, if not a revelation from God, is one of the most fascinating inventions of the human spirit; a construction erected by the best minds of many generations."
> [Kenny 1985, pp. 77-78]

Whether one accepts or rejects what has been called the postmodern condition, it is clear that some such phenomenon forms an actual cultural circumstance that should not be neglected in any such discussion. Now postmodernity is a slippery notion, but as far as I can see there are two aspects to it:

(1) A recognition that we now (in the Western world) definitively live in a pluralistic and relativistic culture,
(2) The rejection of 'foundationalism' and/or the existence of absolute truths.

To (1), it must be added that this kind of relativism has only recently had its decisive breakthrough, and moreover, that the relativism and pluralism are now seen as irreversible. To (2) one could add a language theoretical observation, namely that the rejection of 'foundationalism' is deeply interwoven with a denial of the fixity of linguistic meaning.

Clearly, one could entertain one of these two tenets without holding the other; for the first aspect is rather a description of a cultural state, which may be accepted as correct without subscribing to the second tenet; and conversely, for that matter – one may accept (2) and yet believe that (1) is not – at least not yet – an adequate description.

Recently, the notion of 'postmodernity' has fallen into some disrepute – it has, as it were, succumbed to one of the phenomena that it itself has diagnosed and lived on, namely the ever-increasing speed of changing fashions and convictions. But in a way, that is a pity – for I do think that at the end of this century and millennium, something decisive has indeed happened, and that this prolonged event was rather nicely rendered or conceptualised by the idea of postmodernity – however much we may disagree with so-called postmodernism on some other points, to which I shall come back.

The happening to which I am referring is what should in my opinion above all be seen as a culmination and conclusion of secularisation, or more specifically, the transition from the Christian era into a post-Christian era. It is certainly true that secularisation has been going on for a long time, and that various forms of relativism have also been entertained for a long time. But the thinkers within modernity all took over a number of Christian tenets and sustained them in a secularised form; especially the idea of absolute truth. Moreover, such truth was seen as being far from evident, rather it had to be revealed – although not by divine revelation, but rather by diligent empirical work as well as theory-building. It is only very recently that relativism has truly become the order of the day.

Now there is a remarkable analogy – almost a symmetry – between postmodernity and the pre-Christian Roman world. Certainly a number of postmodernists have themselves observed a similarity between their way of thinking and that classical Rhetoric, which in many ways formed the mind of the educated Roman citizen. Later, the basic ingredients of Rhetoric will be discussed, but there is one point that must be anticipated here: on a Roman rhetorical conception, different convictions – or narratives – are seen as a variety of different myths, none of which aspires to be *the one true* conception. Historians may warn us about going too far in comparing Roman mentality and convictions with present day discussions, but it is safe to say that the kind of rivalry later seen among different religious persuasions was by and large alien to the Romans. As we all know there was no demand that one religion – or any other kind of conviction – should be accepted as *the* truth (except for the political requirement that the Emperor must be worshipped). And the co-existence of many peoples, philosophies and religions apparently seemed to be a quite natural matter, which did not call for deliberations on which way of living and what kind of conviction was *the* true one.

The breakthrough of Christianity within this cultural setting ushered in a new idea of there being one absolute truth – a particular and privileged myth, as a rhetorician might have put it. The story of St. Jerome is very telling in this connection. A famous church father and a rhetorically educated Roman, he himself experienced this intense conflict. We shall come back to his story in detail later.

So, to put it in a crude form, we may depict the symmetry between the advent of Christianity and the 'postmodern' transition into a post-Christian era as in Figure 1.

The idea of absolute truth is interwoven with another idea, that of the 'fixity of meaning': the conception that all words have objective and fixed meanings (literal senses), which form the basis of language use. This idea was almost always implicit in various forms of foundationalist thought, and often not recognized at all, but it seems to be an integral part of both theory and practice within foundationalist theorizing. In our century, Wittgenstein in his *Tractatus*, Chomsky with his Transformational Grammar, and Montague with his Logic Grammar all tried to make systematic sense of the idea of 'fixity of meaning.' I do think that all these attempts have decisively failed, but I hasten to add that in my opinion they were all of outstanding intellectual merit. For it was exactly because they realized and systematized common-place assumptions about language that the impossibility of the foundationalist programme for the semantics of natural language could become clear. In spite of this intellectual merit, the outcome was disenchanting: these theories build upon the sands of notions such as 'atomic proposition', or 'deep structure'. Of course, something at least resembling such units does exist within formal logic, but in natural language, they have proved to be utterly elusive.[115]

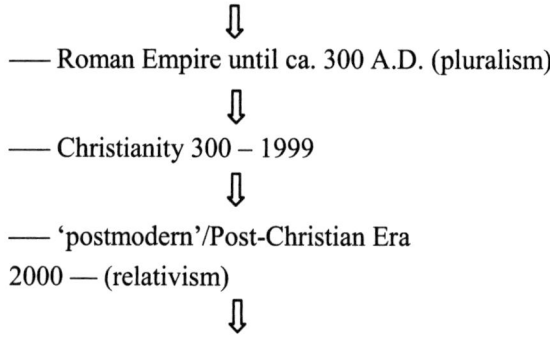

Figure 1.

The failure of these 'semantic foundationalism' programmes has largely been recognized by their progenitors themselves. But it must be added that the failure is only obvious in so far as these programmes are seen as attempts at a faithful empirical description of language. The experience is, in short, that from an empirical study of language no fixed foundation, no deep structure, no atomic propositions are seen to exist. However, there is a deeply entrenched imagination in Western thought that understanding and communication would be impossible without *reference to a common*

---

115 This of course does not rule out the use of such theoretical constructions in the science of linguistics, as long as their nature of being exactly this – theoretical constructions – is not forgotten.

foundation. So there could be another way out, a 'Platonistic' way. For it might be assumed that atomic propositions, deep structures or whatever are *objective ideal*-entities, which sometimes occur or manifest themselves in language use, making it rational and intersubjective in these cases. On this account, logic is not something that can be 'extracted' empirically out of language, it is the other way round: logic exists, a priori and objectively, and language may sometimes be used accordingly, and sometimes not. Indeed the continued insistence on a semantic foundation, in view of the failure to establish it empirically, reintroduces metaphysics to the point of looking almost as a 'proof of God.' This has not gone unobserved – one of the greatest semanticists within Transformational Grammar, Jerrold J. Katz, could in 1971 make the following observation (at a time where the empirical claims of Transformational Grammar were becoming problematic, but where work and hopes within the paradigm were still intense):

> "There is a rather ironic turn of events in store for philosophy... We may see the philosophies of language of Logical Empiricism and Ordinary Language Philosophy replaced by a philosophy of language... concerned with uncovering properties of knowledge and mind on the basis of philosophically relevant aspects of the underlying reality of natural languages. If this happens, *the linguistic turn taken by philosophy in the first half of the twentieth century will have turned back on itself, reintroducing the very metaphysical issues* whose banishment from philosophy was initially proclaimed as the rationale for the turn to linguistic philosophy." [Katz 1971, p. 1899]

For further discussion on this subject I must, however, refer to other works.[116] I mention it because that rhetorical conception of comprehension that will now be discussed is exactly an anti-thesis to the idea of the 'fixity of meaning'.

---

116 See for instance the discussions in (Harris 1996), (Harré 1993) and (Katz 1992).

2. Rhetoric

In trying to make clear what kind of insight into language meaning and language comprehension Rhetoric brings about, I shall be highly selective. Firstly, in the context of this paper it is of course impossible to give a thorough introduction to Rhetoric in general. I shall focus only on those aspects that seem to me to be immediately relevant for my general purpose, which is to show how the rhetorical conception has crucial – and admittedly controversial – implications for the notion of language understanding and text interpretation, and how this may relate to Christian thought as seen through St. Jerome and St. Paul. Secondly, I shall focus on what may be called Ciceronian Rhetoric, and in so doing I shall be heavily indebted to one particular work, namely the 1995-volume *An Ideal Critic* by Karsten Hvidtfelt Nielsen, a book, which is to a great extent an interpretation of Cicero's main rhetorical work, his *Orator*.

For rather obvious reasons, Classical Rhetoric was concerned especially with the speech, and preoccupied in particular with political speeches and speeches in courts of law. But clearly the deliberations on these subjects carry over to quite general questions of how to investigate an issue, how to present it and, perhaps most importantly in our context, what a process of comprehension may be said to consist in. I shall stick to the conventional terms and examples, but bear in mind that the deliberations have far wider implications than simply the speech etc. In general, speech should be understood as any kind of exposition.

Quaestio, Oratio, Mythos

In Roman Rhetoric, the speech was seen not as the stream of words emitted by some speaker, and not even primarily the meaning which could be attributed to those words, but rather as an inseparable unity of three elements: some issue, the speaker, and an audience. The process of making a speech involves a process of investigating the issue at hand, which in fact also involves the idea of comprehending the issue – indeed a whole theory of comprehension is implied.

Time, Reality, and Transcendence in Rational Perspective

The process is described as a quest – *Quaestio*, centered upon available documentation about the issue in question, i.e. the domain at hand. The domain was thus seen as constituted not by indisputable facts, but rather what was called *endoxa*,[117] that is, generally accepted propositions on the relevant issues. A *quaestio* by its very nature deals with some controversial issue, i.e. some case on which there is no universal agreement beforehand. Nevertheless, when building an argued position, one should in general base one's case on what is already well documented, and accepted in general as facts. This means not least that the person who examines the case should be well informed about the *endoxa* – documents, law, testimonies, theories related to the issue, and so forth. On the other hand, it has to be realized that the process of examination is highly selective. Having a purpose, for instance that of defending an accused person in court, one would have to select some recognized facts at the expense of others. Moreover, as soon as one has selected some statements on which to focus, a pattern will begin to form. That pattern will influence the further process of investigation, itself in the next steps of the investigation giving more relevance to some facts than to others.

This idea is nicely rendered in Cicero's *De Oratore*, where one of the characters, the lawyer Antonius, describes his rhetorical quest when asked to take a case, as follows:

> "...when [my client] has departed, in my own person and with perfect impartiality I play three characters, myself, my opponent and the arbitrator." [De O. 2,120]

Succinctly, the quote points out three thing: firstly, the plain observation that a case has several sides to it, and allows for different interpretations, or narrations. Secondly, there is a call for a disciplined and instructed search: one should not rush to conclusions, but should try one's own arguments in a critical process. This refines and partly leads the *quaestio* – the search is not

---

[117] Or in Latin, *exempla*. The latter term is, however, especially used about anecdotes or stories featuring illustrious men, an unfortunate connotation or restriction in this context. For that reason I shall use the greek *endoxa*.

an arbitrary thing, but contributes to constructing a pattern, determined by one's own purpose as well as by possible objections to it. Thirdly, and more implicitly, there is an ethical demand associated with this picture: for if one ends up finding the possible narrations by one's opponent and the resulting images in the eyes of the arbitrator, or audience, more persuasive, then one should not take the case. That is, the lawyer or any other rhetorician should never adopt a case in which he does not believe. If the lawyer believes that the better argument is in fact that the client's claim is invalid, he should not take the case. This means that on a Ciceronian conception of Rhetoric, it is *not* a discipline concerned with how to best achieve *persuasio*, persuasion - or simply to manipulate others, as the detractors of Rhetoric might describe it. Its insights may be abused for such purposes, but so may an insight into, say, formal logic, or traditional grammar.

So far it should be clear that in investigating a certain case with a certain purpose, one is not simply finding the truth. Indeed, one is not even in principle *trying* to find *the* truth. Rather, one is constructing a narration – in Greek, a *Mythos* – which is only one among many possible ones. The narration is not a picturing of incontrovertible facts, but a rendering of established documentation. (In some cases, though, it may of course be necessary to attack already formed opinions and assumed truths, but that only calls for an even higher degree of involving still more documentation.) It is quite clear that this conception implies a kind of relativism, but it is a relativism which is in some senses very moderate. Let us recapitulate the major concepts so far:

1. The *speech (oratio)*, as a unity of speaker, issue, and audience
2. The *quaestio*, as the constructive process of investigation
3. The domain (theme, issue), as an open-ended set of *endoxa*
4. The *Mythos (narratio, fabula),* as the selective but well-informed and arguable point of view of the issue at hand (which is the same thing as a comprehension of the issue).

The relativism consists mainly in these two points: 1) the notion that the investigative process is *constructive,* in its pattern-forming selection and its purpose-oriented character,[118] – the term *Mythos* spells this out very well – and 2) the idea that even the 'facts' selected are not absolute events and relationships in the world, but rather *accepted opinions* (even when these are seen to be accepted for very good reasons). Thus there is *no absolute grounding* of any narrative.

On the other hand, the relativism is tempered by at least two demands: firstly, by the demand that one must be disciplined and well-informed, and secondly, by an ethical demand that one does not deliberately manipulate in order to conform to the purpose of the investigation. Moreover, the crucial role attributed to text and documentation should not be identified with a well-known radical postmodern claim, that 'everything *is* text' – or, speaking with Baudrillard, that reality can not be pictured, because reality itself is nothing more than these pictures [1996]. The idea that a domain consists of *endoxa* does not necessarily imply – indeed I am convinced that for instance Cicero would have thought no such thing – that no extralinguistic reality exists. But it does say that texts and our readings of text are not picturings of reality, but a constructive and selective and interpretative process, for which no absolute decidability procedure exists or even could exist.

Logos, ethos, pathos

In relation to the audience the speaker has three tasks or duties, his so-called offices (*officia*), known as *logos*, *ethos*, and *pathos*. These three duties or functions throw further light on the rhetorical conception. The logos-function of the speech basically consists in instructing the audience about the relevant facts and their logical relations – i.e., in giving information on the case, structured in a coherent manner. The logos-function also demands

---

[118] Since it is purpose-oriented, it is partial. Two traditionally acknowledged senses of 'partial' here nicely recombine: the Mythos is partial in the sense 'incomplete', because it is partial in the sense 'selective with a certain purpose' (quite apart from the practical impossibility of giving a complete account).

consistency and coherence within the speech. In Latin, this obligation of the logos-function is also called *'docere'*, to instruct when giving a speech.

The pathos-function is a demand that to some degree the speech should also relate to the emotions of the audience, and induce appropriate feelings into it – as when a lawyer calls for sympathy with a defendant, or a politician tries to stir our conscience in some matter. The obligation of the speaker is here to move his audience, in Latin *permovere*. It is the function that most easily lends itself to abuse and manipulation, and whose role within the overall rhetorical conception has contributed to its sometimes bad reputation. It is true that Rhetoric is concerned also with how to make speech persuasive, and therefore inevitably has a place for the role of emotional influence. (Although, as mentioned before, with ethical constraints on this objective.) However, the pathos-function is also cultivated out of a wider acceptance of human emotion as a valid part of human recognition. Set against the ideal of pure, disinterested and objective recognition – a hallmark of early modernity – such an idea of course becomes suspect.

Thirdly, there is the ethos-function. This is arguably the crucial function in Rhetoric, or at any rate in Ciceronian Rhetoric. The obligation can be initially described as an obligation to delight one's audience – in Latin *delectare*. Thus a certain immediate *rapport* between the speaker and his audience should be established. But in fact that *rapport* also comprises the matter at hand. For another way of describing this function is to say that the speaker must be, or become, plausible. And this involves his own good faith in his own narration, or point of view. Plausibility in its full sense is not something that one can achieve by skilful deception. We have seen that the rhetorician must be fully aware

1. that one undertakes an investigation and constructs a speech with a purpose – in truth with a *partial* purpose,
2. that one goes about this in a highly selective manner, and
3. that it results in a narration, which is just one out of many possible ones.

Such relativistic awareness notwithstanding, one's case can only be put ethically if one can oneself truly stand up for it and believe in it. We have already seen this with the lawyer Antonius. Another way of putting it is this:

> "... the consummate – and efficient – speaker never tries to prevail upon his audience unless stirred himself 'by the very feelings to which' he is 'seeking to prompt them'. He will adopt the case of another person, shape his speech and self accordingly, and perform in a way which has no use for or any similarity to 'make-believe and trickery'" [Nielsen 95, p. 31]

Even though this quote deals especially with feelings (*pathos*), it is clear that its idea extends to *ethos* and *logos* as well. So the ethos-function requires three things: firstly, *honesty*, that is, good faith in your own speaking. Secondly, the *rhetorical awareness* of all those relativizing aspects just mentioned, that is, the recognition of the relativity of one's own narration. Such awareness gives rise to openness, to possible dialogue, and to tolerance. And thirdly, there is one more thing: a *devotion* to one's audience, that is, respect and commitment. Therefore, *persuasio* is *not* the ultimate goal of the rhetorician's speaking. Rather, the goal is in general to put one's case as well as possible and so to establish a dialogue, hopefully leading to the enrichment of everybody's understanding – and, by the corrections received through a dialogue, to the future improvement of the speaker's own performance.[119]

---

[119] Another way to illuminate the place of the ethos-function is to refer to the following three-way distinction; the distinction between 1) ascertaining, 2) vindicating, 3) persuading. In (1), the objective is to prove conclusively (and thus to end discussion), in (3) the objective is to achieve persuasion, with a slight note of coercion or manipulation. 'In between' one finds the objective of 'vindicating.' One might see 'ascertaining' as the result of an undue emphasis upon logos, and 'persuading' as the result of an undue emphasis upon pathos, whereas the objective of 'vindication' ideally corresponds to giving primacy to the ethos-function.

Actually, the role of the ethos-function establishes yet another striking analogue between Rhetoric and postmodernity, or if you prefer it, the modern media society. Personal plausibility has become a crucial parameter on a par with one's informedness and actual argumentation. Quite a few deplore this as a decline in rationality, a 'closing of the Western mind.' But whatever one thinks of it, it seems to be an inevitable consequence of developments within recent years, and rhetorical thought provides a systematic role for it. Observe also, however, how remote the rhetorical ethics is from a postmodern relativism, wherein 'anything goes.' Neither *ethos* nor *logos* would allow any such thing. But one might ask, of course: after all, why not? If knowledge is insecure and any narration relative, why must one accept some kind of ethics? To reflect on this crucial question we shall in due course bring in some observations on St. Jerome and St. Paul. But first, let us recapitulate what further concepts have been discussed:

- *logos*, the task of instructing (*docere*)
- *pathos*, the task of appealing to emotions (*permovere*)
- *ethos*, the task of delighting (*delectare*), and the obligation to be plausible.

Together with the notions of *Quaestio*, *Mythos* and *Speech* as a unity of speaker, audience, and theme, this makes up a certain idea of 'comprehension.' For not only the making of a speech, but also the process of investigation and the process of comprehending the speech by and large follow the same principles: all of them are selective, constructive, and involve rationality, emotionality and ethics.[120] As for the audience, it should be noted that it need not be a present audience of listeners – it can be intended, actual, or indirect as when you write a book or design a multimedia-system. It can even be oneself, when one is having a conversation with oneself – the *conversio ad se* – for instance, when one is forming an image or ideal of oneself, which we intend others and in

---

[120] Or perhaps it would be better to say that human rationality itself involves emotionality and ethics, as well as logos-oriented thinking – thus avoiding tying up the notion of rationality merely with logos.

particular ourselves to adopt. The bottom-line in our context is this: comprehension is not the uncovering, or the grasping of some absolute truth.[121] Rather,

> "comprehension is a constructive and creative act to the point of dissolving all inherent demarcations between meanings past and present, alien and proper..." [Nielsen 95, p. 91]

3. Perspectives: temporality and internalism

There are two aspects of the rhetorical conception of comprehension or meaning that should be noted.

Firstly, it is what one may call an 'internalist' conception.[122] It is true that the rhetorician would in many cases not hesitate to consider one speech superior to another one. But the truth value, the ethical value, and the beauty of a speech are intrinsic values to that speech, not something that can be decided by referring to any kind of external entities or objective procedures. That does not mean that the way in which a speech – or a theory, or a story, or an argument – is evaluated is radically subjective. But it does mean that the evaluation would itself have to be argued and put forth subject to exactly the same rhetorical uncertainties as that which is being evaluated.

This leads on directly to the second point, the essentially temporal character of the rhetorical conception. 'Meaning,' in so far as we stick to this conventional term, is not a fixed entity. It is something that *happens* in time,

---

[121] Not even in the more cautious sense of fallibilism, where truth is assumed to exist, but where some uncertainty must always be allowed for due to human fallibility.

122 Or immanent conception. I say 'internal' rather than 'immanent,' because a certain kind of transcendent thought is possibly compatible with the rhetorical conception of comprehension or meaning (see section 5).

as it were – subject to an ongoing negotiation, interpretation and reinterpretation.[123] The constructive character of comprehension implies

> "...the idea that understanding does not iterate or depurate a former meaning but 'adds it own' to the extent of effacing any effective demarcation between meaning and action." [Nielsen 95, p. 69]

There is an interesting and striking similarity between these two points about Ciceronian rhetoric and Arthur N. Prior's tense logic. Prior considered the modalities, especially the tenses, to be primitive and irreducible. Thus a 'statement' like for instance *Fp* is according to Prior *not* to be understood as:

$$\exists t.\ now < t\ \&\ p(t).$$ [124]

The latter expression involves the idea of time as objective entities, 't's that can be quantified over.' However, according to Prior such objective time entities do not exist. The latter formula should be understood in terms of the former, *Fp*, and temporal entities should be seen as *conceptual constructions* out of temporal modalities.[125]

This is a conception of time which can be described as understanding time 'from within,' rather than with any reference to external entities ('from without'). Moreover, in tense logic *all* propositions are considered to be

---

[123] Another term for it is 'enchainment' (Lyotard), the idea that 'a meaning' is not a fixed thing, but rather that a speech act produces a chain of interpretation or new speech acts, a chain which has no necessary end to it.

[124] *Fp* may be read as 'it will be the case that *p*'. Thus if *p* stands for 'John smiles,' *Fp* stands for 'it will be the case that John smiles,' or equivalently and more naturally, 'John will smile.' $\exists t.\ now < t\ \&\ p(t)$ can be read as 'there exists some time *t*, such that '*now*' is earlier than *t*, and 'John smiles' is true at time *t*.'

[125] Prior's own term was 'logical constructions' (See [Prior 1968], p. 64 and p. 86). He had in this connection also a quite specific formal notion in mind; see [Prior 1968], chapter XI.

'tensed;' that is, all 'meaning' is temporal, albeit perhaps in a sense which is more restricted than the rhetorical idea I have here tried to espouse. On the other hand, Prior's view that all propositions are tensed (including the propositions of logic and mathematics, such as 2 + 2 = 4) is truly a radical one. The question about which kind of formula is more basic:

$$Fp \text{ or } \exists t. \, now < t \, \& \, p(t).$$

may at first glance seem rather hair-splitting, but it is not: Prior's view is a breach with a very long atemporal tradition within logic, and a radically new conception of both time and logic. (For a fuller treatment of these questions, see Øhrstrøm & Hasle 1995, especially chapters 2.5, 2.9 and 3.1.)

It is true that Prior might not have been happy to be involved as a witness for Rhetoric, at least not in its full implications, but that is not decisive here.[126] The point in the current context – and given that our theme is 'Time, Reality, and Transcendence' – is twofold:

1) There is not necessarily any opposition between logic and rhetoric, even if there exists an ancient quarrel between them. This may allay some of the worst fears among logicians that Rhetoric invites imprecision and intellectual irresponsibility. And conversely, it may open the eyes of rhetoricians to some surprising potentials of logic.

2) What an 'internalist' conception of meaning really says is hard to grasp under the weight of a massive foundationalist tradition. But tense logic provides a lovely example of an 'internalist' conception, at least with respect to time. It is inscribed into the logical tradition but without being foundationalist; that is, the logic of time should

---

[126] Along with 'tense logic,' Prior also argued for a substance metaphysics; but on this point there is arguably a tension within his thought, as already observed by Cocchiarella (1971). The relation between tense logic and Rhetoric is worthy of a much more thorough investigation.

not be understood by reference to any external (and un-tensed) reality.[127]

The attempt at approximating tense logic and Rhetoric would, in my opinion, further the internalist project of Prior and enhance the understanding of Rhetoric. But the radically temporal character of Rhetoric could also be taken in an opposite direction: it was indeed used in an argument for radical relativism by Paul de Man in his famed paper 'The Rhetoric of Temporality' [de Man 1971]. Herein he argued that the temporality of understanding actually meant that rationality – and communication, for that matter – were mere illusions. Along with these theses he put forth an almost postmodern reading of Rhetoric, which may in my view form an obstacle to understanding what the rhetorical conception of comprehension means.

The difference between 'postmodernism' and Rhetoric is this, in a nutshell: according to postmodernism, all narratives are equally good, equal in value (or equally worthless). According to Rhetoric, this is certainly not the case: some narratives are better than other, aesthetically, ethically and alethically (i.e. with respect to truth). On the other hand, Rhetoric agrees with postmodernity 1) that there is no single privileged narrative (or equally, there is no one absolutely adequate narrative); and moreover, 2) there is no absolute grounding of, or foundation for, any narrative.

4. The performative consistency problem

It has just been accepted that for Rhetoric, some narratives *are* better than other ones, aesthetically, ethically and alethically. But how can one assess the relative values among narratives? How can it be maintained that one narrative is superior to another one, in one or more respects – given that there

---

[127] Hence this line of thought may provide a bridge between a modified logical tradition and the present-day cultural condition of a widespread and revitalized scepticism. But admittedly, here I speculate.

is no absolute grounding, or other objective methods of comparison? In short, if one speech is deemed superior to another one, is that not like saying or presupposing that some fixed standards must, after all, be available? And hence, is the rhetorician when making such judgments not being inconsistent in a manner much like the Daddy in a cartoon aggressively shouting 'I am not the least excited'? The point is, of course, that there seems to be an inconsistency between *what* you say and your actual *performance* – what you *do* by saying it. Much like somebody trying to communicate that all communication is in reality impossible. For these reasons this kind of tension is often called performative inconsistency.

The performative consistency argument is in fact the basis of a standard argument against all kinds of relativistic conceptions, and you see it in many varied forms. Its bottom-line is in any case that any assertion of relativism is necessarily 'performatively inconsistent.'

I think that the argument is in fact a serious objection to postmodernist thinkers. Some of these, when charged with 'performative inconsistency,' openly answer along lines like these:

> "yes, we are inconsistent in this manner, but that is simply the result of the weight of a massive foundationalist tradition. We are so tied up with this tradition that we can only speak and even think within it, when trying to promote our relativist ideas aimed at bringing us out of it. So yes, we are contradicting ourselves. That can not be helped, there is no other way to express our point."

Such an answer would, however, be contrary to the ideals of Rhetoric. It violates the requirement of speaking in compliance with the demands of *logos*, and worse still, it is unethical to the extent that it is intellectually implausible – at any rate, unsatisfactory. From a rhetorical position, there are some more qualified answers to the charge of being performatively inconsistent.

A standard riposte against the charge of performative inconsistency is this: the objection raised is (a priori) based on that assumption of fixity of meaning, which it is designed to defend (a posteriori) (defend indirectly, by dismantling its adversary). That seems to me to be an obvious point of departure also for a good rhetorical answer, but it is not fully satisfactory by itself; it must be supplemented.

Let us look more carefully at the argument: when the rhetorician considers one speech to be more plausible than another one – or let us just go all the way and say *truer* than another one, is he not after all reintroducing some foundation, although unwillingly? Indeed, when he considers for instance a report on some event to be actually true – and without doubt he sometimes does so – is he not reintroducing a belief in correspondence, and hence also, some fixity of meaning?

Here it should be noted that if one reinstates 'fixity' and foundationalism on these grounds, then that whole process that lead to their abandonment is bound to start all over again. That is, all the objections which foundationalism is bound to raise, and which lead from semantic foundationalism to rhetorical relativism could be repeated, landing us again in the latter. Whereafter the charge about performative inconsistency could be raised again, and so on infinitely. That situation, however, is far more destructive for the foundationalist than for the rhetorician. An ongoing process as sketched here is almost rhetorical in nature, whereas it is completely irreconcilable with the aspirations of any kind of foundationalism. For *its* very purpose is to find that which is absolute and so ends discussion, at least in principle.[128] What becomes evident here is a basic *asymmetry* between Rhetoric and semantic foundationalism. They are not just two different conceptions on a par, one of which may be right, and the other one wrong. They are, in a sense, incomparable (if you will forgive this slight performative inconsistency from my side, since I have been comparing them for quite some time by now).

Perhaps an example would be helpful. Wittgenstein realized a number of grave objections to the kind of foundationalism represented in his Tractatus.

---

[128] Further discussion being seen as necessary revisions caused by human fallibility, not by the idea of an absolute foundation being inadequate.

He conceived instead the notion of language games, and rejected the Tractatus-ideas. Language games were seen as utterly relativistic and undecidable. Therefore, the things that Wittgenstein said about language games could, by an argument similar to the 'performative inconsistency' argument, not itself be a 'language game' in the same sense – after all, here was something that Wittgenstein considered to be right. But if that observation leads back to Tractatus-like ideas, then evidently these ideas are now subject to that criticism, which lead to their rather conclusive downfall, and to language games. As already argued, such a pattern undermines the principal goals of foundationalism.

What underlies the charge of performative inconsistency against Rhetoric is, as I see it, an incapability to imagine or to grasp that anything can be *right* at all without being so in virtue of some other thing; an almost obsessive compulsive idea within the history of Western thought that truth can only exist in virtue of something else. (And similarly, that communication presupposes some underlying semantic system, beyond Speaker and Hearer themselves.)

On this point the example set by Priorean tense logic is a useful demonstration to the effect that this intuition is dispensable. Of course, Prior in this case deals specifically with time, and nothing else, but his approach can illustrate a general internalist conception. Within his rigorous and formal strand of thought, time is understood from within and is not defined in terms of anything else. In an analogous way one may try to think of truth, and even ethics and aesthetics, as internal to the speech.

Another version of the performative inconsistency argument, directed against relativism in general, is this: the relativist rejects absolutism. But by his own hypothesis, his arguments are relative. Hence, in the very least he must concede that the absolutist can be right. (And hence, there is probably something wrong with his arguments, since they for these reasons must be said to fail to invalidate absolutism.) When directed against an aggressive and over-confident relativism, I do think that the argument carries some weight. But against the more benign scepticism of Rhetoric, I hope that the above discussion has already given some idea about what is wrong with this otherwise persuasive thought: the argument foregoes a basic asymmetry between the two kinds of thought involved. (It also seems to depend on a presupposition of fixed foundation, the very idea that it is designed to demonstrate.)

In an interview some time ago, Richard Rorty defended the idea that concepts such as 'truth,' 'nature,' and 'rationality' would eventually lose their fundamental role within Western thought [Rorty 1997]. Rorty makes a provocative comparison: until less than one hundred years ago, practically any philosopher felt obliged to relate to the concept of God, even if his own philosophy was very remote from, or contrary to, Christian theism. The point was not that this was expected in those days, but rather that the concept of God was seen to be of crucial philosophical importance. Well, those times are over, and most present-day philosophers happily go about their business without any notion of having to relate to God, whether positively or negatively. Only thinkers 'of particular interests' still devote significant work to the concept of God. In a sense, then, according to Rorty the question about God has disappeared rather than been settled. The present-day rhetorician may expect something similar to happen for the twin ideas of the fixity of meaning and absolute truth.[129]

Indeed the problem of absolute foundation versus Rhetoric and related conceptions does not have to do only with 'truth.' Rorty's observations may be followed up by pointing out a phenomenon from the realm of ethics. Until not very long ago, it was thought that the eclipse of religion would mean the erosion of ethics and morals. In fact, also devout atheists were truly worried about this. This thought is obviously related to the other kind of foundationalism: that for something to have validity and viability, there must be some fixed foundation. In the case of ethics, this has arguably proved

---

[129] Of course, this does not imply that the rhetorician *thereby* endorses Rorty's thought in its particular form. Rorty's picture is useful for understanding how concepts may fade away. The classical insistence upon fixity and truth may be expected to go exactly that way in what appears to be an increasingly rhetorical culture, quite regardless of one's own sentiments about this development.

wrong. Similarly, and in line with Rorty's observation, it will probably show that there can well be truth and talk of truth without there being any foundation in the traditional sense for it.

My goal so far has been to show that the charge of performative inconsistency does not establish any conclusive evidence against the rhetorical type of relativism. It is not irrelevant, though – on the contrary, it helps bring out some essential features of the rhetorical conception. Nevertheless, that is not the same thing as saying that this defence of Rhetoric and its particular kind of relativism settles all questions. Indeed the internalist view may leave us with a rather difficult question, which I shall try to elucidate below, with reference to St. Jerome and St. Paul.

5. Cicero, St. Paul and St. Jerome: Christianity and Rhetoric revisited

With the rejection of foundationalism and the moderately relativistic outlook of Rhetoric depicted so far, we can now turn our attention to its role when faced with Christianity.

St. Jerome's story tells us about a formidable obstacle which early Christianity faced. An obstacle with which Christianity or any other belief in absolute truth again finds itself confronted: the rejection of the claim of the privileged myth. It may be added that such rejection is not necessarily a consequence of a conscious relativistic stance: the idea of any privileged myth seems again to be acquiring a quality of being highly implausible (perhaps almost unintelligible) to modern, or postmodern, men and women.

St. Jerome (ca. 347-420) was the principal translator of the first complete Latin version of the Bible which was based directly on the available original Greek and Hebrew manuscripts. His translation is known as *Vulgata*, or the Vulgate.

Jerome was actually born into a Christian family, but the chief influence on him as a young man – in fact even while he was still a boy – was the spirit and learning of Roman Rhetoric, and in particular, of Cicero's writings. When he was about twelve years old, he went to Rome from his native city of Stridon in Illyria. In Rome he was educated by the famous – and non-Christian – Grammarian Donatus. He read the Greek and Roman classics, and the spirit of Roman Rhetoric and especially Cicero permeated his entire education, as he himself was to make very clear later on. He was in fact baptized during this period of his life, but it was only some years later, while he was staying in Trier, that he experienced a personal conversion to Christianity. He became a monk and was also later ordained as a priest, but I shall leave aside all further details of his turbulent life. What concerns us here is the struggle he had in both *combining* his Ciceronian background with his Christian faith and at the same time *separating* them from one another. For, as we have already noted, the idea of a privileged myth is alien to Rhetoric, or in the very least highly mystical from a rhetorical point of view.[130] Christianity came into the Roman world with exactly such a claim of being *the* truth, the one and only valid *Mythos*. And moreover, the Bible could have only one true interpretation, regardless of how much it was debated exactly what this interpretation should be (a discussion still going on, as everybody knows).

Roughly one could say that as a translator Jerome stuck with Cicero, while spiritually he eventually rejected him. In his letter (57) to Pammachius on the best method of translating, *De optimo genere interpretandi*, Jerome states his adherence to Cicero:

---

[130] This 'mystical element' is not an antagonistic observation on Christianity, as seen from the side of Rhetoric. For there was indeed – at that time, at any rate – a strong idea also within Christianity that the truth of Christianity would reveal itself to a person, not through an argument or a discussion, but only through a mystical experience, which was to be achieved above all through an ascetic life, an 'imitation of Christ.'

> "I not only confess but freely profess that in the rendering of Greek texts... I write not word for word but sense for sense. My authority in this matter is Cicero, who translated Plato's Protagoras, Xenophon's Oeconomicus and the two very beautiful speeches of Aeshines and Demosthenes against each other. This is not the moment to say how much in these works Cicero passed over, how much he added or how much he changed in order to explain the characteristics of the Greek in the idiom of the Latin." [Letter 57.5]

Obviously, St. Jerome is conscious of questions such as "how much in these works he passed over, how much he added or how much he changed". But that is not meant as an implicit criticism of Cicero's approach. On the contrary, these were liberties on which St. Jerome insisted, the liberty of addition or deletion, and for which he argued in the course of this letter. Even the name of the letter, *De optimo genere interpretandi*, is a clear allusion to Cicero's work *De optimo genere oratorum*.

Cicero had characterized his own work as a translator by stating that he himself translated not like an interpreter, but as an orator, a speaker – *nec ut interpres, sed ut orator*. [De Opt.]. What that means should be fairiy clear by now: the translation process is constructive and imitative rather than a – more or less succesful – transfer of some absolute literal meaning. Similarly, Jerome argued not only that he was free to translate according to sense rather than 'literally' – *ad sensum* rather than *ad verbum* – but in fact, that it was necessary to do so. That is, that an attempt at literal meaning transfer would yield a distorted text.

Jerome also worked as a commentator on Biblical texts. In an apology for himself against charges raised in the books of Rufinus he describes the task of writing a commentary as a process of presenting and weighing opinions against each other, in a manner highly reminiscent of the rhetorical process of investigating an issue and making a speech:

> "We have to do now with Commentaries... what is the function of a Commentary? It is to interpret another man's words, to put into plain language what he has expressed obscurely. Consequently, it

> enumerates the opinions of many persons, and says, some interpret the passage in this sense, some in that; the one try to support their opinion and understanding of it by such and such evidence or reasons: so that the wise reader, after reading these different explanations, and having many brought before his mind for acceptance or rejection, may judge which is the truest, and, like a good banker, may reject the money of spurious mintage.
>
> "Is the commentator to be held responsible for all these different interpretations, and all these mutually contradicting opinions because he puts down the expositions given by many in the single work on which he is commenting?... Will you find fault with those who have commented on these writers because they have not held to a single explanation, but enumerate their own views and those of others on the same passage?" ['Rufinus', BOOK I, 16]

In fact, at the very opening of St. Jerome's letter on the best method of translating, he calls on the authority of St. Paul, referring to Paul's own rhetorical practices as follows:

> "The apostle Paul when he appeared before King Agrippa to answer the charges, which were brought against him, wishing to use language intelligible to his hearers and confident of the success of his cause, began by congratulating himself in these words: "I think myself happy, King Agrippa, because I shall answer for myself this day before thee touching all the things whereof I am accused by the Jews: especially because thou art expert in all customs and questions which are among the Jews." He had read the saying of Jesus: "Well is him that speaketh in the ears of them that will hear"; and he knew that a pleader only succeeds in proportion as he impresses his judge." [Letter 57.1]

On another famous occasion, when St. Paul gave his speech on Areopagus in Athens, he also used rhetorical insight and practice, when he began his speech as follows (Acts 17, verses 22f.):

> 22. ... Ye men of Athens, I perceive that in all things ye are too superstitious.
> 23. For as I passed by, and beheld your devotions, I found an altar with this inscription, 'To the Unknown God'. Whom therefore ye ignorantly worship, him declare I unto you.

Nevertheless, it could be argued that Paul sometimes characterized his own speech as almost the opposite thing of that rhetorical approach, which we have just seen attributed to him by St. Jerome, and which indeed seems sufficiently evident in the above examples. In 1. Corinthians, Chapter 2, verses 1-2, Paul says:

> 1. And I, brethren, when I came to you, came not with excellency of speech or of wisdom, declaring unto you the testimony of God.
> 2. For I determined not to know anything among you, save Jesus Christ, and him crucified.

But this apparent contradiction can be understood when taking seriously that what Paul preaches is not a *doctrine*, but a *person* – *"Jesus Christ, and him crucified."* On this point, a remarkable and unexpected kinship between Christian thought and the rhetorical conception of comprehension could actually be suggested; I shall soon elaborate this thought.

On the whole, the rhetorical influence on St. Jerome's work as a translator as well as a commentator does seem great. Nevertheless, since ideally the biblical texts have only one true interpretation, clearly a conflict is looming here. As already mentioned, this was evident even in his letter (57), where he acknowledged his debt to Cicero. The conflict was indeed clear to Jerome himself and caused a severe crisis, and he had a dream that dramatized the conflict. In his letter (22) to Eustochium, St. Jerome reports it like this:

> "And so, miserable man that I was, I would fast only that I might afterwards read Cicero. After many nights spent in vigil, after floods of tears called from my inmost heart, after the recollection of my past sins, I would once more take up Plautus. And when at times I returned to my right mind, and began to read the prophets,

their style seemed rude and repellent. I failed to see the light with my blinded eyes; but I attributed the fault not to them, but to the sun.

...

"Suddenly I was caught up in the spirit and dragged before the judgment seat of the Judge; and here the light was so bright, and those who stood around were so radiant, that I cast myself upon the ground and did not dare to look up. Asked who and what I was I replied: *"I am a Christian."* But He who presided said: *"Thou liest, thou art a follower of Cicero and not of Christ. For 'where thy treasure is, there will thy heart be also.'"* [Letter 22.30]

This dream had a profound impact upon St. Jerome, and caused him – apart from severe penitence – to become much more wary of influence from the rhetorical tradition upon his own thought. He nevertheless stuck to Ciceronian principles for translation.

Apart from the rude and repellent style of the prophets, Jerome experienced another and more daunting obstacle to fully accepting the Christian faith. In my opinion, the ultimate difficulty consisted in having to accept the idea of absolute truth, and of the one privileged *Mythos*. This obstacle is mirrored today in that resurging common scepticism, which seems to me epitomized in the postmodern critique of 'grand narratives.' Such scepticism comes in many shades and varying degrees, but I do think that a major shift towards a renewed rhetorical awareness is evident – and moreover, that it is probably irreversible. We may accept as a 'diagnosis', then, that we live in a pluralistic and rhetorical society. But what about that other important claim that there is no fixity of meaning and no absolute truth?

If it is accepted that the charge of 'performative inconsistency' is not a conclusive argument against the rhetorical conception, it can still be said that Rhetoric leaves us with a kind of question. For after all, the demand for consistency is not fully explained by saying that we must speak in compliance with the demands of *logos*. Which *logos*? Is it an arbitrary thing, or constructed in quite the same sense as the *Mythos* is constructed, as comprehension is constructed? Similarly, why or how can there be said to be an ethical demand involved with Rhetoric? If that demand is *constructed*, why should it be heeded, or why should it be privileged when compared with, say, Hitler's use of speech?

These observations are in my opinion entirely relevant, but they can not lead to the re-introduction of classical metaphysics or for that matter modernized versions of substance metaphysics. Then the whole story would repeat itself, at any rate a malign paradox for those who seek fixity – and that, of course, is what these kinds of metaphysics were thought to bring. It may be recalled, however, that in the rhetorical conception there is a kind of coherence, but it is a coherence from within. The coherence and sincerity of the speech can not be measured towards any objective external touchstone, but are intrinsic to the speech.[131] And it does seem, to me at any rate, that on this point we are brought to the brink of intelligibility of the rhetorical conception of comprehension – and of truth and of good.

Now there are some famous words by St. Paul which pertain to speech and communication, and which as I see it address this question about their curious intrinsic qualities. In 1 Corinthians, chapter 13, verses 1 ff., he writes:

> 1. Though I speak with the tongues of men and of angels, and have not charity, I am become as sounding brass, or a tinkling cymbal. 2. And though I have the gift of prophecy, and understand all

---

[131] It must be recalled that 'speech' comprises not only the speaker, but also the theme and the audience. In so far as one would speak of a 'touchstone,' it should rather be sought in the reactions of the audience: *"Ars rhetorica, therefore, is dedicated to the transient character of human knowledge... it urges anyone... to conceive of himself and his verbal activities as the conscious result of an ongoing process of mental stylizations of which no other touchstone can or should be supplied than the manifold reactions of a surrounding community of speakers."* [Nielsen 95, p. 36]

mysteries, and all knowledge; and though I have all faith, so that I could remove mountains, and have not charity, I am nothing.

St. Paul here states a startling thought: even if informed by all earthly knowledge, and heavenly wisdom, speech without love is shallow. Or, if you allow for an even more far-reaching interpretation, the essence of communication is neither factuality nor for that matter beauty, but an ethical element – the *utmost* ethical element: love.[132]

Rhetoric, as will be recalled, calls for openness, tolerance, and devotion to the audience. But this could easily seem to be a mere postulate, conveniently aligning Rhetoric with cherished values. However, he or she who studies Rhetoric may experience a strange cogency about this rhetorical ethics. Similarly, she may experience a cogency about an argumentation, which appears to be over and above the consent of an audience – its coherence and its truthfulness.[133] This experience cannot be grounded in any procedure, but it does seem to call for a 'content.' For those willing to relate Christianity and Rhetoric to each other, this content may be identified with that essence of love, of which Paul speaks so beautifully in 1 Corinthians.

There remains, of course, a genuine difference between on one hand the rhetorical conception (as narrated here), and on the other hand the insistence upon absolute truth within the Christian tradition. But it may be that this claim derives from a misconception, namely that Christianity is a doctrinal system. Surely that conception is well entrenched within the Christian tradition itself, but the Biblical texts also contain another line of thought,

---

[132] I take it that this may be inferred, without going into the discussion of the concept of charity, *caritas* – or for that matter the classical theological discussion of *eros* and *agape*.

[133] A similar perception is at play (in an otherwise rather different sort of communication theory), when Habermas speaks of *"der zwanglose Zwang des besseren Arguments"* (Habermas 1971, p. 137) (with loss of style, the meaning can be rendered in English as *"the uncoercive cogency of the better argument"*).

which is strangely kindred to a rhetorical conception.[134] In John, chapter 14, verse 6, Jesus says:

"I am the way, the truth, and the life."

On an immediate interpretation, this could be understood as a typical metaphor, a positive predication on Christ, to be taken in a 'pictural sense.' Thus, if we focus just on the part restatable as: *Jesus is the truth,* this could be taken to mean plainly that Jesus is truthful, or that what he says is true. But I, for one, think that more is at stake here. In my opinion, this is not a metaphor in this relatively trivial sense. It is much more revolutionary: its main effect is not so much to say that 'Jesus is truthful,' but rather to revolutionize the very idea of truth. The idea here is that truth is ultimately a person – not correspondence, not factuality, but a person. Now a person is exactly that kind of entity which we shall never fully grasp, but which we can only understand through an ongoing dialogue.[135] Without glossing over the important differences between Rhetoric and Christianity, respectively the Christian tradition, I do think that on this reading there is also an interesting point of contact.[136]

---

134 I do not deny that a tension within Christian thought itself seems to follow from these observations. Clearly much theological discussion in our century has centered upon the rift between a 'conservative' interpretation of Christianity and an existentially orientered, so-called 'immanent interpretation,' as championed not least by Rudolf Bultmann. From my point of view, an especially interesting recent development in these discussions has been developed by Gianni Vattimo (1999). Vattimo fully accepts (indeed welcomes) secularization as well as the downfall of classical metaphysics, but from this point he manages to re-establish a positive reading of Christianity along lines very kindred to rhetorical thought.

135 This thought was first pointed out to me by Peter Øhrstrøm in a discussion of the passage just quoted, John 14, 6.

136 This point of contact is further illuminated by the rhetorical emphasis on the importance of *actio*, wherein the meaning as well as the comprehension of

6. Conclusion

If Rhetoric and the Christian faith are opposed with respect to the idea of absolute truth, they seem nevertheless to meet in a crucial emphasis upon the role of the person, or the Self, in the creation of truth. This works both ways – in telling as well as in comprehending truth.

One may accept (and I do) not only as a diagnosis that we now live in an increasingly Rhetorical culture, but also that this development is interwoven with a valid and irreversible insight, namely the recognition of the social and constructive character of human comprehension, and the transient temporal character of human knowledge. That insight does as far as I can see leave no room for the postulation of any single absolutely true *Mythos*. In particular, this means that a belief in Christianity as a doctrinal system cannot be sustained. But that does not imply a wholesale rejection of metaphysics. It is surely a rejection of a classical metaphysics with absolute postulates about 'external' truths, but since Antiquity, 'metaphysics' has another sense, too. In that sense it refers to the *experience* that within thought and thinking, one can encounter that of which one cannot make oneself the master. That is, something which one is not at liberty to accept or reject at one's own discretion or inclination, but which must be 'honoured' in one's thought and speech – for instance, by making it a premise of further thought and investigation.

In a similar spirit, the ethical example put forth by the sayings and doings of Jesus might be seen as an epitome of that intrinsic quality of plausibility, which is acknowledged within Rhetoric. When for instance the parable of the good Samaritan (Luke 10, verses 30-37) is related, it ends up in the direct statement: "Go, and do thou likewise." (Luke 10, verse 37). This parable and its directive can be rejected like any other narration, but alternatively, it can

---

speech are 'created.' In the Biblical texts there is an analogous thought to the effect that truth is something which is not an objective value 'out there', but rather something which is being done (created): *"For he that doeth truth cometh to the light..."*, John 3, 21).

be accepted as a culmination of internal plausibility and ethical cogency. The room for such an experience is surely an integral part of a Rhetorical conception.

It is also clear that the reply to the exhortation of the parable is a deeply existential matter, which decisively involves the 'Self.' The Rhetorical decision to accept ethical and intellectual standards for speech, and for the concomitant development of the Self, can, I think, be informed crucially from Christian thought on this point. It does not *explain,* let alone provide a foundation for, the experience of validity, but it potentially gives an understanding from within of that indispensable value.

When we communicate, what we communicate is in a decisive sense ourselves.[137] Hence the primacy of the ethos-function. This communicated self is inseparably interwoven with the plausibility of our narration about the theme, and even the validity of the emotions, which we may stir. However, it must be realized that the self communicated is no more absolute than 'meaning.' Like 'meaning,' it is an interpretation and imitation of a tradition as well as of our own ideals, of that which we strive to become.

References

Baudrillard, Jean. *The Perfect Crime*. Verso, London, 1996.
Cicero:
    - *De optimo genere oratorum (De Opt.),* ed. Loeb, London 1949
    - *De Oratore,* ed. Loeb, London 1948
    - *Orator,* ed. Loeb, London 1939
Cocchiarella, Nino B. *Review of 'A. N. Prior: Papers on Time and Tense',*
    The Journal of Symbolic Logic, Vol. 36 (1971), pp. 515-518, 1971.

---

[137] But for the Christian believer, of course, there is this addition: to preach the gospel is to communicate along with oneself an imitation of Christ, however imperfect.

Habermas, Jürgen. *'Vorbereitende Bemerkungen zu einer Theorie der kommunikativen Kompetenz'*, in: Habermas, J./Luhmann N., *Theorie der Gesellschaft oder Sozialtechnologie*, Frankfurt, 1971.

Harré; Rom; Harris, Roy (Editors).*Linguistics and Philosophy*. Pergamon Press, 1993.

Harris, Roy. *The Language Connection*. Thoemmes Press, London, 1996.

St. Jerome:

- *Letter 22*, to Eustochium (written A.D. 384)

- *Letter 57*, to Pammachius (written A.D. 395)

- *'Rufinus'*: Jerome's apology for himself against the books of Rufinus. (written A.D. 402. BOOK I)

– *All Jerome quotes taken from: Christian Classics Ethereal Library. Electronic version. New Advent, Inc. 1996. (http://www.newadvent.org/fathers/)*

Katz, Jerrold J. *The Underlying Reality of Language*. Harper and Row, New York, 1971

Katz, Jerrold J. *The Metaphysics of Meaning*. The MIT Press, 1992.

Kenny, Anthony. *A Path from Rome*, Sidgwick and Jackson, London, 1985.

de Man, Paul. 'The Rhetoric of Temporality'. In de Man, Paul (ed.) *Blindness and Insight*. Methuen & Co., London, pp. 187-228, 1971.

Nielsen, Karsten Hvidtfelt. *An Ideal Critic*. Peter Lang Verlag, Bern, 1995.

Prior, A. N. *Papers on Time and Tense*. Clarendon Press, Oxford, 1968.

Rorty, Richard. An Interview with Richard Rorty in *die Zeit* and *Weekend-avisen,* brought in Weekend-avisen, 12.09.1997, p. 6, 1997.

Schaff, Philip (Ed.). *A select library of the Nicene and post-Nicene fathers of the Christian church*. 1st-2nd series. Grand Rapids. Vol. 6, Letters and select works / St. Jerome, 1978-1979.

Vattimo, Gianni. *Belief*. Polity Press, 1999.

Øhrstrøm, Peter; Hasle, Per., *Temporal Logic - from Ancient Ideas to Artificial Intelligence*. 'Studies in Linguistics and Philosophy' (57), Kluwer Academic Publishers 1995.

The Rhetorical Pyramid

PEDER A. TYVAND

Rhetoric is an old discipline. The ancient Greeks emphasised this "science of speech." Rhetoric was considered to be a fundamental skill for the educated and cultivated person.

In modern times, rhetoric has usually not been counted as an academic discipline on its own. The lack of general scientific recognition implies a somewhat reduced status. To be recognized as a rhetorically clever person does not yield high prestige.

In my opinion, rhetoric deserves a higher academic status. Rhetoric could become a common reference point and meeting ground for such diverse fields as mathematical logic, semantics, theological hermeneutics and homiletics, pedagogy, sociology, political science, law, psychology, commercial marketing, communication, and media science. A sign of our times is that the academic status of rhetoric is again increasing. Several American universities are now offering study programmes in rhetoric.

Most people know at least one thing about rhetoric: It can be abused. But this danger is not reduced by ignoring it as a discipline or by letting it be fragmented apart. An established public awareness of rhetoric is the best defence against public rhetorical oppression. One does not become a gangster by mastering the art of self-defence. Rhetorical self-defence is desperately needed in our time, because the tyranny of manipulated opinion is upon us more than ever in the free world. Another sign of our times is that public interest in rhetoric is increasing.

A common rhetorical analysis accessible for non-specialists should satisfy some basic requirements:

(i)   It must be up-to-date in the sense that it must be able to cope with the media.
(ii) It must be able to analyse the manipulation of context, setting, and presuppositions by the media.
(iii) It must be able to analyse the concept of power and its structures.
(iv) It must be able to analyse emotional factors.
(v)   It must incorporate metaphysical values and ethics.
(vi) There must be room for historical lines in the rhetorical analysis.

Below I will describe "the rhetorical pyramid," which I believe is able to satisfy these six requirements. The rhetorical pyramid is a classification system and an analytical tool which can be applied immediately in many contexts where there is debate, opinion-making, or propaganda, in the public as well as in more private arenas. Before describing this pyramid of rhetoric, I will criticize an established view: The positivist argumentation philosophy of the Norwegian professor Arne Næss (born 1912). I refer to his book "Interpretation and preciseness: a contribution to the theory of communication" (Oslo 1953).

On positivistic argumentation-philosophy

A positivist tries to get rid of all metaphysics, and tends to consider all religious and ethical categories as primitive and outdated attempts at objective knowledge. But any positivist applies his own personal will when he chooses to neglect all metaphysics, and in doing so he is acting metaphysically in an inconsistent way.

The word "metaphysics" originates from Greek and means "beside" or "behind" the physical reality. It covers the parts of reality that are not directly observable.

Positivists feel in general that their thinking is scientifically founded. This is a false dream. Positivists need to misinterpret natural science to be able to get a starting point for their thinking. Positivists recognize as real only things that can be measured, observed and classified in categories of natural science. But this is a closed loop of circular reasoning: The circular argument is that all epistemological categories follow from the experiments. But all experiments are based on ideas on what to look for and how to classify and measure it. Without starting from the bias of comprehensive ideas there are no experiments. Scientific categories have arisen because one had ideas of what to look for, and scientific instruments have been developed because one had ideas on how to look at these things. To say that everything followed after the experiments is similar to a Stalinistic revision of the history books. Based on political power, one defines out of history all events and persons that are not flattering for the ideology and the propaganda. Based on scientific power, positivists have claimed the philosophical ownership of many scientific breakthroughs that could never have been made on the basis of positivist philosophy.

The positivist revision of scientific history is that all knowledge is based on objective experiments performed by a neutral observer without any bias. The ideal is a cynically mechanistic process of reasoning without any emotions, without any ethics, without any history, without any metaphysics. This positivistic ideal has had a very high reputation, but it is in essence the utmost naïveté. A human being is considered to be a slave trapped within mechanistic cause and effect. A well-known positivistic statement is the following: "The brain secretes thoughts in the same way as the kidneys secrete urine." An old positivistic daydream is to find the "consciousness formula" which gives the ultimate mathematical representation of consciousness as well as proving the consciousness of human beings. The great drawback for these daydreamers is that any such "proof" has to assume consciousness. This implies that one has not proved anything whatsoever. One cannot assume something to start with and then proceed to proving the same thing, if a proof is supposed to be more than just an abstract escape from reality.

One fatal flaw of positivism is that it has to assume that the concept of causality is rationalistic. Our human reason is assumed to guarantee that effect follows from cause. This point of view requires that human thought is able to penetrate the reality of natural laws, and human reason is hoped to know for certain that the laws of nature are in action from moment to moment. This is absolutely wrong, because the natural laws are metaphysical. The laws of nature rank above the visible nature. The relation of the human mind versus natural laws is based on habit, not on control. The human mind is able to be blinded by its own habits: If we see one event repeat itself sufficiently often, we may lose our natural ability to acknowledge the metaphysics in its cause. If somebody for many years has brushed his teeth just before going to bed, it does not mean that the toothbrush will do the job by itself next time. An established habit does not rule out the metaphysical will of the person in question. Our will is superior to the toothbrush, and is a necessity for the toothbrush to do its job. It does not make any sense to apply "the positivistic method" of pulling apart the toothbrush in order to detect the real cause behind the regular brushing. The regular tooth-brushing cannot be explained if one rules out metaphysics. This example of the tooth-brushing man with his toothbrush is very simplistic as a picture of God and the created physical world. But still it gives a basic illustration of how misleading and dangerous it is when Christian scientists say that "natural science is methodologically atheistic." This is a metaphysical statement, and it is self-contradictory because it denies the relevance of metaphysics. But I have heard it several times from respected Christian intellectuals.

A related claim is the following message: "According to natural science there is no meaning or purpose in the universe. All that ever existed are blind meaningless mechanistic processes according to strict natural laws." These two sentences are in essence the worldview of millions of people. Still I dare to say that this message is utterly absurd. Indeed absurd, although it sounds like being highly intellectual. The absurdness lies in the fact that a non-metaphysical worldview is here presented by the metaphysical concepts "natural," "law," "meaning," "purpose," "exist," "blind," and "strict" as vehicles. Without these borrowed alien concepts of metaphysics, there would be no way to present this opinion. If I say that the universe is void of meaning, I reserve the one singular free spot for myself. The spot of meaning in an environment of no meaning. It would improve clarity if it was said: "Excuse me for just a moment, but I badly need to borrow meaning to be able to say that there is no meaning." Sadly, I doubt that the atheists will ever reach this type of self-awareness. This intellectually self-contradictory position of atheism is one of the greatest paradoxes in our culture. It appears as a stronghold, even though it lacks substance. God's creation and maintenance of reliable natural laws is perhaps the strongest witness of meaning in the universe. But our culture has turned it against God and perverted it into a witness of no meaning in the universe.

In Norway the "logical positivism" of the 20th century is linked to the name Arne Næss. It is described in several of his books (see references). I will avoid linking his argumentation-philosophy to the word "logic." It would generate a metaphysical aura of rationality, objectivity and neutrality. I will now discuss the positivistic argumentation philosophy of Næss. But I have to mention that he has seemingly modified his doctrines somewhat by making room for emotional factors. This has been done in his recent book "Life Philosophy" (printed in Norwegian 1998).

The basis of Næss' doctrines is his program for making statements objective. This program is based on the three metaphysical concepts "interpretation," "preciseness," and "definition." Næss shows great zeal in concealing the metaphysical basis of these concepts. But we can disprove his positivistic basis quite simply by posing the following requirements to Næss: "Please interpret your concept of interpretation!" "Please make precise your concept of preciseness!" "Please define your concept of definition!" These self-references are fatal. The positivist is trapped in a loop of circular reasoning where his concepts must be assumed before they can be defined. It is impossible to escape. This means that the concepts of interpretation, preciseness and definition are undoubtedly metaphysical. Næss' positivistic program of making statements objective has metaphysical stowaways already before its launching. The starting point for all argumentation is metaphysical because it is given by God (John 1:1).

After having described his attempt at making statements objective, Arne Næss presents his scheme for generating an individual opinion: "Pro aut contra," which is a scheme for pro-arguments and counter-arguments to a given assertion. The scheme for opinion-making is constructed as follows: First one basic assertion is formulated: The postulate. The following work has the aim of generating a choice of opinion pro or contra the postulate. This is done by writing two lists: One list of arguments in favour of the postulate, and one list of arguments against the postulate. One then makes a calculation where the weight and relevance of each argument are multiplied together. In the end these results are summed up. This gives two sums, one concerning the pro-arguments and one concerning the counter-arguments. This is the basis for a choice in favour of or against the basic postulate. The idea is that this is opinion-making in a reproducible and objective way. This opinion-making happens individually, with a single person. This person shall according to the scheme "Pro aut contra" be able to make up his mind on an issue in an attemptedly objective manner.

Objectivity according to Næss

Næss also discusses the generation of opinion where two sides are represented. In this case, it is not sufficient to measure the weight and relevance of each argument. This is because not only generation of one person's opinion is involved, but also an exchange of opinion. In a discussion between two parties the concept of objectivity comes into play. Arne Næss formulates some basic criteria for objectivity, which can be summarized as follows:

(A) Do not diverge from the subject of discussion
(B) Make sure that other people's opinions are presented correctly
(C) Avoid ambiguities
(D) Avoid constructing fictitious opponents with artificial opinions ("straw men")
(E) Avoid a biased selection of facts
(F) Present your viewpoints within a neutral framework

Below I will argue against the objectivity criteria A, C and F given by Næss. The criteria B, D and E seem to be acceptable. But it is important to note that these criteria are formulated as various commands that some authoritative person "I" gives to his pupil "you." There is no mutuality, and there is no

Time, Reality, and Transcendence in Rational Perspective

self-criticism made by this safely protected "I" who proclaims these objectivity criteria. I can almost hear some of my the readers protest and say that it is an obvious underlying condition that these six criteria of objectivity are bilateral: they are meant to be applied by "you" versus "me" just as much as by "me" versus "you." This is a too friendly interpretation of Arne Næss, as it is demonstrably wrong. The "issue" (criterion A) and its "framework" (criterion F) are assumed given by some invisible authoritative "I," already before this great director "I" starts posing his objectivity judgements against "you." Any non-directed objectivity where both parties start from zero in absolute equality is impossible because all of the debate fades away. There is no issue to discuss, no frame to place the issue in relation to, and there are no facts that one may have any reason to extract at the expense of other facts.

I will now check these principles of objectivity presented by Næss against the six criteria that I posed for a modern rhetorical analysis.

(i) The objectivity doctrines of Næss are not in touch with reality according to modern media. These doctrines make you close your eyes in confrontation with the way public opinion is generated today. Næss shows nostalgia more than realism when he constructs an abstract setting where issues can be decided by multiplying together weight and relevance of arguments pro and contra. Without reference to metaphysical and ethical values, there is no other option than brute force on which to base the judgement of the weight of arguments.

(ii) The objectivity criteria are the only point in Næss' doctrines which is of any use for analysing the way modern media direct public debates. But his objectivity criteria are not good enough, because the requirement of objectivity is only posed within the borders of the directive power. In practice this means that the objectivity criteria of Næss either are a vain hope that everybody be kind to one another (criteria B, D, E), or even worse: Serve as oppression tools from the strong party who directs the debate (criteria A, C, F). When a Christian leader is confronted with the militant question "Are you an opponent of homosexuals' rights?" he cannot get any help from Næss' objectivity criteria. These criteria cannot reveal the falseness of the underlying dogma that the admission of an ungodly sexual life is an ethical absolute. A defence must have a much stronger basis than the criteria of Næss. First of all, one should point to the personal judgements that the definition-power poses on its opponents. In this case, one is defined as an "opponent" unless one answers the way that the power requires. One should instead characterize oneself positively as somebody working in favour of God's good will for the life of human beings. This is the right starting point for further debate, instead of starting from being against something. However, this may soon lead to a statement from the homosexual side of the debate that we have extreme views. The best reply to such an accusation is that this is a personal judgement of me. An extremely solid documentation is in fact needed to explain away the personal attack that is built into an accusation of having extreme opinions.

(iii) The doctrines of Næss do not include the dimension of power. It is tacitly assumed that all statements are placed on the same level of power, as far as they meet his criteria of objectivity. But the sad fact is that these criteria of objectivity often reinforce the directive power behind the whole discussion. This is particularly the case for the criteria A, C and F. It should be admitted that these criteria still are of some use, even though they are limited and with a short range. They never reach the arena of debate direction or the landscape of dogmas, where the essential part of the battle takes place. The objectivity criterion E immediately looks like a healthy principle. Nevertheless it can be turned against the weakest side in a discussion, as an exclusion from stating premises.

(iv) The original argumentation-philosophy of Næss aims at being completely void of all emotionality. But this is no advantage. It is rather a lack of ability to classify or judge the emotionality that exists within any debate. Arne Næss is now trying to improve his doctrines in his recent book "Life Philosophy" (so far only available in Norwegian). I cannot see that he is successful. There is no specified self-criticism in his new book. The static positivistic foundation in his old philosophy is kept alive. In this system all emotionality is strange and alien. Næss has still not developed any tool for classifying or judging emotionality in a context of rhetoric.

(v) Any consistent philosophical positivist like the young Næss will in theory deny all metaphysical and ethical absolutes. But full consistency as a positivist is never attainable. There will always be loopholes, where the positivist relates to the real world of true and false, good and evil. As an example, the positivists of today usually confess an explicit ethical absolute of a so-called "right" to homosexual lifestyle. There are also many implicit metaphysical absolutes in positivism, to be considered below. In his recent book "Life Philosophy," Arne Næss takes the step of calling his criteria of objectivity "ethical norms," which is an explicitly metaphysical concept. This turns his objectivity criteria into dogmas, which is in conflict with all positivism. To argue in favour of these dogmas, Næss claims that they protect your opponent from being oppressed (page 63 in his recent Norwegian book). This is an obvious exaggeration. These six objectivity criteria are posed by an "I" person as requirements from a "you" person. Who is the one that is protected? It is the "I" person who is subject to protection. The person in charge of governing the whole discussion is also the one who protects himself against oppression. This metaphysical trick in positivistic disguise is more egoism than charity. This actually shows that the weakest party in a discussion is also the one who is met with the most massive requirements of objectivity.

(vi) The ideal for the argumentation-philosophy of Næss is that it be completely void of history. Arguments are hoped to be weighted pro and contra in an atmosphere of neutrality and objectivity, void of tensions, controversy, and metaphysics. This idealized anti-historical approach is the same as the one we meet in a fully axiomatic mathematics, where all historical and empirical background-material is swept under the rug. However, there exists no completely axiomatic applicable mathematics, even though the majority of natural scientists seem to believe in it. All fruitful axiomatic systems are incomplete, in the sense that no axioms can ever prove or disprove all meaningful statements within the system (Gödel's incompleteness theorem from 1931). Mathematical proofs undoubtedly rest on metaphysical conditions, whether one likes it or not. Mathematics can no longer be considered a paradise for atheists, inaccessible for metaphysical judgements.

The original argumentation-philosophy of Arne Næss was based on a purification program of making statements objective. In this original version the word "objective" was meant to be neutral and self-evident. In his recent book on "Life philosophy" (in Norwegian), Næss removes the whole word "objective" and tries to replace it by the less ambitious words "factual" and "unbiased." In my opinion this is more a kind of escape than a solution. The concept of objectivity according to Næss' six criteria tends to hide abuse of power more than it opens up for healthy emotionality. As I see it, Næss tries to supplement his program for objectivity-purification by a vague program for emotional purification. But he achieves nothing but exposing the lack of objectivity in his own argumentation-philosophy. Since he could no longer use even the word objective, his program for making statements pure and objective failed completely. Næss' palace of objectivity was a castle without a foundation.

On the metaphysical dogmas of positivism

Our intellectual climate has been dominated for a long time by this positivistic kind of reasoning that is represented in the argumentation-philosophy of Arne Næss. This is a self-confident thinking which feels that it is neutral and objective. Thereby one tends to neglect the classical rhetoric as something subjective and emotional. One meets the metaphysics of the opponents with disgust, but cuddles one's own metaphysical dogmas. It requires some amount of work to dig out the metaphysical dogmas of positivism to be able to display them in daylight. Some of these positivistic dogmas for opinion-making can be formulated as follows:

(a) There is an ideal process of opinion-making based on objective judgement of weight and relevance for each argument.
(b) This process of ideal opinion-making is ahistorical in the sense that it happens here and now, without bias and presuppositions from the past.
(c) There exist no metaphysical or ethical absolutes with relevance for ideal opinion-making.

(d)   Ideal opinion-making assumes the total absence of emotional factors.

(e)   Positions of power must not disturb the ideal opinion making. By applying objectivity criteria in the correct way, it is possible to remove all imbalance in power behind different statements.

None of these propositions are provable. They have not even been made plausible by any documentation. So they are clearly dogmatic. One argues on a metaphysical level if one assumes their validity. This metaphysical castle is converted into a stronghold with the ambition to annihilate all other metaphysics. This colourless and often invisible positivistic metaphysics is in fact intolerant in dealing with conflicting metaphysics. It is often undemocratic and oppressive in the way it treats conflicting opinions. Still it applies many words of self-praise like "open-minded," "tolerant," "unbiased," or "well-balanced" when it describes its own role in public debate, combined with chasing the ones who are not politically correct.

Arne Næss has given up the strict dogmas (c) and (d) in his recent book "Life Philosophy." But he introduces a concept of "value" which boils down to containing nothing but subjective emotionality. This stripping of the value concept seems to be motivated by a desire to avoid the danger of assuming metaphysical absolutes which can be associated with divine revelation.

Description of the rhetorical pyramid

I will now describe a tool for rhetorical analysis that is able to include power, historical background, metaphysical values, and emotions. The classification tool is called the rhetorical pyramid. The rhetorical pyramid consists of five different levels. Each level is characterized by increased power and increased emotional pressure. Although preciseness is not perfect, I claim that any statement in a situation of opinion-generation can in principle be classified as belonging to one of these five rhetorical levels:

Level 5: Imperative commands
Level 4: Unspecified argument
Level 3: Undocumented argument
Level 2: Documented argument
Level 1: Neutral presentation of facts

This pyramid with five levels is the basic classification. But there are gliding transitions between all five levels of the pyramid. The word "pyramid" serves to illustrate that each higher level is superior to all lower levels as a hierarchy. There is similarity between the rhetorical pyramid and pyramid structures in society like the army, the Catholic Church or the freemasonry.

When one climbs from a lower to a higher level in the rhetorical pyramid, one tends to increase power and status, often at the expense of truth. However, all explicit lies are located at level 3, which is thereby a dangerous position. Power is more comfortable when it cannot be arrested in lying. Therefore a power established on level 3 will always seek the higher levels 4 and 5. At level 4 we encounter the definition power. A characteristic level-4 statement cannot be classified as a lie because it is not precise intellectually. At the same time, it contains a very precise emotional arrow. Levels 4 and 5 are indeed beyond true and false. One could also say "beyond good and evil," which is the title of a book by the philosopher of nihilism Friedrich Nietzsche. Levels 4 and 5 fit very well into a postmodern nihilistic time as ours. The strongest manipulation takes place on levels 4 and 5 or at an intermediate level.

Many efficient imperative statements are in between levels 4 and 5 because they are to some extent unspecified. We are commanded emotionally more than to act in a precise way. The trick is to let our emotions follow the power, while we feel subjectively that we choose it by our free will, since the commands sound like encouragements with a lot of freedom. However, as our emotions are slowly being tuned in, it will follow automatically in the long run that our actions will also be as the power wants from us.

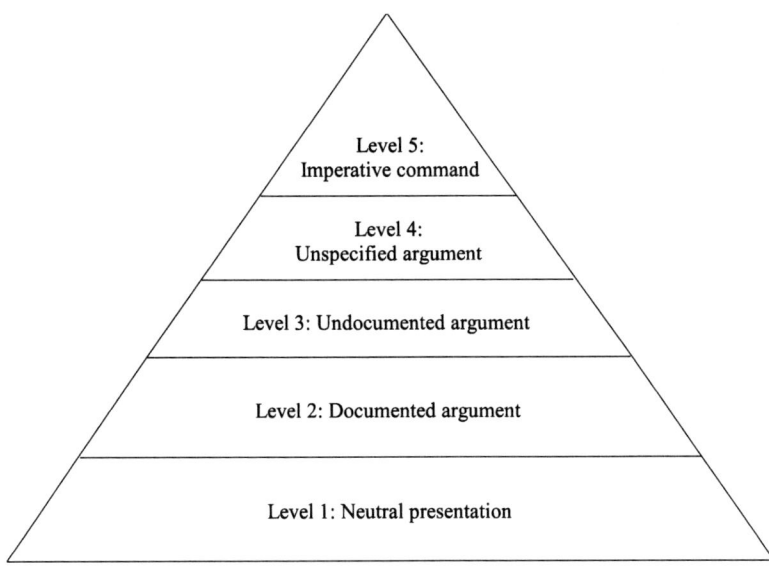

Figure 1: The five levels of the Rhetorical Pyramid

The Norwegian psychiatrist Ingjald Nissen has written a very interesting book called "The Dictatorship of the Psychopaths" (issued in Norwegian by Aschehoug, Oslo 1977). Here he has demonstrated how psychopaths suggestion their victims by fear and sense of guilt. Psychopaths are usually experts at finding suggesting, unspecified arguments on level 4 as lasting attacks on the emotional life of their victims. It is virtually impossible to fight a battle with a psychopath on rhetorical level 4. It tends to end up in a quarrel where we lose our self-control and the psychopath gets an opportunity to restore order by commanding us on level 5. So the goal of a psychopath is to get the victim in a position where he/she can do nothing but follow his arbitrary imperative commands. So it is a bad idea to lose your self-control in a fight with a psychopath. It is much wiser to realize the kind of power you have in confrontation with a psychopath: The power lies in the fact that you can determine to a certain extent the rhetorical level at which you receive the message from a psychopath. So the wisest way to deal with a psychopath under four eyes is most likely to receive his message in a calm and firm way on a lower rhetorical level than it was meant to be. Let us be practical and assume that a psychopath says to me just now: "You will never be able to complete this article. You have not read enough about this subject, and leading experts will no doubt laugh if they read your text." Confronted with such an accusation, I hope that I would be able to answer in a calm way: "I am glad that you remind me that I still want to read a couple of books before I complete this article. I would also be grateful if you could give me reference to a few books that you find important for my work." This way of responding to the psychopath is considerate in several respects. I have confirmed and comforted the lonely psychopath by giving him a real answer with human warmth. I trust in him because I want to hear his list of important books. Most importantly, I do not let him manipulate me. The initiative is mine: I need to read some books that I already am aware of. The psychopath gave me a message almost on level 5, but I take an unexpected grip of peaceful self-defence by misinterpreting him as giving good advice on level 2. Such cool and balanced answers can make a psychopath give up his suggesting, if he does not feel that he is able to reduce my self-control. It is important to appear as a warm human being at the same time. The key to success in dealing with a psychopath is not to follow your instinctive reactions, but the opposite: To suppress your natural inner rage and appear as more and more calm the more he tries to heat you up with accusations and fear. A psychopath is a kind of behaviourist: What he sees is all he gets. So if he does not see any fear or sense of guilt in your reactions, he must give up his manipulations. A noisy quarrel with a psychopath will only happen if he succeeds in stirring up your mind. He cannot take the risk of making noise all by himself. He must do what it takes to avoid being caught as the very one to blame.

Psychopaths rarely use level 3 if there is a danger to be caught in lying. On level 3 there may occasionally be true statements, but lies and half-truths flourish. It is bad to recognize that lies on level 3 have higher emotional status and stronger power than truth on level 2. But it is just this way in this worldly system, as long as the lie is consistent and cannot be disclosed. The Bible says something about this: The world is under the control of evil (1 John 5:19). Therefore I believe that the Christian attitude is to restrict the use of levels 3, 4 and 5 as much as possible. It is not good to use these levels for their own sake. Primarily they must be used to challenge the emotional hegemony of an enemy. But as soon as our opponent is willing to argue on levels 1 and 2, we should also base our arguments on these two levels. The fact that there are four independent versions of the written gospel (although many theologians agree for some strange reason that the three first gospels have the same written source), show that God has been willing to apply level 2 in presenting his most important message to us. In a courtroom, the best way to document historical events is by independent witnesses.

Below I will come back to the army as a very illustrative example of rhetorical levels.

An officer gives a command at level 5. A soldier may do a visible act of obedience at level 1. Or he may have to report back after he has finished his task. He must give his report by means of level-2 arguments. The judgement that he receives for his report will be on level 3 or higher. So there is hardly any doubt that undocumented claims (level 3) have higher rank than documented arguments (level 2) in the pyramid structures of this world. In God's kingdom it is not like that. Jesus says that the one who wants to be highest among us must be the servant of all (Matt 20:26).

One may ask: Is there any substantial difference between levels 1 and 2 after all? Both levels contain obvious facts, truths or things that are easy to document. The conceptual difference between levels 1 and 2 is that only level 2 contains an arrow of emotional direction. One wants to promote a certain act, choice or conclusion, and one chooses an argument that is true, but one still gives an emotional urge in the preferred direction. This is in contrast to level 1, where no emotional pressure is noticeable. A visual act free of power against other people also belongs to level 1.

When we have reached level 5, we have travelled full circle. There is no longer any argumentation, as was also the case on level 1. But on level 1 there was no power, whereas at level 5 there is all power. By power one delivers commands which it is assumed that the receiver follows. A slave operates on level 1 when he obediently follows the level-5 commands from his master. So the giver of the command operates on level 5, while the follower of the same command ideally (seen from above) operates on level 1. Emotionally there is also a great difference: On level 5 great emotional pressure is put on the ones to receive the command. An action on level 1 does not put any emotional pressure on anybody else. It may in fact give emotional relief and support back to the power levels above. Moreover, a fact presented on level 1 does not put any pressure on anybody to reach any specific conclusion. There is a tiny loophole for power on level 1: The very picking of the relevant facts on level 1 can after all be a remnant of invisible directive power. So Næss' objectivity criterion E is relevant here.

In a situation of public debate, each of the sides will carry a load of historical, cultural, and political nature that tends to decide which level of rhetoric is available in the discussion. The stronger side in a debate has the great privilege of denying the weaker side the right to present arguments on higher rhetorical levels than he does himself. The stronger party can thus deliver arguments with higher emotional pressure than the weaker party. This can appropriately be characterized as "emotional hegemony." It is not always wise to keep the arguments on level 2, even though it is safe from an ethical point of view. One should at least try to move the opponent down to level 2. If this attempt fails, it will often be necessary to present arguments on level 3 and 4 to challenge the emotional hegemony of the opponent. An analysis of various public debate situations according to the rhetorical pyramid could be interesting. It would probably show that the leader of the debate often forces the weak side to operate only on levels 1 and 2, while he does not present the same strong requirements against the stronger side. Christian people in Norway have lost many public debates by avoiding challenging the emotional hegemony of the secular humanists. This means to be trapped in levels 1 and 2 while the opponent has a monopoly on levels 3, 4 and 5.

Above I rejected the objectivity criteria A, C and F of Arne Næss. I will now present more detailed arguments for this rejection. Criterion A means to abolish all irrelevant chat and stand firmly with the topic of the discussion. What topic? The definition-power launches the whole topic and its context from level 5. So criterion A is a command that we must stay on levels 1 and 2 in the rhetorical pyramid, a command that we should not always obey. Objectivity-criterion C by Næss means that we shall not give any ambiguous statements. We are not allowed to give unspecified arguments on level 4. Here the power is asking for its own good: "Please stay out of level 4. We want to have that all to ourselves." Let us not obey. Objectivity criterion F by

Næss requires that we do not contribute to the context of the discussion. We are only allowed to submit to the context that the power presents to us. Once more we are met with a level-5 argument that accepts our reply only on levels 1 or 2.

Below I will discuss several topics and construct typical statements that fit in with the five levels of the rhetorical pyramid.

Commercials in the light of the Rhetorical Pyramid

Let us first consider a field where young people's minds are the most vulnerable. Commercial advertisements. Our basic example is Nike, the giant of sports equipment. It started around 1970 in Oregon. At first it was a small firm based on a special product: A jogging shoe with wafer soles. I bought one yellow pair of Nike shoes myself in 1975, from a private backyard importer. These exceptional shoes were not for sale in ordinary shops in Norway. Through two decades this minor company within sports equipment has grown into one of the leading brands in international marketing. You cannot mention many brand names before Nike shows up in your mind. This is also remarkable because Nike has concentrated more on mass products than exclusivity. The logo of Nike is one of the strongest visual logos known to mankind in the year 2000. It is among the select few that can stand on its own without any text. Only the Christian cross, the Moslems' half moon, the five Olympic rings, the Mercedes star in a circle and a few more can compete with Nike's swoosh stripe.

It is interesting to note that giants like McDonald's, Coca-Cola and Ford cannot compete in the same category as the Nike swoosh stripe. Why? Because their logos are all based on a written text, or at least one letter as the big M of McDonald's.

The Nike pyramid:

Level 5:   "Just do it"
Level 4:   "Nike shoes are cool"
Level 3:   "Nike turns you into a more powerful athlete"
Level 2:   "Nike Air protects your feet on paved roads"
Level 1:   Sales statistics for Nike equipment in Norway

The level-5 statement of Nike can be paraphrased naively like this: "Just go ahead and do whatever you want." It sounds like complete freedom. But it is not, because it is a command, an imperative statement. You are commanded to do something, and it seems like you have the freedom to choose what to do. But the point is not to do whatever you want. The point is that you can feel that you do whatever you want. In reality you are urged to become mentally hooked on the dominance of the giant of sports equipment. The message "Just do whatever you want" flatters your ego, although it is a command. But, wait a minute. This is not what is being said. There is no such person "you" in the original statement. "Just do it" is impersonal. This is a smart commercial trick. You do not get any self-respect for free. There is no free lunch where "you" can receive unconditional comfort and respect. You have to buy all your self-respect and self-image. If you buy these fancy jogging shoes, you are transformed from an impersonal amoeba-like creature into a strong and self-confident "I." At least for a while, until your shoes get worn and dirty.

The Nike company used to write "Just do it!" followed by an exclamation mark. Now it is more common to see the slogan ended with a punctuation mark: "Just do it." So the imperative form has been tuned down. This can be afforded with a strengthened grip on the customers. In some American cities there have been serious crimes among teenagers because somebody wanted to take over other people's exclusive footwear. This would never have happened if the commercials had only worked on rhetorical levels 1 and 2. To avoid courtroom trouble, this story of criminal acts is best kept on an unspecified level (level 4).

One more remarkable feature of this emotional marketing is the role of the swoosh stripe. The word "swoosh" in itself is virtually meaningless. However, it has now been established as the name of the well-known Nike logo, which resembles a sickle blade. This logo has followed the company since the early seventies. The swoosh logo was designed in 1971 by the student Caroline Davidson in Portland, Oregon. It symbolizes the wing of Nike, the Greek goddess of victory. Nowadays we see caps, T-shirts, bags, footballs and other products from this company where the Nike name is no longer visible, but where there is nothing but a swoosh stripe. This amounts to introducing an extra level 6 on top of the Nike pyramid: The level of adoration. The power could be said to communicate on level 6 when it assumes adoration by means of the non-verbal power of visual symbols. There is an idol on the top of the Nike pyramid: The swoosh idol of the victory goddess. I do not know if there is any coincidence that the swoosh stripe of Nike resembles both the halfmoon of the Moslems and the symbol of Soviet communism (hammer and sickle). Anyway, the Nike logo has undoubtedly achieved an emotionally heavy status in international marketing. It seems that the Nike logo transcends all differences among people; differences in race, religion, and language. There is no barrier of language when you see only the swoosh. All you need is money to buy the swoosh product.

The levels 1 and 2 in the Nike pyramid contain truth, but nobody would feel that this would be an urge to buy Nike shoes. The competing brands of shoes also protect your feet on paved roads. Levels 1 and 2 are therefore abolished in the modern marketing of Nike. One also seeks to avoid level 3. It is not a good thing to lie. But still the message that you can become a better athlete by using Nike shoes may seep through, indirectly. Pictures of Michael Jordan and other sports heroes may give a feeling that your first step to becoming a better athlete is to buy Nike. What can you lose by trying? However, the explicit marketing statements of Nike are situated on levels 4 and 5 in the pyramid. It is impossible to argue against level-4 statements of the type "Nike shoes are cool." But level-5 statements are even stronger, as long as people follow them.

It is a strange fact indeed that messages on level 5 seem to appeal to modern man, and especially youngsters. Young people prefer to think that nobody ought to tell them what to do. They want to feel free, at least in their leisure time. The typical attitude is the one expressed by Bob Dylan: "Don't follow leaders" (a paradox of a level-5 statement). But take a look at the current slogans in the commercials for the leading brands of soft drinks:

>Pepsi-Cola: "Ask for more!"
>Coca-Cola: "Live your life!"
>Sprite: "Obey your thirst!"

These are not three competing brands but two, since Coca-Cola owns Sprite. There are many reflections to be done about this uniform type of rhetoric. First of all: These are outright commands, level 5. You are told what to do, just like a lowest-rank soldier in the military. No freedom of choice according to the message. Is this really a good message for enjoying your leisure time? (Seemingly so, since young people buy these drinks.) Is freedom of choice a quality that belongs to the past? Why is the slogan "The choice of a new generation" sounding so utterly old-fashioned today?

These brands of soft drinks seem to follow in Nike's footsteps. But it is difficult, and they have not succeeded fully. Coca-Cola's strength lies in its accessibility, its tradition and established design. The classical logo of Coca-Cola is the one common but powerful visual signal in its business. It is comparable to the logos of Ford in the automobile business and Harley Davidson among motorcycles. But when it boils down to the words composing an efficient slogan, Coca-Cola is not as clever as Nike. Most young people know for sure that the short and easy sentence "Just do it" is a Nike slogan. These three words also scare lawyers in marketing departments all over the globe from coming up with something too similar. I was thinking of promoting my rhetoric book by the slogan: "Just forget it." I would be telling the lawyers of the Nike company to forget the temptation of suing me. But what if they did so after all? Perhaps they would win in the courtroom with their accusation: I stole their slogan! It would mean bankruptcy for me.

Time, Reality, and Transcendence in Rational Perspective

But even if I happened to lose a courtroom battle with Nike, the philosophical question would remain: Is it possible for a company to "own" a sentence that any person can happen to say once in a while? Even worse: to claim ownership not just to one sentence, but also to many similar sentences? Were nobody saying or writing "Just do it" before Nike grasped the sentence for their own promotion? Of course people did, but nobody thought of spending dollars on it in order to claim ownership. Coca-Cola still has a long and extremely costly way to go before they own their relatively new slogan "Live your life" in most people's (and lawyers') minds. This sentence is nevertheless smart in offering the fake freedom of "do what you want as long as you buy our product." Just as Nike's slogan does, in spite of being commands on level 5. But it seems less smart to let the buyer of Coca-Cola be called a personal "you" already before buying the drink. He does not have to buy it to experience himself as a true person. He is called a "you" before he buys. However, the difference is that a new soft drink is bought very frequently compared with a new pair of jogging shoes. So it is not so important to insult the buyers with the claim that they are non-personal beings if they do not buy our product. It may be a better and more durable strategy to confirm their self-esteem on the basis of last time they bought the drink. "You are acknowledged as a personal being because you have already bought our drink before. As long as there is some taste left of your previous Coke, you live your life." Compared with Nike, Coca-Cola relies more on people's habits, so it is not a primary strategy to attract new customers all the time. It is smarter to be good at keeping the ones that are already used to the product.

It is interesting to compare Norwegian soft drink campaigns with the American ones. Our leading brand of orange soda pop has formulated its newest slogan as follows: "Solo. Probably the only soft drink that cures nothing but thirst." This is a plain level-3 statement. Its truth may be somewhat doubtful. Still I would say that it respects the customer's integrity and freedom of choice much more than the Coca-Cola type of command slogans on level 5. The Coca-Cola product Fanta has not had a chance until now of kicking Solo out of its Norwegian home market. But could anybody imagine a campaign in downtown Los Angeles with the slogan "Solo. Most likely the only soft drink that cures nothing but thirst"?

A well-known example of drinking rhetoric with its origin in Denmark is: "Probably the best beer in the world." It used to be: "Carlsberg. Probably the best beer in the world." But now you have to search through the picture to find the logo of the Carlsberg truck. The name Carlsberg is not in the commercial text anymore. This is the secret of rhetoric repetition: When most people know already that Carlsberg has the "probably best beer," one just has to press a button, and he is immediately able to find out for himself. This is conditioned learning, like Pavlov and his dogs. But the full original message itself is an undocumented argument: "Carlsberg. Probably the best beer in the world" belongs to level 3, not very high. It is a dangerous sentence, because it may be false. Without the Carlsberg name, however, it climbs higher up in the pyramid. The message "Probably the best beer in the world" is on level 4, unspecified without the name of the beer. When the customer himself makes his Pavlovian link to Carlsberg in his mind, he moves the message even higher up in the pyramid, almost to level 5. So it is indeed smart of Carlsberg to claim very implicitly the definition power of being the best beer in the world. This is true postmodernism - beyond false and true. No competitor can sue Carlsberg anymore.

Various examples of pyramids of rhetoric

Our examples so far have been important for just convincing the reader that there is some value in constructing the rhetorical pyramid. The most important element is the power of definition on level 4 and the emotional pressure that can follow unspecified arguments. Such arguments are impossible to argue against verbally, even though we can feel in our body how they urge us emotionally to do, to think, or to feel in a programmed way. I claim that arguments on level 4 are highly emotional not just with the receiver, but also with the sender. The emotions with the sender of the unspecified message can be hidden very well. They can be a concealed or even sealed emotionality, where the powerful person manipulates things silently the way he wants, leaving no visible trace of emotions on the surface. However, if we succeed in tempting or forcing such a person down from level 4 to level 3 where he has to deliver messages with an intellectual content, we will often be met with seemingly unmotivated aggression. The explanation is that the emotionality that used to be sealed and hidden, all of a sudden materializes itself in a rather scaring way.

Below I will give various examples of rhetorical pyramids. I do not discuss all of them in detail. So I suggest that the reader follows up some of these examples with his/her own thinking. The principles that I present here do not have much value as knowledge in a passive meaning of the word. Their value comes into being only by active applications. I will show characteristic statements from various controversial issues, and classify them according to the rhetorical pyramid. If there are lawyers among my readers, I have to say that I disagree deeply with most statements on level 3. Very often these statements are just plain lies.

Conscious ambiguities on level 4 arise in politics when one seeks to satisfy both religious voters and the media power at the same time. It is also very common in theology, when a professor seeks goodwill from his own conservative audience of laymen and his militant antinomist colleagues at the same time. ("Antinomism" means to rule out the Holy Law of God.)

A rhetorical pyramid in politics:

Level 5:   "Vote for me!"
Level 4:   "If I am elected, I will give you more freedom"
Level 3:   "Your personal economy will improve if I am elected"
Level 2:   "Our party voted against the latest tax increase"
Level 1:   Results from the previous election

A media-rhetorical pyramid:

Level 5:   "It is obvious that the press must be its own ethical control authority"
Level 4:   "The leading newspapers fight for your freedom of speech"
Level 3:   "Nobody has ever been chased to death by journalists"
Level 2:   "Thanks to media, people around the world could follow Princess Diana's funeral"
Level 1:   "The World Cup final in football was watched by about two billion people on TV"

Rhetorical pyramid on divorce:

Level 5:   "I decide to break free from a stagnant marriage"
Level 4:   "We simply grew apart"
Level 3:   "Our divorce will benefit our children"
Level 2:   "The divorces in Oslo put an extra pressure on the real estate market"
Level 1:   "Roughly half the marriages in Oslo end in divorce"

Rhetorical pyramid on homosexuality:

Level 5:   "The church must plead with all homosexuals/Gypsies/Lapps for forgiveness"
Level 4:   "Homosexual partners experience true love"
Level 3:   "Practising homosexuals have exactly the same life expectancy as anybody else"
Level 2:   "A homosexual life style implies hazardous exchange of body liquids, bacteria and viruses."
Level 1:   "The Norwegian Law of Homosexual Partnerships was ratified 30 April 1993 and has been legally valid from 1 August 1993."

Rhetorical pyramid on abortion:

Level 5:   "I terminate my unwanted pregnancy"
Level 4:   "To criticize an abortion is to attack a person's freedom"
Level 3:   "The foetus is just another part of its mother's body (if so, an abortion is perhaps an amputation of her body and lobotomy of her soul?)"
Level 2:   "The population increase in Norway has been dramatically reduced because of abortions"
Level 1:   "About 15000 legalized abortions are done in Norway each year"

A common accusation against the Christian people in Norway now is that they have given up the battle against abortion. How can this be true? Mostly because the media never brings any news about people working against abortion. In May 1986 there was a big protest with 15000 people in central Oslo walking in a long line with banners against abortion. Feminists raged against it. But the journalists did not care. The whole event was defined in the media as a non-event. If 500 people protest against nuclear weapons, they may easily get the front page on leading newspapers, but 15000? "No," the media seemed to think. "We cannot write about that. This is just too much, and it is symbolically too strong, with one living person for each unborn child who died." So there was a "gentlemen's agreement" in the media to kill the whole abortion protest by silence.

What happened to the Christian protest against abortion, confronted with this massive media silence? The whole abortion protest faded out. Most of us thought in retrospect that our action did not communicate. We did not realize that the opposite was true: We communicated too well! The secular media were scared. We should have taken their silence as an encouragement: "They don't dare to write about us" (instead of being manipulated into thinking: "They don't really care about us"). I am certain: In May 2000 the journalists would have given up and finally written about us, if we had demonstrated 15 years in a row against abortion with 15000 people each year. But we did not. We gave up immediately. We are the ones to blame, since we were fooled by people who actually were much more scared of us than we were of them. No newspaper could have silenced to death such an event 15 years in a row, because common people in the streets of Oslo might have got their eyes opened: What is this? A big yearly event that we hear and read nothing about? Isn't the Norwegian press a free press after all? Is it filtering and distorting important news before they reach us?

I have recently heard several people blame the Christians for having given up and quit working against abortions, instead working only against homosexuality. But in reality this is a projection of the priorities chosen in the secular media. It is true to a certain extent, but basically as a self-fulfilling prophecy. At present, the media focuses enormously on homosexuals and the church, basically as a campaign to open up all positions for the homosexuals in the church. If they succeed (which I hope they do not), this theme will probably also fall into silence. Then people may start to blame the church for not speaking up against homosexuality anymore. In any case the fact is: People's judgement of the church and its priorities repeats the arbitrary constraints put on the church in the public by secular journalists. But people blame the church, not the journalists. Why are we not so concerned with abortions now? Because the secular press does not allow us to give the impression of being concerned with abortions. The sad thing is that this also manipulates us to worry less about abortions. Even if we care about aborted foetuses in theory, we do not do it so much in practice, if you compare with a situation in the past where we got media coverage for our protest against abortions.

Various comments on rhetoric

Most of the above examples are concerned with the presentation of a subject in the media. Some general advice may be of value. First of all, it is not wise to trust media when they give arguments on levels 4 and 5. Is there any point in trusting in a message which is meant as an emotional message without precise content? It is of course also dangerous to trust media when they give arguments on level 3, where lies and half-truths flourish. But a reader does not have the capacity of digging into all sources of information. So it is impracticable to require that all messages must be on levels 1 or 2. However, why would somebody try to hide your access to documentation if what they tell you is actually true. Be especially alert when arguments that should belong to level 2 are presented on level 3 with an implicit wish that documentation is inaccessible for the receiver.

When a student writes a thesis, it must as far as possible contain arguments on level 1 and 2. Quick arguments on higher rhetorical levels will weaken the impression of the thesis. What is the content of the judgement of the thesis? Will the student receive arguments on levels 1 and 2? Usually not. The mark itself considered as an argument belongs to level 3, seen from the student's point of view. To fail at an exam will be received as a message on level 5.

As soldier in the army one will receive a lot of commands on the top rhetorical level (5). These must be followed either as visual actions (level 1), or one has to report back to the officers after having implemented the command (level 2). If a soldier responds to a command on level 4 or 5, it can be received harshly. But if one chooses to command back on level 5, one can be certain to be taken out of service and punished severely. But the officers themselves can apply all levels 3, 4 and 5 to discipline the soldiers. Level 2 is also used by the officers within formalized teaching situations in a classroom. But level 2 is never used in the battle field in the sense that the officers report to the soldiers. The authority of the officers could not survive if they applied levels 1 and 2 outside a safely formalized teaching situation.

At the moment, Norway seems to be the most narrow-minded country in the world with respect to homosexual propaganda. We are overwhelmed with surveys and statistics on all possible subjects. Still there is no useful statistics available concerning average health condition, frequency of diseases, and average life span of Norwegian homosexuals. The basic propaganda goes like this: "The homosexuals must be allowed to live as they want to (level 5), because they do not do any harm to anybody (level 3)." But is it really true that homosexual activities never does any harm to people not taking part in them? Very doubtful indeed. Many heterosexuals suffering from AIDS must have received this "virus relay" through one or more homosexual links.

Peder A. Tyvand

Evolution in the light of the Rhetorical Pyramid

Our last example of a rhetorical pyramid is concerned with the theory of evolution. There is hardly any example that is made more transparent by the rhetorical pyramid than the theory of evolution. Evolution has become a focus of all human vanity, while it is encapsulated in the greatest possible intellectual prestige. This is a bizarre combination. The rhetorical pyramid is useful in exposing the psychological mechanisms that are busy defending the fortress of evolution. If your aim is to avoid performing rhetoric, you should rather leave the whole scene of evolution debate, because rhetoric is what it is all about. If you do not get to grips with the rhetoric of evolution, you have hardly any chance of success in criticizing the theory of evolution. So we have to take seriously the accusation from the evolutionists that we are making rhetoric noise. We have no choice other than compete rhetorically with the evolutionists. If we are too modest to do so, we achieve nothing but leaving the whole emotional arena and the definition power for the evolutionists. What is the point of winning the battle of the crumbs if we refuse fighting for the bread?

Here are some characteristic statements on the five rhetorical levels:

Level 5: "It is illegal for a university biologist to show any doubt on evolution in public"
Level 4: "Evolution is a fact"
Level 3: "All human skills originate from evolution by natural selection"
Level 2: "Natural selection can be observed in the species *biston bitularia*"
Level 1: An exhibition of fossils at a museum

Let us first see how it is possible to meet these arguments. Levels 1 and 2 are rather unproblematic. Natural selection means that the individuals with best fitness in a given environment will survive and breed most efficiently. This is true to a considerable extent in nature, but does not cause any evolution from one species to another one. On level 3, natural selection is applied as a confession of belief, a kind of religious mantra. It is a belief in a fate called natural selection. No matter what a living creature is doing, natural selection is the deepest cause behind its actions. Nobody can escape the almighty fate of natural selection.

One of the paradoxes with this belief in a deepest cause is that it is indeed very shallow: Natural selection is a very primitive principle: It just selects away and dumps from the genetic pools the varieties of a population that are not sufficiently fit. There is nothing subtle in this. There is no reason to believe that the most subtle mechanisms in the natural world owe their existence to such a primitive principle. No river can flow to a higher point than its source.

Still I would say that it is an attempt at a scientific statement (on level 3) to say that natural selection can explain all human skills. It can easily be attacked on the same level (level 3): So far natural selection has not evolved a single new property. It is impossible to develop anything new by just selecting out things, which is all that natural selection can do. This concise statement has proven to have a very provocative effect among evolutionists.

To argue against the statement on level 4 one can first ask for a precise definition of "evolution" and "fact." Any definition must be at lower levels. If no definition is given, and the rhetoric continues on the same level, this shows that there is no reality behind the claim of evolution as a fact, just emotions. We may also go to counter-attack and talk about our belief in a supernatural act of creation. In this context this is a level-3 statement. But in general one will often have to apply rhetorical levels close to the ones we are arguing against.

On level 5 the command is given that it is prohibited to be an anti-evolutionst university biologist in Norway. Since this command has been operative for many years, this is indeed true. There are no openly anti-Darwinist biology professors in Norwegian universities, and it is a flaw in our democracy. We can argue against this command on level 2 by saying that freedom of opinion is a basic human right according to the Declaration of Human Rights from 1948.

Evolution is not just a theory, but a paradigm (a concept introduced by Thomas Kuhn 1962). The concept of paradigm encompasses the totality of generally accepted ideas, models, presuppositions, frameworks, interpretations, methods, and established insights in a scientific field. There are also paradigms in art and human lifestyle. A relevant example in Norway is the paradigm of homosexuality that has been established here during the last ten years. The distorted view on reality imposed by this paradigm has made a public taboo out of all health problems connected with homosexual lifestyle.

The paradigm of evolution is a fortress with an emotional foundation built by rhetoric. Evolution is not founded on facts. Above we have seen that Nike would not have been a leading commercial brand today if its marketing had stayed on levels 1 and 2. The same is true with evolution: It would not have been a dominating doctrine if it had presented itself on the rhetorical levels 1 and 2. In most public debates on evolution where I have been involved, somebody has at one point in the discussion uttered the sentence: "Evolution is a fact." This is an unspecified argument on level 4. Emotionally it means something like the following: "The idea of evolution feels good for me. Moreover, it is accepted by all influential people." This is no doubt true, subjectively and emotionally. Everybody can choose whom they want to characterize as influential people. To any atheist, the idea of evolution is an emotional umbilical cord. There is simply no atheistic life without it. We should note that the idea of evolution is primarily emotional, only secondarily intellectual. So evolution cannot be as important intellectually as it is emotionally for an atheist.

The word "evolution" transmits an emotional experience of mankind as a link in a natural web of development. But scientifically there exists no documentation to support the claim of a continuous genetic relay race of natural descent from a primeval cell all the way to man. Evolution in this basic meaning is far beyond all verification. But instead of being caught in a trap of faith beyond reason, evolutionists find their way out by playing a trick of words: The whole word "evolution" changes its meaning as soon as it is going to be documented: Then it is interpreted as "small changes within a species." This is ambiguous rhetoric on level 4, two levels higher than most of decent science.

I have to protest when I meet an evolutionist saying "Evolution is a fact" (level 4) in a public debate. But this evolutionist may have a seemingly kind way of dealing with my objection. He will often answer with the obliging comment: "Please show me findings that stand against evolution." "Findings" are on rhetorical level 1. My opponent seems open and willing to consider all possible findings that I might be able to present. But he reserves all the keys of interpretation of these findings for himself. So in reality I am being caught in a trap. The debate is completely asymmetric, as I stand on level 1 while he stands on level 4. It is like a football match between two teams: His team "Unspecified" versus my team "Data." "Unspecified" leads 4:1 even before the match starts. "Unspecified" controls the rules and the referee. After the battle, the evolutionist may often be considered as the winner. But what kind of battle was it, when one side could give all kinds of arguments while the other one was only allowed to present findings? This kind of debate where arguments never are allowed to meet on the same level is not an intellectual battle at all, just an emotional one. The intellectual content in such a debate boils down to being equivalent to shouting "blah, blah, blah" back and forth at one another.

One more trick of evolution rhetoric on level 4 is the question: "Are human beings and apes related?" This question is a rhetorical trap, because we do not know what it means to be a relative. So one should refuse to answer "yes" or "no" on such a question. A "relative" may mean either (1) "someone with anatomical and physiological similarities" or (2) "a being with the same natural descent." These two meanings are utterly different. The first one may embrace a special act of creation for mankind, while the second one denies it explicitly. So this rhetorical trap of a question cannot be answered at all if one wants to stand firmly on the belief of creation. If one answers "no," it will be interpreted by evolutionists as a denial of interpretation (1), which is a blunder. On the other hand, the answer "yes" will be interpreted as accepting interpretation (2), which is also a blunder. In both cases, one has lost much integrity as a scientist believing in creation. It has been given up because of the strong definition power of evolution.

People tend to embrace the definition power of evolution as something self-evident in our culture, as it penetrates the schools and media. A fortress that is never challenged will appear as balanced, safe, well-founded, self-sufficient, perhaps even neutral. But if we challenge this evolution power, we will soon experience its militant emotionality that is latent below the surface. The massive emotional pressure of evolution is concentrated at levels 4 and 5. It is worth noting that documented empirical facts usually play no role at all in the rhetoric of evolution.

Summarizing views

This article has come into being gradually as it has grown after each of the seven or eight talks I have given on it so far. The response given by the audiences has been so good that it has highly influenced the written text. So this material has not grown out of pencil notes or literature studies in peace and quiet. It is primarily a discussion-material which has grown by its own dynamics in the various situations of presentation. A judgement and classification of this material from an academic point of view may be of course be done by anybody who feels so inclined. The only condition I would like to state from my point of view is that I want the freedom to perform a rhetorical criticism of the critics afterwards.

The danger of being put down completely on level 4 by experts in classical philosophy and history of ideas is obvious. I have already heard the judgement: "This is nothing but classical rhetoric from ancient Greece." Typical unspecified argument. Still there is something true in it. I should not attempt to reinvent the wheel when I emphasize the emotional basis in rhetoric. The classical Greek philosophy had the concept "pathos" incorporated as one of the building blocks of rhetoric.

Rhetoric can be considered as the "art of convincing other people." It is the very basis of many professions. The man who is able to sell sand in Sahara is good at rhetoric. Generally it is hard to be a successful businessman without feeling comfortable with a basic rhetorical handicraft. A religious preacher is also skilful at rhetoric, as far as we consider his natural gifts and not his spiritual gifts. Moreover, rhetoric is basic for the political handicraft and for the courtroom performance of lawyers.

What is the relevance of the male and female sex in rhetoric? I have no doubt that it plays a role, even though I may thereby risk provoking feminists. Men have been and are still brought up to be more rhetorically active and more rhetorically oriented than women. In the old days this was more obvious than today. Old-fashioned courtship was an advanced art of rhetoric. In war and love men have taken all rhetorical level in use, especially the highest ones. The woman that was the subject of the old-fashioned courtship did not need to perform any rhetoric. All she had to do in the end was to answer his proposal either by "yes" or "no." Today this is a little bit more complicated. Feminism urges the modern woman to perform rhetoric on higher levels than before, whether or not it feels natural for her as a woman. But when politically correct feminism says that female company leaders are better leaders than men, this is at best an undocumented argument on level 3. It may even be a level-4 statement, if the feminist possesses the whole definition power of the concept of "a good leader." The unsolvable dilemma is that the same feminists try to say at the same time that there is no difference between men and women. The difference between the sexes is reduced the higher up in the pyramid one gets. Pure power manifested as imperatives on level 5 will only be weakly dependent on sex. Whether Margaret Thatcher was the one to say "bomb the intruders in the Falkland Islands" or Harold Wilson had said the same thing, it would not make any significant difference.

I have mentioned courtship. When a man proposes to a woman, he asks a question. So far in this article I have avoided classifying questions rhetorically. Questions in general have a good rhetorical reputation, perhaps better than they deserve. It is common to consider a person that keeps on asking to be open-minded, liberal, listening, and free of bias. His contrast is a person who never asks, but keeps telling people what to mean and what to do all the time. The person who asks tends to have a better media image than the person who gives clear answers.

But reality is not that simple. A question can in itself give a strong rhetorical constraint. It can even be a way of being thoroughly biased. Anybody who tries to go into details behind surveys will see that. When somebody asks a question, he may restrict the permissible answers severely. He hides himself by avoiding the requirements of documentation. Moreover, his definition power puts the load of documentation on the poor shoulders of the victim of his questions. The person that is asking does not need to expose his personality and weak points. He just stimulates or forces the other person to do so. Questions may be difficult to classify rhetorically, but will always belong to relatively high levels in the rhetorical pyramid. One can start from level 3 when one poses questions, and one will often go up to level 4 and 5. My suspicion is that media has given questions such a positive rhetorical image because they need it so badly themselves: A journalist asks questions all the time.

I will end this article with a clear message to those who still possess a doubt that a question can be an explicit command on level 5. It is in fact very common in English. If I want to urge somebody to study the present article, I may put it this way: "Why don't you read my article thoroughly?"

References

Næss, Arne. *Interpretation and preciseness: a contribution to the theory of communication.* Norwegian Academy of Science, Oslo. 450 pp, 1953.

Næss, Arne. *Communication and argument: elements of applied semantics /* translated from Norwegian by Alastair Hannay. Universitetsforlaget/Allen & Unwin, 135 pp., 1966.

Is Being a Theist More Rational than Being an Atheist?

A Debate between

WILLIAM LANE CRAIG
and
LENNART NØRREKLIT

This text is based on a transcription of a debate between Dr. William Lane Craig (WLC) and Dr. Lennart Nørreklit (LN). The debate took place at the conference on "Time, Reality, and Transcendence", Aalborg University, March 20, 1999. Professor Niels Henrik Gregersen (NHG), Aarhus University, served as a mediator. Only minor editorial changes have been made in the text.

NHG: It is a privilege for me to welcome our two panelists Dr. William Craig from Atlanta and Dr. Lennart Nørreklit. I do not think any of you need any further introduction, but the rules will be the following: We will first have two presentations of 15 minutes each by each of the presenters; followed by 10 minutes of response allowing for some reply on the position of the other person. Then we will have a third round for last replies before this interesting debate will be opened for the floor. The first to present his case is William Craig, please.

WLC: Thank you. Now, in asking the question "Does God exist?," we need to actually ask ourselves two fundamental questions: 1) Are there good reasons to think that God exists? 2) Are there good reasons to think that God does not exist? Now, with respect to that second question I will leave it up to Lennart to present the reasons why he thinks that God does not exist. But note that although atheist philosophers have tried for centuries to disprove the existence of God, no one has been able to come up with a successful argument. So rather than attack straw men I will just wait to hear Lennart's answer to the following question; "What good arguments are there to think that God does not exist?"

So let's ask instead: Are there good reasons to think that God exists? Let me present four reasons why I think that theism is more plausible then atheism. Taken together these arguments furnish a powerful cumulative case for believing in God's existence.

1. The Origin of the Universe

Have you ever asked yourself where the universe came from? Why anything at all exists instead of just nothing? Well, typically atheists have said that the universe is just eternal and uncaused. But is that a plausible position? If the universe never had a beginning, that means that the number of events in the past history of the universe is infinite. But mathematicians recognise that the existence of an actually infinite number of things ultimately leads to self-contradictions. For example, what is infinity minus infinity? Well, mathematically you get self-contradictory answers. This shows that infinity is just an idea in your mind, not something which exists in reality. David Hilbert - perhaps the greatest mathematician of this century - states: "The infinite is nowhere to be found in reality. It neither exists in nature nor provides a legitimate basis for rational thought. The role that remains for the infinite to play is solely that of an idea." But since past events are not just ideas but are real, the number of past events must be finite. Therefore the series of past events cannot just go back and back forever. Rather the universe must have begun to exist.

This conclusion has been confirmed by remarkable discoveries in astronomy and astrophysics. The astrophysical evidence indicates that the universe began to exist in a great explosion called the Big Bang, 15 billion years ago. Most people do not understand that according to the Big Bang theory, not only were all matter and energy, but physical space and time themselves, created in that event. Therefore as the Cambridge astronomer Fred Hoyle points out, the Big Bang theory requires the creation of universe from nothing. This is because as you go back in time you reach a point at which, in Hoyle's words, the universe was "shrunk down to nothing at all." Thus what the Big Bang model requires is that the universe began to exist and was created out of nothing.

Now, this tends to be very awkward for the atheist. For as Anthony Kenny of Oxford University urges, a proponent of the Big Bang theory, at least if he is an atheist, must believe that the universe came from nothing by nothing. But surely, that does not make sense. Out of nothing, nothing comes. So why does the universe exist instead of nothing? Where does it come from? There must have been a cause, which brought the universe into being. We can summarize our argument thus as follows:

Premise 1: Whatever begins to exist has a cause.
Premise 2: The universe began to exist.
Therefore: The universe has a cause.

Now from the very nature of the case, as the cause of space and time, this cause must be an uncaused, changeless, timeless, beginningless, immaterial being, of unimaginable power, which created the universe.

2. The complex Order in the Universe

During the last 30 years or so, scientists have discovered that the existence of intelligent life depends upon a delicate and complex balance of initial conditions simply given in the Big Bang itself. We now know that life-prohibiting universes are vastly more probable than any life-permitting universe like ours. How much more probable? Well, the answer is that the chances that the universe should be life-permitting are so infinitesimal as to be incalculable and incomprehensible. For example, Stephen Hawking has estimated that if the rate of the universe's expansion one second after the Big Bang had been smaller, by even one part in a 100.000 million million, the universe would have re-collapsed into a hot fireball. P.C.W Davies has calculated that the odds against the initial conditions being suitable for later star formation, without which planets cannot exist, is one followed by a 1000 billion billion zeros at least. There are around 50 such quantities and constants present in the Big Bang, which must be finely tuned in that way if the universe is to permit life. So improbability is added to improbability to improbability, until our minds are reeling in incomprehensible numbers.

There is no physical reason why these constants and quantities should possess the values that they do. The one time agnostic physicist Paul Davies comments: "Through my scientific work I have come to believe more and more strongly that the physical universe is put together with an ingenuity so astonishing that I cannot accept it merely as a brute fact." Similarly Fred Hoyle remarks: "A common sense interpretation of the facts suggests that a super intellect has monkeyed with physics." And Robert Jastrow, the head of NASA's Institute for Space Studies, has called it the most powerful evidence for the existence of God ever to come out of science. So once again the theistic view that there is an intelligent designer of the universe seems to make much more sense than the atheistic view that the universe, when it popped into being uncaused out of nothing, just happened to be by chance fine-tuned to an incomprehensible precision for the existence of intelligent life. We can summarize this second argument as follows:

Premise 1: The fine-tuning of the initial conditions of the universe is due to either law, chance or design.
Premise 2: It is not due to either law or chance.
Therefore: It is due to design.

3. Objective Moral Values in the World

If God does not exist, then objective moral values do not exist. Many theists and atheists alike agree on this point. For example, Michael Ruse, a Canadian philosopher of science, explains: "Morality is biological adaptation, no less than are hands, feet and teeth. Considered as a rationally justifiable set of claims about an objective something, ethics is illusory. I appreciate that when somebody says: 'Love your neighbour as yourself,' they think they are referring above and beyond themselves. Nevertheless such reference is truly without foundation. Morality is just aid to survival and reproduction, and any deeper meaning is illusory." Friedrich Nietzsche, the great atheist of the last century who proclaimed the death of God, understood that the death of God meant the destruction of all meaning and value in life. I think that Friedrich Nietzsche was right.

But we have got to be very careful here. The question here is not: Must we believe in God in order to live moral lives? I am not claiming that we must. Nor is the question: Can we recognise objective moral values without believing in God? I think that we can. Rather the question is: If God does not exist, do objective moral values exist? I must confess that I just do not see any reason to think that in the absence of God the herd-morality evolved by *homo sapiens* is objective. After all if there is no God, then what is so special about human beings? They are just accidental by-products of nature which have evolved relatively recently on an infinitesimal speck of dust called the planet Earth, lost somewhere in a hostile and mindless universe and which are doomed to perish individually and collectively in a relatively short time. On the atheistic view some action, say rape, may not be socially advantageous and so in the course of human development has become taboo. But that does absolutely nothing to prove that rape is really wrong. On the atheistic view there is nothing really wrong with your raping someone. Thus without God there is no absolute right and wrong which imposes itself on our conscience.

But the problem is that objective values do exist and deep down I think we all know it. There is no more reason to deny the objective reality of moral values than the objective reality of the physical world. Actions like rape, torture and child abuse are not just socially unacceptable behaviour. They are moral abominations. Some things at least are really wrong. Similarly love, equality and generosity are really good. Thus we can summarize this third argument as follows:

> *Premise 1*:   If God does not exist, objective moral values do not exist.
> *Premise 2*:   Objective values do exist.
> *Therefore*:   God exists.

4. The Immediate Experience of God

This is not really an argument for God's existence. Rather it is the claim that you can know that God exists wholly apart from arguments, simply by immediately experiencing Him. This was the way that people in the Bible knew God. As professor John Hick explains: "God was known to them as a dynamic will interacting with their own wills, a sheer given reality as inescapably to be reckoned with as destructive storm and life-giving sunshine. God was not an idea adopted by the mind, but an experiential reality which gave significance to their lives". Now if this is so, then there is a danger that arguments for God's existence could actually distract our attention from God himself. If a person is sincerely seeking God, then God will make His existence evident to him. The Bible promises: "Draw near to God, and He will draw near to you." We should not so concentrate on the external proofs that we fail to hear the inner voice of God speaking to our hearts. For those who listen, God becomes an intimate reality in their lives.

In conclusion then, we have yet to see any argument to show that God does not exist, and we have seen four reasons that God does exist. Together these constitute a powerful cumulative case for the existence of God. And unless or until we are given better arguments for atheism, I think we can agree that theism is the more rational worldview. Thank you.

LN: My task is to defend atheism and I will do so on the following grounds. When we look at the concept of reason, it has at least two aspects to it. The first is a question of inference, of logic, and of clear rational thinking. From that perspective I think that the concept presently under debate, the concept of God, is not sufficiently clear to be maintained as rational, that is, for theism to be rational. The other aspect of the concept of reason has a kind of social component, to be reasonable. This is a very central element in the concept of reason, and also based on this aspect I think it is very important to stick to atheism in order to avoid dangerous fundamentalism amongst people. On the other hand, we could say that there is a personal element involved. Reason goes for the objective, the social, and the intersubjective. The personal element goes for the subjective side and very much I think religion is a very personal question, which one basically should let it be. So I will not so much concentrate on that personal side, but put my efforts on the others.

The concepts of Theism and Atheism

We are debating the question: Is it more rational to be a theist than to be an atheist? Well, bound up in this question, we have the concept of rationality as I started by pointing out. We also have the concept of theism; and finally we have the concept of being (not to forget the importance of knowing what it is to be something in this context). I hope that I can get the time to dig into all these concepts.

Let us take first of all the concept of theism. We have to point out that we can operate with theism and deism as two different concepts. According to theism, which we are debating here, God is a personal God. God is someone outside the world or over the world, who created the world, who is maintaining its existence, and who is the guidance of the development of this world, so to speak. To some extent the deist agrees with the theist, but the deist does not think that God interferes with the world. So in order to be theist we should not only prove the existence of a transcendent God, we should add to it that this God interferes with the world and is concerned about what is happening in the world. So there is a tremendous difference between how theists and deists are looking at the matter. For instance, in Christianity we would have the debates about the status of Jesus, and about God's interference in the process and development of the world. This interference would be in contradiction with the concept of deism. In this case it has to be theism.

In relation to the analysis of the concepts I will forget about pantheism, which is not the question here. I would say that atheism, which I defend here, states that in a rational, objective context, we should do without the concept of God.

Reasons can be given for that in several ways. One is the question of meaning: Are the concepts clear enough to be handled rationally? Secondly, there is the question of truth. We cannot debate the concept of truth unless the concept of meaning is clear, if it has no clear meaning, we cannot discuss the question of truth. It is not possible to have a rational debate on that, if the meaning is unclear. But I will then go a little further. What kind of statement is the claim: "I am a theist"? According to modern language-philosophy, this claim should probably be seen as a so-called "speech act." It is not simply a statement of a normal truth as "I wear a tie" or something like that. It is a very different statement. To say "I am a theist" is somehow to make a kind of commitment. We are touching upon what it is to be a theist. I am not simply saying "I believe." I am saying that "I am a theist." In my opinion, to make a speech act, like "I am a theist," "I am a believer," is not simply a rational statement. It is a commitment. But what is the alternative to this theistic position? I think that the negation of theism would simply be the claim that I will not make the theistic commitment.

So atheism is not necessarily an alternative metaphysics. When we make negations of statements, we basically open up for a number of alternatives. For instance, what is not right can be anything, and what is not a theist may be a variety of things. So in this sense, I think, I have a simpler task. I have to defend an atheism, which can in fact be very many types of things. It is just to say that I do not make the theistic commitment and to defend the view that in a number of contexts we should – for logical as well as social reasons - not make such commitments.

I would like to comment a bit more on the idea of being a theist. Since I am not a theist myself, I may do it a little rudely. It is of course complicated to debate such things, which are very personal. One may easily hurt people's feelings or something similar; and that is why I think one has to keep it quite personal. We should note that there are various beliefs. Are we sure that we all believe in the same God, if we believe in God? At least some people believe that they can talk with God. Some even hear voices. But what does it mean to speak with God? I think it is very difficult to answer such questions. When my grandmother was 85 years old, I was a boy and she said to me: "I think am soon going to die. I hear the angels. They are playing for me, and they have also started singing for me." So that was her way of telling that she felt she would die soon. Whether or not she really heard the angels sing, I do not know. I think she heard some angels singing. That is okay at a personal level. In fact, I think it was a very fine and beautiful way for her to experience the last time of her life. But that is a kind of personal experience about which it is certainly very difficult to communicate. We hear all kinds of personal experiences. Some say that they have been seduced by UFOs etc. But how can we rationally communicate about such very personal experiences? From a rational, scientific point of view we have to treat such experiences as something very subjective. We should not try to make them stand for something objective. Of course, we should not say that it is nonsense that my grandmother could hear the angels sing. We have to show such experiences respect. They may count for something very essential in human life.

Finally, I will move on to the concept of God, but maybe I will open up the issue of being a theist later.

The concept of God

Typically we have a mythological concept of God, which we have got from our childhood, from the stories in the Bible etc. We may also get ideas of God from the study of metaphysics, which is the main issue. But as far as I understand it, Dr. Craig is also mentioning the mystical experiences which I to some extent I have alluded to here and which in my opinion must be seen as something very subjective and not very relevant with respect to the question about the objective existence of God. When it comes to the metaphysical way of approaching the concept of God, there are also a lot of problems. Are we really sure that we know what we are saying, when we say God is the absolute necessary being, the absolute perfection or the Almighty?

We know what it is to be, to have some power, or to have some degree of perfection. We know what it is to love. We know what it means that something is relatively necessary or relatively not necessary. But when we talk about the Almighty etc., we make precisely the type of generalisation which has been criticised through the history of philosophy. One can, for instance, mention the famous criticism by the famous philosopher Kant, according to whom we cannot be sure that they make sense.

Let us think about the concept of the Almighty. Does it make sense at all? I do not think that any of us can understand what it means to be almighty. It seems to mean that the Almighty has all power, so that nobody else has any power. But what about us? It seems that we have some power at least. But then it is not the case that God has all power. Then he has only got all power minus the power we have, but that sounds kind of arbitrary and does not really sound like smart metaphysics.

We can also ask which power we are speaking about. The power to do what? Maybe we are speaking about the power to do anything, which is logically possible. OK. Can God create a being which is stronger than himself? Can he do that? Questions of this kind are part of the analysis of what this concept means. If God cannot make a being stronger than himself, we run into problems. Development in history is basically creating something, which improves and gets stronger and stronger. The nature of development is always to create something stronger than oneself is. I can create something stronger than myself. We all can do that. Maybe my children get smarter then me. I can at least create a machine which is smarter than I am. We have calculators which are smarter than we are, and so on. So is it logically impossible for God to create a being stronger than himself? If yes we'll question the notion of evolution. Development of power will be an illusion.

Let us turn to the idea that God is all-knowing. That is, he knows everything. He cannot be wrong. It is not just that he has superstitions. His ideas must be true. They cannot later on be proven to be false. So do we know what it is to know everything? Do we understand the concept? What is it to know? Well, one aspect of knowing is that I can ask some further questions. That is always part of knowing, as we know the concept. But when we say all knowledge, that has stopped. So it is surely not the normal concept of knowledge we are talking about here, and if it was not the normal concept, then what is it? Then we have no clear concept.

I will also comment a bit on the idea of God knowing the future. If God's knows the future, my will disappears. I believe I have a free will, but on the assumption of the all-knowing God, my free will turns out to be an illusion. And if it is not an illusion, then God cannot know what I will do in the future, because it depends on my free will. And in addition: Does he know that he knows everything? That would give rise to an infinite regress. I agree with Dr. Craig that there cannot be an actual infinity. Therefore God cannot be all-knowing. Does God know what he will do in the future? What will he do in the far future? Suppose he knows everything, then he cannot change anything, because if he could change anything then this would not be a real valid knowledge, then he has lost his power. And on the other hand if he has to maintain his power, then he must say it is uncertain what will happen in the future. I do not know the future because it depends on what I will decide in the future. So I think there are consistency problems involved here. Of course the arguments from harm or from love (or what we would call it) could be debated in similar ways, and we can take these problems up later on. Thank you very much.

WLC: You remember that I said that there were two questions that need to be asked in today's debate. 1) Are there any good reasons to think that God does not exist? 2) Are there good reasons to think that He does?

Now, with respect to his argument for atheism, Lennart first says that atheism is just non-theism and that therefore he does not have any burden of proof to prove that God does not exist. Now, I submit that that is simply a misunderstanding of what atheism is, and let me simply appeal to the *Encyclopaedia of Philosophy* and the article there on atheism by Poul Edwards. He says: "According to the most usual definition, an atheist is a person who maintains that there is no God, i.e. that the sentence 'God exists' expresses a false proposition. In contrast, an agnostic maintains that it is not known whether there is a God." Now, Lennart has clearly confused agnosticism with atheism. The atheist maintains there is no God. That is a claim to know something, that is a knowledge claim, and it therefore requires justification. It is the agnostic who simply is the non-theist. He does not know whether God exists or not. So if Lennart is going to defend atheism, we need to have positive arguments for that.

Now, Lennart does give one positive argument in his first speech, namely that the concept of God is ambiguous. He says, do we really know what we are saying when we say that God is almighty or all-knowing? Now, notice in general, it is not a disproof of God's existence to say that the concept of God's attributes requires closer definition. It is true that the Bible does not give close definitions of what it is to be almighty, for example, but that is no disproof of such a being. Rather this is just a call for those of us who are Christian philosophers to attempt to formulate more carefully a definition of the attributes of God. Having that task is no proof that there is no such being.

But can Lennart in fact show us that there are contradictions in these concepts? Then he would be right. Then it would be a disproof, if he could show that there is a contradiction in the concept of being omnipotent. I would argue simply that he has not been able to show any contradictions. For example, what does it mean to say that God is almighty? Well, I would refer to the excellent article by Alfred Freddoso and Thomas Flint called *Maximal Power* in their book *The Existence and Nature of God*, where they give a very careful and clear definition of omnipotence, which I think is perfectly coherent. Roughly speaking, it has to do with God's ability to actualise any logically possible state of affairs. And therefore the answer to the question "Can God create a being stronger than himself?" is simply "no" because the state of affairs with a being stronger than the omnipotent God is not a logically possible state of affairs. So that does not count against divine omnipotence. In general, I think, if he reads this article Lennart will find that

Flint and Freddoso solve all of these traditional conundrums about stones heavier than God can lift and other such things. So I see no problem with the definition of omnipotence.

What about the concept of God's being all-knowing? Lennart says that knowing involves the ability to ask questions, and God cannot do that because He knows everything. Well, I simply deny that is what knowing involves. Epistemologists say that to know a proposition p is to have a justified true belief that p, and certainly God has that. I would say that God's omniscience means 'for all p: if p, then God knows that p and he does not believe not p' and that is a perfectly good definition of omniscience. God knows only and all true propositions. Does God know the future? Yes, I think, because future tense propositions are bivalent. They have a truth value, and God has the essential property of knowing only and all true propositions. In virtue of knowing future tense propositions, He thereby knows the future. Now, Lennart says that if God knows the future then He cannot change the future. That is, I think, a confusion on Lennart's part. It is logically impossible to change the future, because the future by definition is what will be. So to change the future would be to make what will be not be, which is a self-contradiction. Rather what God has, and I believe we have, is the power to determine the future, and that is all that freedom requires. So God knows the future. He has the power to determine the future, and the future is contingent, because God could act differently than He will in fact act. So I see no difficulty in the concept of either omniscience or omnipotence, and therefore no difficulty with the concept of God. So I do not see any good reasons to think atheism is true. It seems to me that the concept of God has not been show to be incoherent.

Now, what about my reasons for theism? Lennart says in general, that I have not proved theism because all I have proven is deism. Well, I would say that deism is a sub-category of theism. Deists are theists but they just do not believe that God is active in any special revelation in the world. Moreover I think that there are good reasons to believe that God has specially revealed Himself in the world. We have evidence in the New Testament for a divine revelation in the person of Jesus.

Now what about my specific arguments? First the argument from the origin of the universe. Lennart agrees that you cannot have an infinite regress. So there must have been a beginning. So the only question is, is it true that whatever begins to exist has a cause? Well that seems to me intuitively obvious. Even Kai Nielsen, an atheist, writes: "Suppose you suddenly hear a loud bang, and you asked me 'what made that bang?' and I reply, 'nothing, it just happened.' You would not accept that. In fact you would find my reply quite unintelligible." Well, what is true about the little bang, is true about the Big Bang. It must have had a cause, and therefore I think we have good grounds for thinking there is a creator of the universe.

As for the argument from complex order in the universe, let me just reinforce the point by quoting from Barrow and Tipler and their book *The Anthropic Cosmological Principle*. They say: "We have no explanation for the precise numerical values taken by these numbers. They are not subject to evolution or selection by any known natural or unnatural mechanism. The fortuitous nature of many of their numerical values cries out for explanation." And this explanation cannot be given in view of chance, given the literally incomprehensible odds against such a thing happening.

And then of course the arguments for moral values and personal experience, it seems to me, also justifiy me, at least, in believing in God. Lennart admits that it is rational for me to go on the basis of my experience, if I have such experience and therefore, I think, theism is rational for me.

LN: I also looked the concepts up in a dictionary before I came here. I used terms in the way in which they were represented in this dictionary of philosophy. This only shows that we have to rely on the clear thinking we make ourselves, and that appealing to authority is a problem because authorities disagree. And we can easily define the concepts here. I accept we can say that I should define atheism in a stronger sense than just being agnostic. Therefore I tried to give you the argument which you called for. I argued that there is a contradiction involved in the concept of all power combined with the concept of all knowledge. I do not think that the problem can be solved in the way you tried to solve it. You tried to make it a statement simply about the future, but this was not my point. My point was that God decides the future and that he cannot know what he is going to decide before he has made the decision. After he has made this decision his powers are limited because then he cannot change anything. So God's knowledge is relative to God's own decisions. When he has made the decision, then he knows what the future is going to be. Before he has made the decision, he cannot know the future. Maybe he made the decision from the early beginning on, but then he limited his power from the early beginning on. If he did not do that, he would not have the knowledge, because then later on he might change his mind. That was, I think, the point I tried to put up here.

So I think it is very contingent how this world is structured, whether something good or something bad happens. The argument from harm is well known and you have surely debated it many times, but I think it is also has its good points. Since it is contingent whether people get hurt, get killed or what ever, what happens not a logical truth. Therefore things can be changed. And what does a loving and caring person do, when he sees something terrible happening and he has the power to prevent it. Of course the Almighty has the power to prevent it. And if he has the power to prevent it, why does that not happen? It is not easy to dismiss this question.

I will try to dig a little more about into the concept of how we have to base things on our own reason. We can think about objective values in many ways. I think Kant has some very good considerations on categorical ethics. He connects it also with postulates of God, but I do not think that is necessary. We have seen many societies, which are not theistic, but which have had very high moral standards. In these societies people have felt very strongly about moral values and they have wanted to stick to them and to keep them in a rational manner. But where do we do have our reason from? That is, I think, an essential question. Basically, we get it by upbringing and we get some intelligence from birth, so we think. But of course if there is an almighty reason, intelligence then that would be the one intelligence we should obey. If there is an almighty power, and we can know that power, then of course we have to realise that maybe it is not my reason, which I have to follow. In that case I have to follow the higher insight. God is so much more than I am. He is so much more powerful than I am, so how can I know what is really right and wrong. I would have to try to rely on finding out what God's statements are in order to find out what is right and wrong. Now how can I do that? I look for God. I can dig into the depth of my mind and into the depth of the universe looking for God. I want to know what is right and what is wrong and what the world is like. Maybe I hear a voice, I get a vision and hear it saying: 'I am God. Listen to me.' Then I have to make a judgement, is this God or not. It could be the devil! How can I know? Maybe there is simply something bad inside of me, which is making this vision for me and the devil tries to seduce me. How can I know? I have to make the judgement. I must say 'yes' or 'no', so I have to rely on my own reason, even if I give up my own reason. What could come out of that? I think that if we are to communicate between religions and between cultures, we must assume a common reason. We are communicating, not because God commands us to do it. That would lead to fighting, because different cultures may have different gods. Then there would mighty commanders on each side, which could easily lead to war. I think that is really a bad thing, to lift it into this level, and to accept a god as such a mighty commander. That is why I think that religion has to be kept at the personal and subjective level. That it is very important. We cannot raise it to the common level. We cannot have a multicultural society based on that. That is why the decisions in the universities, in the governments and so on are not based on the God's commands. It has to be rational on these common levels. Otherwise we would be put into an area that is subjective, where we cannot make a reasonable decision among each other. That is my social argument. I think we should add, that for us in this country it is especially important to remember today in a situation, where Denmark is starting to become a multicultural society - in the sense that Christianity is not anymore the only religion represented in Denmark.

WLC: Now in my closing remarks let me try to draw together some of the threads of our discussion. First what good reasons have we heard to think that atheism is true? Well, in his last speech Lennart brought a new argument, the problem of harm, and he suggested that if God is all-powerful, He can create a world without harm. And if He is all-good, He would want to create a world without harm. Therefore there should be no harm and since there is, God must not exist.

The problem is that neither of these two premises is necessarily true. First of all, if God wills to create *free* creatures, then He cannot guarantee that they will always do what is right. It is logically impossible to make someone freely do something, and God's being all-powerful does not imply that He can do the logically impossible. Lennart would have to prove that there is a world of free creatures, which God could create, which has as much good as this world but without as much evil as this world. How can he possibly prove such a thing? That is pure speculation. Moreover, I think his second premise is not necessarily true either. Certainly God wants the best for us, but that raises the question "what is the best?" We tend to just assume that if God exists, His purpose for us in life is to make us happy in this life. But, you see, on the Christian view of God that is false. The purpose of life is not happiness as such, but rather it is the knowledge of God and His salvation. And many evils may happen in life, which are utterly pointless with respect to producing human happiness in this life, but they may not be pointless with respect to producing the knowledge of God. It is possible that only in a world that has gratuitous moral and natural evil, would the maximum of people come to freely know God and His salvation. So Lennart would have to prove that there is another world, which has this much knowledge of God and his salvation, which involves less evil. And again how can he possibly prove that? It is pure speculation. And therefore I think the argument from evil simply fails.

As for the argument based on the incoherence of divine foreknowledge, what I would say here is that God logically prior to His foreknowledge of the world has what theologians call middle knowledge. He knows what free creatures would freely do under any circumstances God could place them in, and by then actualising those creatures in those circumstances He knows exactly what will happen in the future. So I do not think any problem there. So basically these arguments for atheism, it seems to me, are quite inconclusive and not sound.

What about my arguments for theism? Well, we have seen no refutation of the first argument, based on the origin of the universe, and there has been no refutation of the second argument based on the complex order of the universe. What about moral values? Here I think Lennart really confused the argument. He said: "How do I know what is right and what is wrong? I must judge. I must be rational." As I said in my opening statement, the issue is not, can we recognise objective moral values without believing in God. I certainly think that we can. That is an epistemological question. My question is ontological. What is the basis of those values? And I see no basis for objective moral values, if there is not a transcendent anchor for them. Everything becomes socio-culturally relative. In his book *Morality after Auschwitz* Peter Haas asked how an entire society could have participated in the mass genocide of Jews and gypsies for over a decade without any serious opposition. His answer is that the holocaust was possible only because a new ethic was in place which did not define the arrest and deportation of Jews as wrong, but in fact defined them as ethically good. And Hass's point is that the Nazis' ethic could not be discredited from within, because it was internally consistent and coherent. That is the problem if you do not have a transcendent anchor point for your moral values. Everything becomes socio-culturally relative, and there is no way to say that the Nazi ethic was wrong, and that the ethic of our liberal democratic society was right.

Finally as to personal experience the point here is that in the absence of cogent arguments for atheism I am certainly in my rights rationally to believe in God on the basis of my personal experience of God. God is real to me. So why should I not go on believing in God, in the absence of any overwhelming argument for the atheistic view?

LN: As to the creation of the universe, I think the universe is a mystery, and it is a paradox. I do not think it is possible to explain it with any concept of explanation we have today. To me it does not help very much to say there is a God. That will only give rise to a new question. It actually adds to the problems rather than helping the problem of explanation. So I do not think it really helps. Dr. Craig argued from the concept of complexity and he considered the issue of how likely it would be that a universe would be created like ours where there can be life. I have no real knowledge about these things, but how many universes are there? Our universe is life-permitting, and maybe there are many other such universes. I do not know. Maybe there are other types of universes with other types of life. I have surely no idea. As to the foundation of morality I would agree with you on one point: We need an ontology on which morality can be based. I mentioned Kant because he based it on reason and that is for sure a rather solid foundation and of course the Nazi system could not stand for that. That is absolutely out of the question. The reasons include considerations for all human beings, and that they surely did not do. So I think there are very strong types or ways of founding morality, but it needs an ontology in addition, namely an idea of what human beings are and what life is about. Therefore, I think it needs more foundation than simply an idea of reason. It needs an idea of what a human being is and what life is about. And of course one possible proposal is, as you mentioned, to base it on a belief in God, but we could also suggest other types of foundation, and others have done that.

I would like to say a little about what it is to be. What is to be a theist or to be an atheist? Is it simply to say "I am an atheist" or "I am a theist."? Is being a Christian simply to believe, when Jesus says you have to believe? Is it simply to say that I believe something to be true? To believe in Jesus is much more than that. It is really a commitment when we relate ourselves to such major issues. And who makes this commitment? When I look around in the Danish society, I would basically think many people say that they are Christians unless they come from another culture. But that is just a statement like saying "I belong to this culture" or "I belong to this society" and to much more people would not like to commit themselves. I would not really say I am a Christian, because what would that really mean when I consider what Jesus says? He says: "Well, you are wealthy people, and wealthy people cannot get in heaven." It is really difficult at least - very difficult as far as we know. So maybe he meant much more. He demands much of us in order to be a believer. He demands much more than this lip service we pay. So the question of being a theist is not the question of the lip service we pay. It has to be something much more solid.

NHG: Thank you very much. Even if it was relatively easy to be a timekeeper this afternoon, it is very difficult to be a moderator between these two views, which seem to be so divergent, but have been proposed here so in a manner so lively and so concise. Perhaps we should remind ourselves of the benefit of discussing these matters in a university setting, where we can stick to general rules of fairness, but also can allow ourselves to bring in our commitments and our non-commitments into the discussions. And I think this has been very obvious from both our speakers. Now the floor is for open questions to both of our presenters.

Question: Lennart, why don't you want to accept creation as a possible explanation to the problem of the origin of the universe?

LN: When we work with explanation, we try to work out concepts of "how do we explain things?", for instance. And basically we have this structure of cause and effect. And we normally assume that cause and effect are basically different. But here it seems that we are confronted with the idea of a cause that causes itself. I do not think it is easy to understand what that means. Furthermore, we have to add on a number of properties to this cause of knowledge.

The idea of creation out of nothing is a very bold hypothesis. There is no evidence for that. Normally we assume that things come out of development and the statement about a creation in this massive manner would be far from any understanding from any known concept of explanation. We do not have a concept of explanation that really allows us to say that this is an obvious way of explaining the things.

Question: This is again a question to Lennart. As far as I can understand it, you are actually taking the illocution out of the statement "I am a theist." Very often statements can have more than one function, so when we are comparing these issues, we should consider the context in which we are actually saying these things. Do you think it is fair to take it out of the referential aspects of the statement?

LN: I fully agree with you that we cannot only look at the speech act type. The reason why I take it up here is the way the question has been formulated. It is not only the question "Is it true that there exists a God" The question of being something is also involved. To say "I believe in God," that may be one thing, but saying "I am" that seems to me not simply to accept a statement as true or false. It seems to me to be much more.

We are talking about something absolute, the absolute power. Do I really think that God's absolute power of God's absolute reason has to control what I am going to do, or do I have to keep to my own reason and say I have to find out myself and be responsible. May be I can let God decide for me, but how will I really stand up if he then comes like Khomeini telling children to go into the mine fields which Iranians have placed there. When you go out there, he says, then you'll go directly to heaven. That is really a big problem when it comes to transforming personal religious beliefs from the personal level to 'objective' statements which are supposed to control the society. The decision making process then gets out of your hands and you have given permission for this to happen. You have said: In the end I will let it be decided by somebody else and then I am in the pocket of those who decide.

Question: This is a question for Bill Craig. I cannot think of one single act, which a human being could perform which has not been acceptable to some human moral system. If this is so, how can you still believe objective moral values?

Question: C. S. Lewis argues much along the same lines as you do I believe i.e. that the existence of moral values in a way points to God. But he also points out a problem with that thought. He states that it is not enough to say well we can place moral values on the existence of God. Because God said so, we will be punished if we act in a certain way. In the worst case that would make a tyrant or even a demon out of God, Lewis says. So in some sense there must be an intrinsic relation between this goodness and God. The question is not fully answered by saying, well God said so. There must be some more intrinsic reason to something being good.

WLC: In essence the last question raises the old dilemma: Does God will what is good or is what is good good because God wills it? What I do is split the horns of the dilemma and say that God's moral commands flow necessarily out of the divine nature. God is essentially loving, holy, just, kind, merciful and so forth. Thus His commands are not arbitrary, and they are not based in sheer acts of will. I am not a voluntarist in that sense, but I think that God's moral commands are necessary expressions of God's own moral nature. So God is what Plato called the Good, the moral nature of God. And his commands flow necessarily from it. Now on that basis that enables me to answer the first question, namely that I am not at all reluctant to condemn other cultures because of these sorts of practices that you say. There is no reason to take the politically correct view that just because some practice is accepted in some culture, we have to think that it is alright. I think it is heinous, for example, that in Hindu society, they burned women alive, on the funeral pyres of their husbands. In ancient China they bound the feet of women like lotus blossoms, crippling them for life. In other cultures, as you say, there are examples where rape of young girls is accepted. What I want to say is that these cultures are wrong. But you cannot do that without a trans-cultural anchor point in God to say that the Nazi culture was wrong, apartheid was wrong, terrorists are wrong, etc. Therefore I am not at all bothered by the fact that there are these abnormal cultures and societies that are proofs of what I think are moral abominations. It is precisely because I am a theist that I can consistently condemn such actions. Apart from that the Nürnberg war trials would have been impossible. There is no such thing as intrinsic human rights unless you have some transcendent anchor point.

I do not think that moral values have to be universal in order to be objective. I mean if we take the Christian doctrine of sin seriously there are some people who are terribly warped. So I am not at all disturbed by the fact that some Nazi war criminal who thinks it is allright to send people to the gas chambers disagrees with me. I do not see that I should doubt that there is a difference between red and green because some colour blind person cannot see it. In the same way there is no reason to doubt my moral intuitions that anti-semitism is objectively wrong. There is no reason that I should doubt what is, I think, my clear moral intuition about certain things because some people are so morally blind or crippled or handicapped that they cannot see, for example, that torturing children is wrong. So do not let the fact that there are people who are evil in any way undermine your confidence that objective moral values actually exist.

Question: My question is for Bill Craig. I tend to agree with your first four arguments. Would you label any of those as being specifically Christian? Or could they just as well have been put forward by a Muslim scholar or any other person belonging to another theistic religion?

WLC: These arguments are consistent with any of the great monotheistic faiths, but I could add other reasons why I believe in the Christian faith.

Question: That is a question for both of you. I am glad that you have accepted the idea that the issue of God is not beyond rationality. But how far would you be ready to rely on your own rationality. Could there in principle be rational arguments, which would make you change your minds in the question about the existence of God?

WLC: How far would I rely on rationality? Would one change one's mind? I do not think we should try to answer this question personally because that might have to do with personal failure or faith or sin or something. But the question is: would it be rational for one to change one's mind? My religious epistemology is that belief in God is actually a basic belief, which is guaranteed to me through the witness of the Holy Spirit and that witness is an intrinsic defeater of any ostensible defeater brought against it. So that I think that a person who attends to the witness of the Holy Spirit will be rational to remain with that witness even in the face of arguments which he cannot answer. The Holy Spirit's witness will have more warrant for him than the ostensible defeater brought against it.

Question: Bill Craig, I was a bit worried about your linking belief in God with the belief in the Big Bang theory. Do you think that other cosmological theories will be inconsistent with belief in God?

WLC: I used the Big Bang theory as scientific confirmation of a conclusion already reached philosophically. I give a philosophical argument for the premise that the universe began to exist, and this does have empirical confirmation. But obviously the fact that the universe began to exist, does not obligate one to accept the Big Bang theory. You are quite right.

Question: This is a question for Bill Craig. Why should we prove that God exists? Is it not more important to believe in God and to trust him than to find some logical proof of his existence?

WLC: Well, you cannot trust someone unless you believe that person exists. You first have to know that he exists, before you can trust him. And let me just end on a general word here. In European countries and Scandinavia in particular, the forces of secularism in the universities are so strong that Christians would be ill-advised to simply embrace a kind of fideism, a kind of leap of faith in the dark that avoids rational apologetics. I think in times such as these theists need as never before to have a rational apologetic available to give an answer to secularists and naturalists at the university who ask us for the reason of the hope that is in us as Christians. So I think it is vital in a secular society that we have good reasons to share with others even if in the end those reasons are not the basis of our own faith but perhaps merely confirmation of a faith guaranteed to us by the Holy Spirit immediately.

LN: How far do reason and the rational go? I think they have to go all the way. That is the precondition for having a nice way of treating each other and avoiding the dangers that would come out stopping human reason. And what would the alternatives be? Of course if the alternative normally is a nice culture there is no problem, but sometimes it gets wild and it gets messy. So I think it is important that reason goes all the way. It is so to speak the *a priori*, and of course it has to be self-critical and has to be open to the possibility of being refuted no matter what kind of statements we have. No doubt about that. And there I think we really need to look at it self-critically, I think that is very important. And in order to know ourselves and what we are doing to each other and with other people around us, we have to be self-critical. I think for instance that when we consider other cultures, it is OK to criticise. I fully agree that we should not simply to be culturally relativistic. But we also have to be self-critical. We burned the pictures. We made war against the Indians in the name of Christianity.

I have to be open for the arguments from other people to test my intuition. Maybe I would change it. If I cannot listen then maybe the others are right. Then I think I am a dogmatist in the sense that we had better not be.

NHG: Thank you very much to both of the presenters of today for having given us all your passions, your commitments and for having done it in such a beautiful and delightful way. You have shown the reasons that might be given pro and con. Thank you very much.

Contributors

William Lane Craig, Professor, Talbot School of Theology, California.
Niels Henrik Gregersen, Professor, Aarhus University.
Per Hasle, Professor, University of Southern Denmark.
Søren Holm, Professor, University of Manchester.
Lennart Nørreklit, Reader, Aalborg University.
SteinarThorvaldsen, Lecturer, Tromsø University College.
Peder A. Tyvand, Professor, Agricultural University of Norway.
Mogens Wegener, Associate Professor, Aarhus University.
Nicolai Winther-Nielsen, Associate Professor, Copenhagen Lutheran School of Theology.
Peter Øhrstrøm, Professor, Aalborg University.